## EACH OF THEM WANTED SOMETHING . . .

**FAY PARKS**—A beautiful and ambitious reporter for the *Washington Globe*. She was after a Pulitzer prize and the story she stumbled on just might win it for her—posthumously.

**CAPTAIN ALLEN A. KOWALSKI**—A Naval Intelligence officer whose best friend died aboard the *Trident*. He'd do anything to discover the truth—defy his commanding officer, destroy his career—and possibly lose his life.

**DR. PHILLIP GRANT**—A brilliant and elusive scientist with blood on his hands and death in his heart. He wanted something *more* than revenge.

**REAR ADMIRAL "BULL" PULVEY**—It was his job to keep the press from sinking the Trident program. His future depended on everything going smoothly. He never expected he'd have to deal with . . .

# THE TRIDENT TRAGEDY

# THE
# TRIDENT
# TRAGEDY

Stanley C. Monroe
&
Robert J. Szilagye

A DELL BOOK

*For Suzanne Szilagye and Michelle Ruocco,*
*who dedicated themselves unselfishly in our behalf.*

Published by
Dell Publishing Co., Inc.
1 Dag Hammarskjold Plaza
New York, New York 10017

Dell ® TM 681510, Dell Publishing Co., Inc.

ISBN: 0-440-18769-9

Printed in the United States of America

First printing—June 1983

**Prologue**

*December 20th—New York City*

Christmas carols played over the PA system in Grand Central Station. Helen Boyd, standing in the crowd beside the lighted Christmas tree in the main concourse, watched her friend Mary Stagmyer purchase tickets and hurry away from the window to rejoin her.

Mary separated her Amtrack ticket from the Conrail ticket to Norwich, Connecticut, she'd bought for Helen. "You're going to be leaving from track six, Helen. My train is boarding now on track twelve. That doesn't leave us any time to say good-bye." They hugged impulsively.

"I'm going to miss you," Helen said.

"I'm going to miss you, too. All I can say is . . . it was a long haul to graduation, Dr. Helen Boyd."

"It certainly was, Dr. Mary Stagmyer. Boy, it still feels funny calling each other doctor."

"It'll grow on us in time. By the time we finish our internships we'll be quite used to the title. Sure you won't reconsider my offer and come out to the West Coast with me for a couple of weeks before you look for a placement at a hospital in Connecticut?"

"You know I'd love to, Mary . . . but my father's been quite lonely since my mother died," Helen said as she toyed affectionately with the cameo pinky ring her mother had bequeathed her. "I want to spend some time with him before going on to my internship."

Mary heard the PA system interrupt the Christmas carols to announce her train was about to leave. "Well, I guess this is it. You write and let me know what hospital you get work with, and I'll do the same." She kissed Helen. "Have a Merry Christmas and a Happy New Year!" Mary turned and hurried off to her train.

From an obscure alcove in the main concourse Nelson Hobart had observed Helen Boyd saying good-bye to her friend. He had the image of the petite young woman with short cut hair and soft brown eyes fused in his mind from a picture of her he had committed to memory. As soon as she moved off toward the New Haven tracks, he hurried after her.

Helen was about to pass through the boarding gate when she heard someone call out her name. She turned and saw a tall, frail man with graying hair who was dressed in a dark gray vested business suit, pushing his way through the crowd toward her. His neat appearance suggested he might be someone from the college who knew her.

"You don't know me, Miss Boyd," he said when he reached her. "I'm Nelson Hobart. I was sent to New York by Marine Dynamics to get you. I just missed you at the college and was told you were heading home by train." He took out his wallet and showed her his defense plant identification card.

Helen recognized it as similar to the one her father had been issued by the submarine builder.

"What is this all about?" she asked apprehensively.

"I'm very sorry to have to tell you this, but your father was in a serious accident at the plant."

His statement overwhelmed her and her face turned ashen at the news.

"How did he get hurt? What's wrong with him?"

"All I know is he's been taken to New London Hospital, and he's in critical condition. The company sent me to get you because there are forms for you to fill out and sign as his next of kin. I have a car waiting outside the station to take you to your father. May I suggest we get started right away? The sooner I get you to the hospital, the better it will be for your father."

"Maybe we should call the hospital and let them know I'm on my way."

"Please, Miss Boyd. There's no time to lose," Hobart said. "My instructions were to get you to the hospital as fast as possible." He gestured to her suitcase and overnight bag. "May I take those for you?" Given an approving nod, he picked up her luggage, then nodded for her to follow him out of the main concourse toward an exit.

From the rear seat of a black Lincoln Continental Mark IV, one of the three men in the car saw Hobart and the young attractive woman step out of the railroad station doors. "Start your engine, Mr. C," he ordered the driver. He then looked over at the man seated in the rear next to him. "Get your straight razor ready, Mr. B. And be sure to handle her carefully. Mr. Hobart doesn't want an accident."

"Don't worry about it, Mr. A."

"Move the split seat forward, Mr. C. Here they come," Mr. A added, then prepared himself to yank Helen Boyd into the car when the door opened.

The bright late-morning sun glittered off the dark tinted windows of the car, denying Helen Boyd view of its interior as she came to its side. As soon as the long door opened, she stepped down to get in, then felt herself being pulled and pushed into the back seat. A gag was immediately stuffed into her mouth. She stared wide-eyed at the sinister-looking man holding a straight razor against her windpipe.

Hobart threw Helen's suitcase and overnight bag into the front seat next to the driver, then quickly jumped in. "Proceed, Mr. C. Obey every law as we go. We don't wish to be stopped by the police." He looked back at Helen Boyd sandwiched between Mr. A's muscular frame and the stocky frame of Mr. B. "If you'll promise to sit back and not put up a struggle, I can have Mr. B dispense with the straight razor. I'd hate to see what would happen if we were to hit a pothole. Will you agree?" He got a faint nod. "Put your razor away, Mr. B. Helen will behave."

Brilliant blue flashes from arc-welding torches lit the wintry late-afternoon sky above the first behemoth *Trident* submarine's dull black rounded hull. The new submarine was held steadfast by bow, stern, and amidship lines to a long construction pier in the rear of Marine Dynamics Corporation's spacious defense plant facilities in Groton, Connecticut. The pier, with towering construction cranes set on rails to move fore and aft, stretched out over the murky waters of the Thames River from its bulkhead west bank. Across the river, other nuclear submarines, tied in tiers like offspring of their huge tender ships, seemed dwarfed in comparison to the Navy's biggest creature of the deep. Some distance upriver at a Naval submarine base in New London, the Navy brass anxiously awaited the new behemoth submarine's completion.

From his office window on the fourth floor of the plant's six-story administration building, Captain Rudolph Boyd of the Marine Dynamics security police force stared out at the silver-helmeted men wearing heavy quilted jump suits as they roamed the topside decks of the new submarine or hung by safety straps at varying levels of the *Trident*'s tall finlike sail. Other men stood surefooted on the surface of the diving planes that winged the sail, defying as best as they could the brisk wind sweeping inland from the nearby Long

Island Sound. The new submarine was overdue to join the fleet, and he could sense the urgency of the technical engineers as they feverishly went over blueprints on the *Trident*'s topside deck.

Boyd was a tall, narrow-framed man in his early sixties with graying hair that was thick and wavy. He had deep brown eyes that were constantly on the move, suggesting he was suspicious of everything around him. He was; it was his job to be. He had spent twenty years in the Navy doing security work, the last four of which had raised him to the rank of super chief petty officer. His military service had well prepared him for the sixteen years he now had in at the defense plant. He had started as a security police shift sergeant and for the last eight years had enjoyed the prestigious position of captain in command of one of the most stringent security police units in the nation.

The plant whistle sounded for ten seconds to alert Boyd that the day shift was ending. It prompted him to move away from the window and take up his customary position at the rows of TV monitors that lined one wall of his private office so that he could observe his staff maintaining tight security at the highly restricted defense plant. He looked at the main gate monitor and watched two newly hired guards check meticulously inside lunch pails and other hand-carried articles employees were leaving with.

A knock on his office door drew Boyd's attention away from the monitors. "Come in," he said, then smiled, seeing the expected face of Lieutenant Wilbur Brown, his relief.

Brown, a brawny black man in his mid-fifties, slipped out of his uniform parka and joined Boyd at the monitors. "Anything I should know about in the turnover log?"

"Nothing out of the ordinary," Boyd replied as he put on his parka and prepared to leave. "See you tomorrow, Brown. Have a nice night."

The normally thirty-minute drive from Groton to Norwich took Boyd over an hour because of heavy traffic. He felt deep sorrow again as he passed through the intersection of Main and Chestnut, where his wife, Martha, had been struck and killed by a speeding motorist last Christmas Eve.

That Christmas he and Helen had been denied any yuletide spirit, but he planned to make this Christmas as joyous as he possibly could for Helen's sake. Helen had graduated medical school, bestowing the title of doctor to the Boyd name for the first time in the family's history. That was something to celebrate, so he had put up over three hundred twinkling multicolored lights around the outside of their modest Colonial two-story house on Clark Street. And he already had a real Christmas tree set up in the living room.

As he turned onto Clark Street, Boyd searched for the twinkling lights on his house but found it to be swallowed by total darkness. Helen hadn't arrived home yet. He pulled into the driveway and parked. As he removed the mail from the porch mailbox, he smiled at a large envelope he knew to be a Christmas card from his aging Uncle Gunther in West Berlin, but was puzzled by a small box wrapped in brown paper and sealed tightly with cellophane tape. The box was marked urgent and was addressed to him, but it had no postage or return address.

Boyd flicked on a number of switches when he got inside the house, bringing on the Christmas tree and outside lights. He removed his uniform parka, sat down on the living room couch, and read his Uncle Gunther's Christmas greeting. He then turned his attention to the small box. When he'd opened it he found its contents was covered by a wad of cotton that was stained red. The instant he removed the cotton packing, he shuddered and dropped the box and its contents onto the table. There before him lay a bloodstained pinky with a cameo ring still attached to it.

Boyd stared at it, unable to move or even speak. He grew terrified when he realized that the cameo ring was unmistakably the same ring that his late wife, Martha, had bequeathed to Helen.

He finally managed to look away and caught sight of a sheet of white paper with dried blood on it folded tightly inside the box. With trembling fingers Boyd removed the sheet of paper from the box. Unfolding it, he found a message that had been formed from words cut out of newspapers and magazines.

RUDOLPH BOYD, WE HAVE YOUR DAUGHTER HELEN AS HER PINKY AND CAMEO RING WILL VERIFY. WE WARN YOU, WE WILL MAIL HELEN TO YOU PIECE BY PIECE UNLESS YOU DO EXACTLY AS YOU ARE TOLD. YOU ARE TO SAY NOTHING ABOUT THIS TO ANYONE. YOU ARE TO BE AVAILABLE TO RECEIVE A PHONE CALL AND FURTHER INSTRUCTIONS TOMORROW NIGHT.

At the end of the note there was a bloodstained fingerprint that was said to be made by the next finger Helen was to lose if he failed to obey her captors' demands when they called.

Boyd dropped the letter into his lap. Tears began rolling down his face uncontrollably. Helen was all he had in the world worth living for. If she was to be killed, he'd surrender to death, too. But not until there was no hope left of saving her.

Boyd slumped back in his chair and stared up at the ceiling. "Martha, they have our little girl," he sobbed. "What am I going to do . . .?"

# PART ONE

## Chapter One

*Thursday night, some eight months later*

The mammoth creature swam defiantly through the forbidding dark depths of the Mid-Atlantic some six hundred feet beneath the ocean's tossing surface. It was almost two football fields long from its bulbous nose to its trim crisscrossed tail. It stood nearly seven stories high from the top of its winged conning tower to the bottom of its dull black, rounded body. Its nuclear-powered twin propellers, one swirling in the sea behind the other on a single shaft, pushed the behemoth U.S.S. *Trident* submarine quickly, quietly, and effortlessly along its westward course for home waters. It was an undersea city on the move; a mobile missile base on the prowl.

Night had fallen on the surface, but unless a clock or wristwatch was checked, the *Trident*'s crew of one hundred sixty men and officers had no concept of the time of day. During the new submarine's two-month-long maiden voyage taps told them when it was night and reveille announced the start of each new day. Overhead fluorescent lights illuminated the thickly carpeted compartments and passageways, creating an eternal day. Even the monotonous hum of the air conditioning seemed to be a faint, timeless sound.

The *Trident* was the Navy's newest and largest nuclear submarine. Its control room was a marvel of modern technology. Crewmen wearing navy blue jump suits and matching baseball caps manned the spacious and intricately computerized compartment, illuminated by soft white overhead fluorescent lamps, which could be switched to red lighting for night vision. Inside this area related groups of vital stations were partially separated from each other by soundproof side partitions.

Occupying most of the portside bulkhead in the control room were the *Trident*'s CIC (Combat Information Center) stations, which comprised ship's radio communications, satellite communications, telegraph, code ciphering, IFF (Interrogator—Friend or Foe), search and weather radar, passive (listening) sonar, active (contact) sonar, and the *Trident*'s new "top secret" sonar avoidance system, a highly sophisticated antidetection device designed to make the *Trident* virtually invisible to its enemies. This device had undergone stringent testing throughout the submarine's two-month-long maiden voyage and so far had performed flawlessly.

CIC was manned by a dozen men sitting in leather upholstered swivel armchairs. They monitored their electronic sensing and sounding modules, which served as the *Trident*'s eyes and ears that constantly probed the area the submarine was leaving, passing through, or heading toward for a radius of some two hundred miles.

Forward of CIC on the same side of the control room was the helm, annunciator, ballast, and planes stations. As the submarine's propulsion and maneuvering stations, they were manned by a half dozen men who were also seated in leather upholstered swivel armchairs. They faced rows and tiers of square and round-faced indicators, ranks of toggle switches, lines of dials, and numerous sets of multicolored lights that walled their control consoles and told them the systems they were scrutinizing were vibrantly alive.

Occupying the center of the thickly carpeted floor, but favoring the rear of the control room, were the *Trident*'s dual periscopes. They were set on an elevated platform that was about knee high from the floor and were wrapped by a safety guardrail. Swirling up from the periscope deck to an overhead watertight hatch was a spiral staircase that connected the control room with the conning tower that hatted the pressure hull. Inside the conning deck an upright steel ladder climbed to a watertight pressure hull hatch that gave access to the submarine's outer bridge deck.

In a generously allocated walk-around area ahead of the periscope deck was the *Trident*'s computerized navigations plotting table. It was four feet square and topped with a glass viewing window that looked inside the table, where a three-dimensional electronic display simulated the precise subterranean topography the submarine was negotiating while submerged. It worked in conjunction with a series of digital display modules that gave electronic readings on depth soundings, mass and elevation measurements of subterranean mountains, plateaus, ridges, and canyons—even sunken ships and other objects foreign to the ocean's floor, which the sea had claimed and kept locked in its immense depths.

Standing waist high to ceiling and occupying nearly the entire length of the starboard bulkhead of the control room was a computerized, three-dimensional political world map that was in exact detail to the huge world map located in the war room in Washington. It also functioned as a simulator and depicted as miniature green lights in ocean areas of the world map the precise "at sea" locations of all U.S. and NATO military vessels, tracking with precision every change those ships made as they moved through the oceans of the globe. Simulated as miniature red lights in ocean areas of the world map were all the known "at sea" positions of Soviet military vessels, military vessels belonging to Soviet Bloc nations, and military vessels belonging to navies of other nations said to be hostile to the U.S. and its allies. The tiny red lights that burned steady represented ships that had been identified. Those that pulsated represented ships that were being correlated by physical characteristics to a host of intelligence data gathered worldwide and channeled to the war room in Washington.

In a generously allocated area along starboard, at the most forward part of the control room, was the *Trident*'s Systems Aggregate Monitoring computer. SAM, as the Navy had nicknamed the device, was responsible for operating and monitoring all vital stations throughout the submarine. SAM's biggest job was operating and monitoring the captain's command console, which was a central portion of the computer's housing. Standing upright atop SAM's center module, the command console had tiers of four-inch-square repeater indicators set on a forty-five-degree angle at eye level, furnishing the captain with a readout on all of the submarine's vitals at a glance. Atop the captain's command console was a thirty-inch-square viewing screen, which served as SAM's communication link with the captain. A computerized typewriter keyboard allowed the captain to talk to SAM.

When he had first come aboard to take command of the Navy's new pride and joy, Captain Jack Bentsen was in awe of the *Trident*'s control room. He immediately regarded it as a technological masterpiece, a majesty of undersea voyaging. His initial love for the new and highly sophisticated submarine had steadily intensified during the two months he had been aboard, leaving him with a secret desire to spend the rest of his Navy career with her, despite his occasional annoyance with SAM.

Bentsen was a wiry man who stood just under five feet nine and looked like the Navy's exemplification of what a submariner's physical condition ought to be at all times. He kept his thinning blond hair styled in a crew cut, and with his meticulously close-shaven face he looked out of place around his predominantly bearded and longish-haired crew, who took advantage of the new Navy's tolerance of the latest male mod appearance. Bentsen's deep blue eyes were alert and powerful. The crow's-feet siding the sockets of his eyes and the gullied wrinkles across the top of his forehead suggested he had a permanent frown. But the wrinkles were not signs of age or disposition, but rather indications of the persistent pressure of his job.

Standing in front of the command console, Bentsen fit the role perfectly, wearing Navy-issue officer's khakis that were neatly pressed with regulation creases in the pants legs and directly through the center of his shirt breast pockets. Cocked slightly to the right side of his head was a navy blue baseball cap, the peak of which was gold embroidered. Above the peak on the front of the cap were the letters *Co*, which along with the gleaming captain's eagles on the collar of his shirt told everyone aboard at a glance that he was the *Trident*'s commanding officer. He was both loved and respected by his men as a well-seasoned submariner, a veteran officer with over sixteen years of service, eight of which he served as a submarine skipper.

The *Trident*'s passive sonar was scrutinizing the undersea and ocean's surface for miles around the submarine, listening for engine sounds coming from another submarine or ship. But there were no sounds of man-made quality to report. Working in conjunction with listening sonar, active sonar was electronically probing the same areas to make contact with solid forms. Suddenly a return pinging indicated a submerged mass was ahead of the *Trident*.

SAM was the first to respond by triggering a gong that sounded like an airline stewardess's call button. The gong brought Bentsen's eyes up to the viewing screen at once as line after line of information raced across it.

```
ATTENTION:.................................................
APPROACHING SUBMERGED MID-ATLANTIC RIDGE............
SURFACE FORMATION: AZORES..............................
PLOTTED CROSSING: AZORES SUBTERRANEAN PLATEAU ......
BEARING: TWO-SEVEN-ZERO.................................
RANGE: TWENTY MILES ......................................
ELEVATION BELOW SEA LEVEL: FOUR HUNDRED FEET ........
PRESENT DEPTH BELOW SEA LEVEL: SIX HUNDRED FEET ......
RECOMMEND ASCENDING TO THREE HUNDRED FEET, BSL.....
URGENT:...................................................
```

```
APPROACHING DETECTION RANGE OF AZORES, ASW . . . . . . . . . .
RECOMMEND SECURING ACTIVE SONAR . . . . . . . . . . . . . . . . . . . . . .
RECOMMEND ENGAGING SONAR AVOIDANCE . . . . . . . . . . . . . . . .
RECOMMEND RIGGING FOR QUIET RUNNING . . . . . . . . . . . . . . . .
END . . . . . . . . . . . . . . . . . . . . . . . . . . . . . . . . . . . . . . . . . . . . . . . . . . . . .
```

As quickly as SAM signed off, the active sonarman reported aloud, "Submerged mass. Bearing, two-seven-zero. Range, twenty miles."

Commander Harris, the *Trident*'s executive officer, was next to report on the submerged mass. A muscular black man in his late forties with handsome chiseled features that closely resembled those of the movie star, Sidney Poitier, Harris raised his deep brown eyes up from the plotting table's simulation of the ocean's floor. "It's the Ridge, Skipper."

Bentsen pressed the erase button on the computer's keyboard and SAM's viewing screen display dissolved at once. "I know. SAM just told me." He moved away from the command console and joined Harris at the plotting table. "You've taken over the command console enough times during the maiden voyage, George. Ever get the feeling that SAM's constant reminders and recommendations have some shortcomings built into the computer's design that the Navy failed to anticipate?"

"Sort of a feeling like, with SAM aboard, who the hell needs us?" Harris offered.

"Right. I sometimes wonder if I'm originating orders for the crew or merely relaying SAM's orders. What I really resent in SAM's design," he went on, "is that we could become overly dependent on it. Then all we'd need during a crisis is to have a computer malfunction, leaving us with no time to take evasive action."

"It worries me, too, Skipper," Harris said.

Bentsen nodded, then regarded CIC. "Secure active sonar. Engage sonar avoidance." Looking back at Harris, he said, "SAM recommends that we cross the Azores Plateau at a depth setting of three hundred feet. I'm for giving Azores ASW a sporting chance to defy our sonar avoidance if they can. After all, that's what our orders call for. Let's skim the tops of the Azores submerged detection towers at, say . . . three hundred fifty feet, George."

Harris glanced at the simulator's depth-sounding digital display module set along one edge of the plotting table. "Right, Skipper. That should put their listening microphones right under our keel. It'll be a good practice run for when we penetrate our own ASW in home waters."

Bentsen nodded decisively. "When was the last time you heard from the engine room about that electrical short circuit SAM reported to us?"

Harris glanced at his wristwatch. "About a half hour ago."

Bentsen returned to the command console and picked up the control room phone. He pressed a button that automatically connected him with the engine room. After a brief pause, a crackly voice that he knew to be the engineering chief finally answered. "How are things going with your brownout condition, Chief?" he asked.

"We're still tracing through schematics to find the source of the trouble, Skipper," Chief Brooks reported.

"Has the Marine Dynamics engineering tech rep gotten there yet?" Bentsen asked.

"Aye, aye, Skipper," Brooks returned. "Mr. Hobart is tracing through the wiring diagrams now."

"Well, keep me informed, Chief," Bentsen ordered. "I want the engine room back on normal lighting as quickly as possible." After returning the phone to its cradle, Bentsen picked up the PA system microphone and keyed on. "Hear this. This is the captain speaking. We are about to cross over Azores ASW range. Rig for quiet running. Refrain from making any excessive noises about the decks. That is all."

Bentsen's announcement was Nelson Hobart's cue to make his planned exit. He drew a circle in pencil around some electrical schematic symbols on the wiring diagram, as though he had just come upon a hint of where the trouble might be. Getting Chief Brooks's attention, he said, "This has to be the area of concentration, Chief. I suggest that you make a continuity reading with your test meter on these two electrical bus bars first. If they check out okay, then check these four junction boxes for continuity. If you strike out there as well, then I'm afraid you're going to have to resort to troubleshooting wiring trunks for a short or break."

"Christ! I hope we don't narrow it down to tracing through a bunch of wiring trunks," Brooks said sourly. "We might still be looking for the short circuit when we get back to home port."

"I think you'll find the problem in one of the bus bars or J-boxes, Chief," Hobart said, knowing he was right. Expecting that Chief

Brooks and his men would be kept busy for at least an hour, he moved away from the workbench. "I'll be up in the control room if you need me for anything else, Chief."

"Thanks for lending a hand, Mr. Hobart," Brooks said with a sigh of relief. "If it hadn't been for you, we'd have had to tear into every damn electrical device in the engine room to find the failure. It's amazing how you were able to read through those wiring diagrams so easily."

"There's no real trick to it, Chief," Hobart said. "I was in charge of putting most of these systems aboard when the *Trident* was under construction."

"I'm sure glad Marine Dynamics chose you to come along on the maiden voyage as the builder's liaison to the Navy. I'm buying you a round of drinks when we get back to home base."

"I'll look forward to that," Hobart said, returning the chief's smile. He moved over to the engine room's forward hatch and undogged it. After passing through, he dogged it shut again in compliance with ship's watertight integrity procedures. Heading forward along a well-lighted and carpeted passageway, he passed several repair shops and some living compartments allocated to the engineering department. At the end of the passageway was the dogged-closed aft hatch of Sherwood Forest, the *Trident*'s missile room. Repeating watertight integrity procedures he passed through the hatch and greeted the officers and crewmen manning the missile room. He glanced up at the twenty-four battleship-gray missile tubes towering through four full decks, forming two uniform rows of twelve on either side of a carpeted walkway.

Hobart exited Sherwood Forest through the forward hatch. A short passageway brought him to the dogged-closed rear hatch of the control room. Outside the control room a steel ladder climbed steeply to an overhead hatch, which was that part of the submarine's emergency access to the conning tower deck. Unobserved, Hobart scurried up the ladder, through the overhead hatch, and into the dimly lit conning. Ahead lay another deck hatch that led down to the control room. In its dogged-shut position his presence in the conning would go unobserved by anyone manning that vital compartment.

As he moved forward in the conning and passed around the periscope housings, Hobart felt the sensation of the *Trident*'s ascent in the sea. After locating a mechanic's inspection and repair access panel set about midway up the conning tower's inside bulkhead, he removed a screwdriver from one of his jump suit pockets, already crammed with a selection of commonly used tools. Eight screws held the access panel in place, and after they were removed, the panel opened like a door and hung by its lower hinge. Inside the panel was one of SAM's sound-sensing probes, a small microphone that would register any excessive noises should an electrical or mechanical device in that area manifest a malfunction. Amidst the other devices he found the port diving plane actuator and positioned his screwdriver on the actuator's mechanical linkage tension adjustment screw. He waited.

Within a few minutes the actuator hummed softly as the *Trident*'s diving planes were being returned to their neutral position. Hobart felt the submarine's incline diminish as the *Trident* settled evenly on its fore and aft axis in the sea. He knew the diving planes would be used again when the submarine completed its crossing over the Mid-Atlantic Ridge and made its descent again to its preferred cruising depth. He tightened the tension screw to its fullest setting, closed the access panel door, and replaced the mounting screws.

Commander Harris looked up from the plotting table when Hobart entered the control room. "Good evening, Mr. Hobart."

Bentsen heard Harris greet Hobart. Without taking his eyes off the command console's repeater indicators he asked, "How are the men doing with that short circuit in the control room, Mr. Hobart?"

Hobart stepped over to the command console. "I've managed to narrow down the probabilities to either a bus bar or J-box. I expect they'll have the problem corrected and will be back on normal lighting within the hour, Captain."

"Fine. Thanks," Bentsen said, then looked up at the viewing screen as SAM's gong sounded.

```
ATTENTION: . . . . . . . . . . . . . . . . . . . . . . . . . . . . . . . . . . . . . . . . . . .
CLEAR OF AZORES ASW DETECTION RANGE . . . . . . . . . . . . . . . . . . .
RECOMMEND SECURING SONAR AVOIDANCE . . . . . . . . . . . . . . . . . .
RECOMMEND ENGAGING ACTIVE SONAR . . . . . . . . . . . . . . . . . . . . . .
RECOMMEND DESCENDING TO CRUISE DEPTH . . . . . . . . . . . . . . . .
END . . . . . . . . . . . . . . . . . . . . . . . . . . . . . . . . . . . . . . . . . . . . . . . . . .
```

Bentsen regarded the propulsion and maneuvering stations across the room. "Take us down to six hundred feet. Maintain course two-seven-zero. Ahead two-thirds." He glanced over at CIC next. "Secure sonar avoidance. Engage active sonar."

As quickly as Bentsen's orders to descend had been obeyed, SAM's gong brought Bentsen's eyes back to the viewing screen.

```
ATTENTION:.....................................................
BREACH OF QUIET RUNNING EXISTS ...........................
MECHANICAL/ELECTRICAL MALFUNCTION APPARENT .........
LOCATION OF DISTURBANCE: SENSORS, ONE-ONE-NINE &
ONE-TWO-SEVEN ...............................................
FRAME: P-2. COMPARTMENT: AC-0102: P-2-AC-0102 ............
INVESTIGATE AT ONCE .........................................
END ..........................................................
```

"Now what?" Bentsen said in a tone of agitation.

"May I, Captain?" Hobart asked as he gestured to the computer keyboard. He was given an approving nod. He typed instructions to SAM, and after a few moments, SAM's gong sounded again.

```
ATTENTION:.....................................................
LOCATION: P-2-AC-0102 DEFINED AS: PORTSIDE OF
SHIP, CONNING DECK, ACCESSORIES COMPARTMENT 0102.
PROFILE ILLUSTRATION OF HULL FOLLOWS ...................
```

Bentsen and Hobart locked their eyes on the viewing screen as it displayed a profile diagram of the *Trident*'s hull from stem to stern. In the area of the conning tower, where the diving planes wing the conning, a tiny green light was pulsating to illustrate the exact location of the disturbance.

"It's up in the conning," Hobart offered. "Since you've just used diving planes, I'd say one of the diving plane components is causing the breach of quiet running."

"I'm not that familiar with SAM's functions as a mechanical and electrical troubleshooter, Mr. Hobart," Bentsen said. "Can SAM tell us exactly what's causing the noise violation?"

"I'm afraid we don't have that function programmed into SAM, Captain. It can isolate the disturbance to an exact area where some mechanical and electrical devices are located, but it can't tell us precisely which device is causing the problem. The troubleshooting is left up to us."

Bentsen reached for the control room phone. "I'll get Chief Brooks up here to look around in the conning for the problem."

Hobart grabbed Bentsen's hand to stop him. "No need to bother

Chief Brooks, Captain. He's got his hands full with that electrical failure. As long as I'm here, I'll go up to the conning and see if I can locate the problem, maybe even fix it. I may need to have the planes operated for a functional testing to help me troubleshoot for the noise. I'll take a headset up to the conning with me so I can communicate with you from up there.''

Bentsen removed a spare headset from the center module of the command console and handed it to Hobart. After watching Hobart swirl up the spiral staircase to the conning's hatch, he put on his command console headset and waited to hear Hobart's voice.

Up in the conning, Hobart found a wall jack and plugged in the headset, then slipped it on. He quickly removed the access panel screws again and allowed the panel to drop open. With the port diving plane actuator in view once more, he keyed his headset mike. ''Are you there, Captain?'' He was acknowledged. ''Run the planes through the same ascent setting you called for before.'' The diving plane actuator growled loudly as soon as it came alive.

SAM's gong sounded in immediate response to use of the planes and Bentsen looked up at the viewing screen for SAM's reaction.

```
ATTENTION: . . . . . . . . . . . . . . . . . . . . . . . . . . . . . . . . . . . . . . . . . . . . . . . . . . . .
BREACH OF QUIET RUNNING EXISTS . . . . . . . . . . . . . . . . . . . . . . . . . . .
MECHANICAL/ELECTRICAL MALFUNCTION APPARENT . . . . . . . . .
LOCATION OF DISTURBANCE: SENSORS, ONE-ONE-NINE &
ONE-TWO-SEVEN . . . . . . . . . . . . . . . . . . . . . . . . . . . . . . . . . . . . . . . . . . . . . . .
FRAME: P-2. COMPARTMENT: AC-0102: P-2-AC-0102 . . . . . . . . . . . . .
INVESTIGATE AT ONCE . . . . . . . . . . . . . . . . . . . . . . . . . . . . . . . . . . . . . . . .
END . . . . . . . . . . . . . . . . . . . . . . . . . . . . . . . . . . . . . . . . . . . . . . . . . . . . . . . . . . . .
```

''SAM is still registering a breach of quiet running, Mr. Hobart,'' Bentsen said into his headset mike.

''Yes. I heard a loud growling sound when you used planes,'' Hobart returned. ''Run the planes back to neutral, Captain. Please tell the planesman to pull out the power supply circuit breaker and secure his station. I'll be right down to explain what I've found out.'' He heard the actuator growl loudly again, knew SAM was repeating an alert display on the viewing screen in response to the sound-laden motion. When the actuator fell silent, he placed his screwdriver on the tension screw and backed off the taut setting he had applied to it before.

As Hobart was stepping down to the periscope deck from the

spiral staircase, Bentsen returned his headset to the command console and anxiously asked, "Did you locate the problem? Were you able to fix it?"

Hobart climbed down the steps from the periscope deck. Rejoining Bentsen at the command console, he answered, "Yes to locating the source of the noise. No to getting it fixed at the moment. I thought the problem was the diving plane actuator. Unfortunately, that wasn't it," he lied. "Had it been, our troubles would be over. I've isolated the source of the noise to the diving plane slaving servo. It sounded to me like the slaving servo's clutching mechanism is out of adjustment. If so, it'll be an easy matter to rectify with a screwdriver. But I'm afraid we're going to have to surface to accomplish that adjustment."

"Surface?" Bentsen was surprised.

"Yes, Captain," Hobart replied firmly. "Our only access to the slaving servo is from outside the pressure hull. There's a watertight mechanic's inspection and repair panel on the side wall of the sail, just about eye level up from the diving plane wing. May I suggest that I handle the repair? The slaving servo's clutching mechanism is quite delicate. Also, keep the planes secured. If they're used again, it might cause the unit to burn out, necessitating a replacement of the device."

"I'm for avoiding additional mechanical problems, Mr. Hobart," Bentsen said firmly. "We can't have the damn thing breaching our quiet running, so since you're sure that's the only way the problem can be resolved, I'll get us topside right away." He picked up the bitch box mike. "Hear this. This is the captain speaking. We are going to surface for a minor repair on the diving planes. All personnel not required to assist with the handling are to remain below decks while we are surfaced." He paused, then keyed on again. "Special sea, anchor, and handling detail report to the control room on the double." He returned the mike to the console, then depressed the Klaxon horn, sending its amplified *oogaa* sound reverberating throughout the submarine. Facing propulsion and maneuvering, he said, "Blow auxiliary ballast. Bring us up to periscope depth. Do not—repeat—*do not* use planes!"

Bentsen typed a request for surface conditions on the keyboard, then glanced up at the viewing screen for SAM's response as the computer's gong sounded.

ATTENTION:. . . . . . . . . . . . . . . . . . . . . . . . . . . . . . . . . . . . . . . . . . . . . . . .
SOURCE OF INFORMATION: U.S. WEATHER SATELLITE. . . . . . . . .

```
SURFACE CONDITIONS FOLLOW.............................
SKY CLEAR ........................................
FULL MOON OVER EASTERN HORIZON .......................
AIR TEMPERATURE: SIXTY-EIGHT DEGREES, FAHRENHEIT .....
PREVAILING WIND OUT OF THE SOUTH AT FIVE KNOTS .......
SURFACE WATER TEMPERATURE: FIFTY-TWO DEGREES, F .....
TWO TO THREE-FOOT SWELLS .............................
PREVAILING CURRENTS: WESTERLY AT TWO KNOTS ..........
END .................................................
```

Bentsen turned to Hobart. "Well, at least it's a nice night up on the surface for making the repair. However, the full moon will play down on us like a spotlight. I want to avoid being seen by any high seas traffic while we're topside. How long will this take you, Mr. Hobart?"

"No more than twenty minutes, Captain."

Bentsen climbed the steps to the periscope deck and positioned himself by number one periscope. "Switch to night vision lighting," he ordered. A master switch immediately changed the control room's white fluorescent lighting to red lamps.

Hobart felt the submarine ascending in the sea. He was elated as he looked around the control room and saw the crewmen meticulously preparing the submarine for surfacing. He smiled. It had worked.


## Chapter Two

For a brief moment the full moon's glow illuminated a faint wake on the sea, then the *Trident*'s periscope disappeared beneath the slow-rolling swells. Moments later the sleek conning tower rose to the surface, pulling the diving planes out of the water. Just aft of the bridge deck an electrical humming sound escaped out over the quiet sea as two radio antennas telescoped up to the night sky. A thick mast rose skyward after them and immediately started probing the heavens for its communications satellite. Behind the mast a dome door slid open and released a second, less audible humming sound as a radar scanner climbed out of hiding and instantly began its rotating vigilance of the surface and above.

Engulfed in a frenzy of foamy, hissing white water, the submarine's massive dull black body broke surface, sending seawater rushing down its swollen rounded sides. It brought its tall trim tail up some five hundred feet astern of the conning tower. In another moment the hissing noise stopped and the U.S.S. *Trident* settled on the surface in neutral buoyancy.

The bridge hatch undogged and lifted open, sending a gush of remaining seawater splashing down on two lookouts standing on the bridge ladder inside the hatchway. They climbed out and scurried to their assigned perches on port and starboard above the bridge deck. After opening caps that kept their wall jacks waterproof, they plugged in their headsets and reported that their positions were manned and ready. Acknowledged, they began playing their infrared night vision binoculars on the sky and sea surrounding the submarine.

Bentsen came to the bridge and took up his position at the forward bridge wall. He opened a watertight compartment containing switches and buttons, then plugged his headset into a jack inside the compartment. He keyed his mike. "Control room from bridge. How do you read me, over?"

Commander Harris was at the captain's command console, studying the ranks of repeater indicators for the submarine's vitals, when he heard Bentsen's voice come over his headset. He keyed his mike as he continued his scrutiny. "Bridge from control room, I read you loud and clear, over."

Keying his mike, Bentsen ordered, "Slow to one-third. Send the tech rep and engineering party to the bridge."

Two engineering department crewmen scrambled up to the bridge, and after rendering a hand salute that was returned by a faint nod, they joined Bentsen at the port bridge wall. One crewman switched on a portable spotlight he was carrying, then shined it down the conning wall to illuminate the diving plane. The other man was carrying a safety harness and nylon lifeline. He hooked one end of the lifeline to a stationary cleat atop the bridge wall, gave it a few hearty tugs to insure it was secured to the cleat, then stood by as Nelson Hobart's hatless head appeared in the bridge hatchway.

Hobart struggled through the hatchway, the zippered pockets of his jump suit bulging oddly with tools and other equipment. He took a deep breath of the fresh sea air and moved over to the others. "SAM was right, Captain," he said casually. "It is a beautiful night up here."

"Beautiful indeed," Bentsen returned without looking up from the diving plane. He examined the dripping wet handgrips that descended down the conning wall to form a steep ladder to the diving plane. "Everything is still quite wet down there. Be careful climbing down the handgrips."

"I will, Captain," Hobart assured him as he strapped the safety harness snugly around his thin waist. He accepted the other end of the nylon lifeline and connected it to the front coupling of the harness. After giving the line several tugs, he said, "I'm ready to go down."

With one crewman playing the portable spotlight down on the shiny handgrips, the other crewman assisted Bentsen in getting Hobart over the bridge wall. "We'll keep the lifeline taut so you won't fall far if you do slip," Bentsen said.

Hobart climbed down carefully. Reaching the bottom handgrip, he carefully stepped down onto the plane and tested his footing, then trusted all his weight to its surface. "I'm down. I'm leaving the handgrips."

"Are you going to be all right?" Bentsen shouted down to him.

"I'll be fine. It looks worse than it really is," he said as he walked toward the trailing edge of the plane. Finding the watertight access hatch that accommodated the diving plane slaving servo, he hugged the conning tower wall and began undogging it. It was some ten inches in diameter and crabbed out on its inside hinge when he pulled it open. He folded it back against the conning wall, out of the way, then squinted up at the bright beam of the spotlight shining down on him from the bridge. "You'll have to kill that spotlight. It's blinding me. I have my own light to work with." He removed a wide-beam flashlight from a clip sewn to one side of his jump suit.

Bentsen nodded and the crewman's spotlight switched off. "Be ready to switch your light back on if he gets into any trouble down there," he ordered, then looked back down at the surface of the plane. The submarine's conning tower cast a shadow over Hobart as he hugged the conning wall, depriving Bentsen of a good view of Hobart going about his work.

Hobart could see the faces of Bentsen and the crewmen staring down at him curiously. Not wanting an audience while he worked, he set his flashlight down on the plane and switched it on, then played its bright beam up to the watchful eyes on the bridge. He saw their faces turn away. On one wall inside the slaving servo's access compartment was a light switch, which he switched on to illuminate the compartment. Instantly, a yellow beam of light spilled out to the surface of the plane, then was smothered when he positioned himself in front of the hatch opening. He peered inside the compartment and saw the huge slaving servo, which was accompanied by one of SAM's sound sensors, and ignored them both. As an added precaution, just in case anyone on the bridge could still see what he was doing, he took out a screwdriver from one of his knee pockets and inserted it into the compartment. As though making some adjustments, he staged turning motions for a few moments, then withdrew the screwdriver and put it back in his pocket. He picked up his flashlight and switched it off, then moved over to the handgrips and climbed onto them. Looking up at the bridge, he shouted, "The slaving servo's tension screw was quite loose, Captain. That may have been causing the noise problem SAM detected. I've tightened it, but I'll have to lock it in position when I'm through, so it won't loosen again. Before I do, let's run the planes through a functional test cycling and see if SAM still repeats its breach-of-quiet-running display."

Bentsen keyed his mike. "Control room from bridge. Cycle the planes and advise me if you get a reaction from SAM."

"Control room, aye," Harris said from the command console. He looked across the control room to the planesman. "Cycle planes through a full ascent, but standby to shut them down if I give the word."

"Aye, aye, sir," the planesman returned as he pressed the power supply circuit breaker. He actuated the planes, then watched his indicator needle duplicating their motion. When they indicated full ascent, he called across the room, "Planes in full ascent position, sir."

Harris waited an extra moment in case SAM had a delayed reaction, but the viewing screen didn't respond. He keyed his mike. "Bridge from control room, no display from SAM."

"Bridge, aye," Bentsen returned, then looked down at Hobart. "It seems your adjustment solved the problem, Mr. Hobart. There was no response from SAM that time."

"Fine, Captain," Hobart called back as he looked at the planes pitched up toward the sky. "I think cycling them through a full descent will be a waste of time. Have the planes returned to neutral, and if SAM still doesn't respond, I'll finish my work down here."

"Will do," Bentsen replied, then keyed his mike. "Return planes to neutral and leave them in that position, George."

"Aye, aye, Skipper," Harris said. Looking across the room again, he ordered, "Planes to neutral and secure your station."

The planesman watched the indicator needle as he actuated the planes. When the needle reached the center mark, he shut the planes off and reported, "Planes in neutral, station secured, sir."

Harris had his eyes locked on the viewing screen, but there was no response from SAM again. Keying his mike at once, he said happily, "Not a peep out of SAM that time either, Skipper. Planes secured."

"Bridge, aye," Bentsen acknowledged in a pleased tone. He looked down at Hobart. "Planes in neutral, station is secured. There was no breach of quiet running displayed that time either, Mr. Hobart. You've done it. Thank you."

Hobart was already stepping off the handgrips in seeing the planes straight and level again. "I'll be a few more minutes at locking the tension screw in that position, then I'll be up, Captain." He set his flashlight down on the surface of the plane and switched it on. After readjusting its bright beam to shine up to the bridge, he unzipped the front of his jump suit and removed a cylindrical-shaped device. It was six inches long and about two inches in diameter. On one end were two electrical feed leads with quick-connect clips attached to the ends of the wires. On the body of the device was an adhesive strip that was covered with protective paper. He began peeling off the paper to expose the adhesive for mounting inside the compartment.

Inside the control room, Harris was about to leave the command console and make his routine rounds when a loud, repetitious beeping sound, like that of a vibrant telephone busy signal, got his attention. It brought his and every crewmen's eyes in the room to the viewing screen at once as SAM began displaying information with urgency.

ATTENTION: . . . . . . . . . . . . . . . . . . . . . . . . . . . . . . . . . . . . . . . . . . . . . . . . . . . . . . .
. . . . . . . . . . . . . . . . . . . . . . . RED ALERT . . . . . . . . . . . . . . . . . . . . . . .

As quickly as the display was written across the viewing screen, it began flashing off and on rapidly in unison with the beeping sound. Harris keyed his mike as the beeping sound and flashing display continued. "Bridge from control room, we have a red alert advise and the display does not indicate it is a drill."

Bentsen frowned on hearing Harris's report. Of all the times to pick, he thought, then moved over to the front bridge wall and pressed the GQ alarm button. Immediately the Klaxon horn's *oogaa* sound blared intermittently with the general alarm bell, reverberating throughout the submarine and out over the topside decks.

Hobart had just finished peeling the protective paper off the device and was about to install it when the unexpected blaring of the GQ alarm crashed into his ears. Its sudden interruption nearly caused him to drop the device into the sea.

"General quarters! General quarters!" Bentsen shouted to the engineers and lookouts nearby. "We are at Red Alert! This is not a drill! Repeat! This is not a drill! All hands man your battle stations! All hands man your battle stations!" He keyed his mike and called into it, "Control room from bridge! Retract antennas! Prepare to dive!" He looked down at Hobart, squinting as his eyes met the bright beam of Hobart's flashlight. "Close everything up, Mr. Hobart! We have to dive at once!"

Hobart was stunned for a moment. In confusion he glanced at the device he was about to install, wondering if it had caused the red alert. It was impossible, he reassured himself, realizing he hadn't even hooked the device up yet. With professional instinct, he quickly placed the device inside the hatch and secured its adhesive side to the floor of the compartment. He took hold of the device's electrical leads and attached them to the compartment light switch. The connection immediately gave the device life. With his task done, he left the compartment light on so it would continually feed electric power to the device, then closed and dogged the access hatch shut. He picked up his flashlight and hurried over to the handgrips, then scurried up to the bridge.

"Is everything secured below?" Bentsen asked as he assisted the crewmen in getting Hobart over the bridge wall.

"Yes, Captain," Hobart said.

Bentsen shouted, "Clear the bridge. Now!" His command sent the two crewmen and Hobart scampering through the bridge hatch. "Lookouts below!" he ordered next, then watched them hurry down from their perches and follow through the hatch after the others. He looked at the top of the conning tower to see that the antennas had been retracted and the dome closed. Moving over to the forward bridge wall, he shut off the GQ alarm, then depressed the Klaxon horn button three times. As its *oogaa* sound blared below decks and out over the quiet sea, he shouted into his mike, "Dive! Dive! Dive!" With a quick tug on his headset cord he disconnected it from the wall jack, then closed the watertight doors of the forward bridge wall compartment. He felt the submarine descending into the sea as he hurried over to the hatch. Without delay he jumped down onto the bridge ladder, then pulled the hatch closed and dogged it shut. A red warning light inside the closed hatch turned to green at once, indicating the bridge hatch was battened down. He hurried down the bridge ladder to the conning deck, through its hatch, and finally down the spiral staircase to the control room.

Crewmen were still arriving to man their GQ stations in the control room when Bentsen stepped down from the periscope deck. He immediately sensed the tense atmosphere looming over the room. It was written on every face: confusion, uncertainty, fear. They had turned out for red alerts before, but he could tell by their solemn stares as he walked past them that they knew this time it was different.

Bentsen joined Commander Harris at the command console. "Challenge SAM for verification of the red alert, George," he said.

Harris requested information over the keyboard and SAM speedily wrote new lines of information across the viewing screen.

```
ATTENTION: . . . . . . . . . . . . . . . . . . . . . . . . . . . . . . . . . . . . . . .
. . . . . . . . . . . . . . . PRIMARY CHANNEL-VERIFIED . . . . . . . . . . . . . . .
. . . . . . . . . . . . . . . . . PRIMARY PHASE-VERIFIED . . . . . . . . . . . . . . . .
. . . . . . . . . . . . . . . . . PRIMARY CODE-VERIFIED . . . . . . . . . . . . . . . . .
. . . . . . . . . . . . . . . . . . . . . CONDITION-RED . . . . . . . . . . . . . . . . . . . .
. . . . . . . . . . . . . . . . . . . . . . PRIORITY-ONE . . . . . . . . . . . . . . . . . . . .
STRATEGIC DEFENSE ALERT: . . . . . . . . . . . . . . . . . . . . . . . . . . . . .
. . . . . . . . . . . SET CONDITION FACTOR-SDA17-ALPHA . . . . . . . . . . . .
. . . . . . . . . . . . . . . . . . . . . . . . ISQ-MISSILES . . . . . . . . . . . . . . . . . . . . . . .
```

Bentsen turned to Harris and said stiffly, "Exec, you are authorized to go to my cabin and retrieve the strategic defense alert attaché case from my safe. Muster two armed Marines to escort you back to the control room once you have the case."

"Aye, aye, Captain." Harris headed out of the control room through the forward hatch, keeping his face expressionless.

"Ballast, take us down to missile depth," Bentsen called into his mike. He was acknowledged, then keyed on again. "Missile fire control from command, we are ordered to ISQ, missiles. Purge and flood all tubes."

At the master fire control panel, the senior missile officer regarded SAM's instructions on the missile room's repeater viewing screen. "Roger that," he said into his mike. "ISQ, missiles. Purging all tubes now." He nodded to a junior officer, who actuated a series of toggle switches under a row of twenty-four steady burning green lights. Immediately the green lights went off and twenty-four amber lights under them came on and began pulsating rapidly, causing SAM's gong to respond with a viewing screen display.

ATTENTION:. . . . . . . . . . . . . . . . . . . . . . . . . . . . . . . . . . . . . . . . . . . . .
. . . . . . . . . . . . . . . . . .PURGING IN PROGRESS . . . . . . . . . . . . . . . . . . .

Moments later, the pulsating amber lights burned steady and SAM's gong sounded again.

ATTENTION:. . . . . . . . . . . . . . . . . . . . . . . . . . . . . . . . . . . . . . . . . . . . .
. . . . . . . . . . . . . . . . . .PURGING-DENOTED . . . . . . . . . . . . . . . . . . . .

"All tubes purged," the senior missile fire control officer reported into his mike. "Flooding tubes now," he added, and a similar procedure was gone through. When SAM's verification appeared on the screen, the senior fire control officer keyed his mike. "Command from missile fire control, all tubes flooded. We are at ISQ, missiles."

Studying the viewing screen display in the control room, Bentsen keyed his mike. "Roger that. Standby to arm missiles." He was acknowledged.

"Depth, two hundred feet, sir," the ballastman called into his mike.

"Neutral buoyancy," Bentsen said in response. "All stop. Rudder amidships. Keep active sonar operating," he called over to CIC. "But stand by to secure active and set sonar avoidance when I give the word."

Commander Harris entered, carrying a black leather attaché case. He was accompanied by a middle-aged Marine sergeant and a young Marine lance corporal, both of whom had holstered military .45 automatics strapped to their hips. Harris posted the Marine sergeant in the front of the control room, near the forward hatch, and the young lance corporal in the rear of the room near the aft hatch. At the command console Harris placed the attaché case down on its ledge. He watched Bentsen dial the combination tumblers and open the case.

Bentsen thumbed through several large manila envelopes, all of which had bold red printing across the face of them. He selected an envelope coded: TOP SECRET, CONDITION FACTOR SDA-17-ALPHA. After breaking the wax seal on the back of it, he removed a computer keypunch card from inside and studied the coded notations on it. After showing the notations to Harris, he inserted the card into a scanning slot at the top of the command console, then joined Harris at the viewing screen.

    ATTENTION: . . . . . . . . . . . . . . . . . . . . . . . . . . . . . . . . . . . . . . . . . . .
        STRATEGIC DEFENSE ALERT:        SDA-17-ALPHA-DENOTED
    . . . . . . . . . . . . . . . . . . . . . . ARM MISSILES . . . . . . . . . . . . . . . . . . . . . . .

Bentsen and Harris took out their key rings and selected identical keys, then simultaneously inserted them into dual key slots at the base of the command console. They nodded to each other, then turned their keys to the right at the same time. The action dissolved the viewing screen display and immediately brought up new directives.

    ATTENTION: . . . . . . . . . . . . . . . . . . . . . . . . . . . . . . . . . . . . . . . . . . . . .
    . . . . . . . . . . . . . . . . MISSILE ARMING-DENOTED . . . . . . . . . . . . . . . .
    . . . . . . . . . . . . . . . . . . . . TARGETS  ASSIGNED . . . . . . . . . . . . . . . . . . . .

The huge world map was displaying numerous pulsating red lights, marking strategic targets in the Soviet Union and its Bloc nations. These lights were slightly larger than the steady burning red lights that located enemy vessels on the map.

Bentsen moved over to the world map and studied its pulsating red lights, then began mentally reciting the names of the cities that were targeted for annihilation. Moscow. Leningrad. Stalingrad. Odessa. Kiev. So many others, he weighed as he looked at the cities targeted in the Soviet Bloc nations. It seemed as though that part of the world was to become a void. Defense? he thought.

SAM's gong brought a new display on the viewing screen.

    ATTENTION: . . . . . . . . . . . . . . . . . . . . . . . . . . . . . . . . . . . . . . . . . . . . .
    . . . . . . . . . . . . . . TARGET  ALIGNMENTS-DENOTED . . . . . . . . . . . . .
    . . . . . . . . . . . . . . . . . . COMMENCE  COUNTDOWN . . . . . . . . . . . . . . . .

Looking over at the viewing screen display, Bentsen ordered, "Exec, set the elapsed time to fire missiles to minus ten minutes and advise missile fire control we are commencing countdown."

"Aye, aye, Skipper," Harris replied as he faced the elapsed-time clock on the command console. He adjusted the elapsed-time clock's digital display to read: 00:10.00. "Missile fire control from command, is your digital elapsed-time display monitor synchronized to minus ten minutes and holding?"

"Command from missile fire control, roger that. My display is holding at minus ten minutes to fire missiles."

Keying on again, Harris said, "This is command. Commencing countdown now." The elapsed time clock's digital display began subtracting seconds from the ten-minute setting. With the clock in motion SAM's gong sounded.

ATTENTION:......................................................
................COUNTDOWN IN PROGRESS.................
ELAPSED TIME TO FIRE MISSILES:...........................
...........MINUS NINE MINUTES, FIFTY SECONDS...........
....................COUNTING DOWN....................

Harris verified SAM's viewing screen time display. "Digital countdown synchronized with SAM," he called into his mike.

Across the room, active sonarman Peterson perked up in his seat as two giant blips suddenly appeared on his green-faced scope about twenty miles east of the *Trident*'s position. With seasoned eyes he watched the spread of white light move out from the center of the scope and make contact with the two blips. Using the dials on his digital display, he plotted them and determined they were subsurface contacts, flanking each other at about a thousand yards apart as they headed toward the *Trident*.

Seated next to Peterson, passive sonarman Rudges cupped his hands over his earphones in response to defined propeller sounds. He cranked some dials on his sound-detecting module and established that propeller noises were being generated from two subsurface sources. He looked over at passive sonarman Peterson and tapped him on the shoulder. "I'm picking up engine sounds from two sources," he said.

Peterson nodded, then keyed his headset mike. "Command from active sonar, monitoring two subsurface contacts. Bearing, zero-nine-zero. Range, thirty-nine thousand yards. Heading, two-seven-zero. Speed, forty knots and closing."

"Passive sonar, do you confirm?" Bentsen asked as he spun around to face the CIC stations.

"Command from passive," Rudges replied excitedly. "Confirming, sir. Picking up two separate sources of screw noises. Flanked and bearing, zero-nine-zero. Left flanking contact is twin screws. Right flanking contact is single screw. Submarines, sir. Depth, three hundred feet. Range, thirty-nine thousand yards. Heading, two-seven-zero. Speed, forty knots and closing."

SAM's gong sounded in the background, prompting Harris to look up at the viewing screen.

```
ATTENTION:.................................................
.....MONITORING TWO SUBSURFACE SONAR CONTACTS .....
...............DEPTH: THREE HUNDRED FEET...............
..................BEARING: 090 DEGREES ..................
..........RANGE: THIRTY-NINE THOUSAND YARDS ..........
.......HEADING: TWO HUNDRED SEVENTY DEGREES ........
...................SPEED: FORTY KNOTS ...................
DO YOU REQUIRE IDENTIFICATION DATAM ??????????????????????
```

"SAM confirms the sonar contacts, Skipper," Harris called into his mike. "Shall we challenge for idents?"

"Affirmative," Bentsen replied, then studied the two miniature pulsating red lights flanking each other that just appeared on the world map in the *Trident*'s vicinity.

Harris typed information to SAM over the keyboard, then looked up as the gong sounded.

```
ATTENTION:.................................................
............CORRELATING INTELLIGENCE DATUM ............
........................STAND BY ........................
```

"Standing by with SAM for idents," Harris reported. "We are at minus seven minutes to fire missiles."

"Roger that," Bentsen replied. He glanced up at his targets for an instant, then faced the viewing screen as SAM's gong sounded.

```
ATTENTION:.................................................
........SONAR CONTACT IDENTIFICATION FOLLOWS........
............LEFT FLANKING CONTACT.................
NATIONALITY: SOVIET UNION ...........................
CLASS: DELTA, ICBM-SUBMARINE ...........................
DISPLACEMENT: NINE THOUSAND TONS.....................
```

```
POWERED: TWIN NUCLEAR-STEAM TURBINE ..................
SHIP'S S.H.P.: TWENTY-FOUR THOUSAND.....................
SPEED: FORTY KNOTS-SUBMERGED ...........................
........................ARMAMENT ........................
SIXTEEN ICBM-SINGLE WARHEAD MISSILES ..................
RANGE: FOUR THOUSAND NAUTICAL MILES...................
EIGHT TWENTY-ONE-INCH SUBROCKS.........................
TYPE: SURFACE-TO-AIR, NUCLEAR ...........................
RANGE: FOUR HUNDRED MILES ..............................
........................STAND BY ........................
```

The words *STAND BY* flashed on and off for a few seconds before being replaced by additional data.

```
ATTENTION:.....................................................
................RIGHT FLANKING CONTACT.................
NATIONALITY: SOVIET UNION ...............................
CLASS: LIMA, ATTACK, ANTISUBMARINE ....................
FURTHER DATUM, UNKNOWN ..............................
END .........................................................
```

"Secure active sonar," Bentsen ordered. "Set sonar avoidance. Passive sonar, keep me informed on the engine sounds you're monitoring."

Nelson Hobart stood in the rear of the control room. His face was drawn and pale. His armpits were moist, causing large stains to appear around those areas of his jump suit. He had absorbed all of SAM's viewing screen displays, silently wishing somehow SAM might be wrong about the red alert. He was terrified and he was sure that was obvious to everyone else in the room.

"Command from passive sonar," Rudges called into his headset mike.

"Command, aye," Bentsen replied.

"Contacts now separating, sir! Left flanking contact now bearing zero-eight-zero. Range, twenty-eight thousand yards. Heading two-nine-five. Depth, two hundred feet. Right flanking contact now bearing zero-nine-five. Range, twenty-six thousand yards. Heading two-five-five. Depth, one hundred fifty feet."

"Exec, assign sonar contacts as targets," Bentsen ordered. "Left flanking contact will be target one. Right flanking contact will be target two. Challenge the computer for a subrock strike evaluation."

"Aye, aye, Captain," Harris said, then typed Bentsen's orders on the input keyboard.

```
ATTENTION:......................................................
....................TARGETS  ASSIGNED ....................
STRIKE EFFECTIVITY .....................TARGET ONE: 100%
STRIKE EFFECTIVITY .........................TARGET TWO:
.................CANNOT BE DETERMINED .................
DO YOU REQUIRE A THREAT EVALUATION ??????????????????????
```

Harris keyed "AFFIRMATIVE" into the computer.

```
ATTENTION:......................................................
....................THREAT IMMINENT ....................
....................DESTROY AT ONCE ....................
```

The display began flashing on and off, holding Hobart spellbound for a moment. Simultaneously, he observed the elapsed-time clock: MINUS 05:40.

Bentsen keyed his mike. "Missile control from command."

"Missile control, aye."

"Sonar contacts one and two are now targets one and two. Arm subrocks one through four and flood tubes."

There was a hesitation as the fire control officer passed his eyes over the men in the missile room staring back at him nervously. He felt weak. Cold.

"Missile control," Bentsen shouted with urgency. "Acknowledge!"

"Missile control, aye. Arming subrocks one through four. Flooding subrock tubes," the fire control officer repeated almost mechanically.

```
ATTENTION:......................................................
....................SUBROCKS ARMED ....................
....................TARGETS  ALIGNED ....................
...............PREPARE TO FIRE SUBROCKS ................
```

Harris keyed his mike. "Minus four minutes to fire missiles."

"Adjust the world map to zoom in on grid F-eight-one-seven," Bentsen ordered.

Harris flicked several switches on the command console and the world map flickered for a moment, then focused on grid F-817, enlarging the entire area around the *Trident*'s position and the positions of the two Russian submarines.

"Missile control, stand by for verbal countdown to fire subrocks," Bentsen ordered.

"Missile control, aye," the fire control officer answered, then readied himself at the subrock fire control levers. He envisioned how once he pulled the firing levers the four subrocks would be fired from their tubes, rise to the surface and travel through the air. Once above their targets they would reenter the water and detonate their warheads.

Bentsen keyed his mike. "Missile control from command. Beginning countdown. Five, four, three, two, one. Fire subrocks!"

Without hesitation the fire control officer pulled down the four levers in succession, and four lights above the levers turned to green. "Command from missile control, subrocks one through four away, sir."

In the control room the viewing screen responded.

    ATTENTION:.....................................................
    .................SUBROCKS LAUNCHED ...................

All eyes in the control room saw the display on the viewing screen, then locked in on the world map and watched as four white dotted lines streaked out from the green light representing the *Trident*. The four electronic lines spread apart and headed speedily for their targets, two of them zeroing in on the left flanking target, while the other two attached themselves to the right flanking target.

Twenty seconds after their departure, the four white dotted lines reached their targets. The two red lights flickered, then disappeared off the map.

    ATTENTION:.....................................................
    ...................TARGETS DESTROYED....................
    ..............PROCEED WITH MISSILE LAUNCH ..............

Passive sonarman Rudges had heard a loud commotion over his earphones that lasted for brief moments, then there were no longer any sounds at all. He said into his headset mike, "Both contacts lost, sir."

"Roger that," Bentsen replied. "Exec, return the map to expanded view." He watched as the map's display changed, showing his strategic targets as small red lights, then SAM's gong drew his attention to the viewing screen.

```
ATTENTION:.....................................................
...........ELAPSED TIME TO LAUNCH MISSILES ............
................IS NOW MINUS ONE MINUTE................
...............PREPARE TO LAUNCH MISSILES ...............
```

"Missile control from command," Bentsen said into his mike.

"Missile control, aye."

"We are now at launch minus fifty seconds. At launch minus zero you will have verbal authorization from me to fire missiles. You will follow my verbal countdown at launch minus ten seconds. Acknowledge!"

"Missile control, acknowledging. Understand, will follow countdown at launch minus ten seconds."

"Affirmative," Bentsen replied, his eyes never leaving the elapsed-time display.

An eerie silence engulfed the control room as the last few seconds to fire missiles slowly ticked away. The men monitoring their control stations were experiencing the reality of a nuclear war for the first time. They had drilled for it many times before, but never really expected to be involved in one. They shared the same thoughts and emotions. What would happen after they launched their missiles? What had happened to begin with? Did the Russians attack us? Could we be attacking them first? They thought of children playing innocently in school playgrounds; of mothers holding their babies in their arms; of old people unsuspectingly sitting in parks, feeding pigeons; green trees full of singing birds; a bright sun, a warm breeze. There would be a brilliant flash of light, several times brighter than the sun as the missiles struck their targets. Then, there would be nothing at all.

```
ATTENTION:....................................................
...............LAUNCH MINUS TEN SECONDS...............
```

Bentsen keyed his mike and began the countdown. "Ten, nine . . ."

Below in the missile room, the missile fire control officer counted off the seconds with him. "Six, five . . ."

Nelson Hobart didn't have a headset on, but could see the seconds tick away on the command console clock. Three, two . . .

Bentsen's voice echoed in the room. "Fire missiles!"

In the missile room the fire control officer's sweaty hand gripped the revolver-shaped firing mechanism. He squeezed the trigger. He listened.

A moment passed and he and the other missilemen at their stations turned to stare dumbfounded at the forty-foot-high missile tubes standing silently in the aft section of the four-story missile room. Then, one by one, they turned and looked at each other, the tension leaving their faces. The thumping sensation of the missiles being launched in succession never occurred.

Hobart and the other men in the control room were startled when the computer began buzzing loudly.

```
    ATTENTION:.................................................
    .....STRATEGIC DEFENSE ALERT-17-ALPHA COMPLETED .....
    ...........ALL SIMULATED TARGETS DESTROYED ...........
    .................SECURE FROM ISQ MISSILES.................
    .......................WELL DONE ......................
SAFE VOYAGE HOME ...........................................
    ..........THE PRESIDENT OF THE UNITED STATES ...........
```

Bentsen ejected the computer disc and dropped it into the attaché case, closed the case, and spun the combination tumblers. He and Harris turned the missile-arming mechanism off and removed their keys. Immediately the strategic targets on the world map vanished. He said to Harris, "Exec, you may return the attaché case to my safe," and smiled warmly.

Returning Bentsen's smile, Harris said, "Aye, aye, Skipper." He picked up the attaché case, gestured for the two Marines to follow him, and led the way through the forward hatch.

Captain Bentsen removed his headset and returned it to its hook alongside the command console. He picked up the PA system microphone. "This is the captain speaking. Hear this. You may secure from ISQ missiles, but remain at your GQ stations."

Men everywhere outside the control room were wondering what had happened as they removed their headsets and quietly secured their stations from red alert.

Bentsen gave his men time to prepare for his announcement, then keyed the PA mike again. "Stand at ease," he began. "What you have just witnessed was a first testing of a new type of red alert. It is called a Strategic Defense Alert and differs from the standard

Navy, ISQ, and GQ in only one way. During an SDA exercise, personnel will not be advised that a drill is taking place. You will act under the assumption that a state of nuclear war exists, and you will be expected to proceed to your GQ stations with the utmost urgency and perform your duties and carry out all orders given to you in the highest state of discipline.''

Muttered remarks were exchanged by the crew outside the range of Bentsen's hearing. Was the Navy going bananas? Did the Navy enjoy this morbid way of scaring the crap out of everyone? What in hell did the Navy need a new kind of drill for? Weren't the ones they had enough? They heard the PA speakers crackle again and fall quiet.

''Our first testing aboard the *Trident* today was a complete success. You've all responded par excellence, and I am pleased to pass along to you a *well done* from the President of the United States. You may secure from your GQ stations, that is all.'' He returned the PA mike to the command console.

Nelson Hobart walked over to Bentsen, looking dismayed. ''Captain.''

''Yes, Mr. Hobart?''

''I find it hard to believe this was all a drill. How . . .?''

''It was a computer programmed and controlled simulation,'' Bentsen interrupted. ''All that was real about the red alert was the viewing screen directive we received from the Pentagon. I didn't know if it was an actual alert to go to ISQ missiles or not until I read my top secret orders. The coded information on the computer disc was to advise me it was a drill. I was warned before we left home base that such new types of drills would be implemented by surprise. The computer disc that I inserted into the command console slot not only produced a programmed simulation of all the visual effects on the world map and at other tied in stations, but it also prevented an accidental firing of missiles by overriding the arming circuit. When Commander Harris and I inserted our arming keys, we did so into a circuit deactivated by SAM.''

''I'm astonished, Captain,'' Hobart returned: ''I'm still trying to accept that it was all mere simulation.'' The color began to return to his face.

''I assure you, if it had been the real thing, I'd have ordered you out of the control room,'' Bentsen said. ''Actually, I shouldn't be telling you these things, but I wanted you to see some of the amazing capabilities the Navy has incorporated into this fantastic submarine your company has built for us."

"Thank you for the honor, Captain. However, I must admit . . . it scared the hell out of me. Nevertheless, I'm glad you allowed me to watch it all."

"My thanks to you for your expedient and skillful repair of that diving plane noise," Bentsen said. He checked the propulsion and maneuvering stations. "All ahead two-thirds. Course is two-seven-zero. Bring us down to six hundred feet. We're going home."

## Chapter Three

*Thursday evening, Washington, D.C.*
In the depths of the Pentagon the war room's computerized viewing screen went black for a moment, then a new display materialized.

ATTENTION:. . . . . . . . . . . . . . . . . . . . . . . . . . . . . . . . . . . . . . . . . . . . . .
MR. PRESIDENT, DECDEF, SECNAV, JOINT CHIEFS, CNO: ON BE-
HALF OF THE CREW, THANK YOU FOR YOUR COMMENDATION
AND GOOD WISHES. IT WAS BOTH AN HONOR AND A PRIVILEGE
TO HAVE BEEN CHOSEN TO TAKE THIS MAGNIFICENT NEW
SUBMARINE OUT ON ITS MAIDEN VOYAGE AND DEMONSTRATE
ITS CAPABILITIES
. . . . . . . . . . . . . . . .BENTSEN, CAPTAIN, USN-C.O. U.S.S. *TRIDENT*.

Chief of Naval Operations, Fleet Admiral Richard Preston, a burly man in his early sixties with thinning silver-gray hair, walked to the war room computerized control console, erased the display, and shut off the huge floor-to-ceiling world map. With a gleam in his deep blue eyes he moved over to a podium set to one side of the world map and adjusted a tabletop microphone.

"Mr. President, Secretary of Defense, Secretary of the Navy, members of the Joint Chiefs of Staff, thank you for your undivided attention during this demonstration. What you've just witnessed is an exclusive red alert, involving only the U.S.S. *Trident* and us here at the war room. Everything you saw on the world map and viewing screen was a staged simulation, utilizing the new SAM computer. However, had the *Trident* been responding to an actual red alert, we can readily see by their performance this evening that both vessel and crew would have carried out their strategic orders to the letter. To say the least, this is a very proud moment for us all. The *Trident* submarine, along with the SAM computer and its sonar avoidance system, is a fantastic weapons package."

The President applauded, prompting everyone else in the room to join in, and walked up to the podium. He adjusted the microphone and said, "The new fleet of Trident submarines is a supreme nuclear deterrence and will also arm us with the kind of clout we want to have when we meet the Soviet Union at future SALT accords. I have given the Trident program my full backing. I hope I will continue to have the support of all of you in seeing the program reach completion. Not only as a Navy project, but as a project that will benefit all of our armed forces in many ways. Thank you." He stepped down from the podium and began shaking hands with the members of the Joint Chiefs of Staff. He nodded to the Secretary of Defense and Secretary of the Navy as they left the war room. After the Joint Chiefs filed out after them, he gestured for Admiral Preston to walk along with him. "What sort of media coverage have you arranged for the *Trident*'s return to home port on Monday, Admiral?"

"We've invited a contingent of press people to attend an open-house ceremony for the entire three-day Labor Day weekend at the submarine base in New London. I've instructed Rear Admiral William Pulvey, commander of submarine operations at New London, to roll out the red carpet for the media."

"Is this Admiral Pulvey a good man for the job, Admiral?" the President asked as they rounded a corridor and approached the elevator.

"I think so, Mr. President. 'Bull' Pulvey is a tough old salt, but he has the tact of a diplomat and the charm of a movie star."

The elevator arrived with two Secret Service agents aboard to escort the President back to the Oval Office. He got on and told them to hold the doors open. Facing Preston, he said firmly, "Admiral, I want the media to encourage the public to lovingly support the Trident program. You tell this Admiral Pulvey that's a direct order from me. If he wins over the press, there will be a promotion in it for him."

*Thursday night, Norwich, Connecticut.*

Rudolph Boyd had a lot on his mind as he turned into his driveway at the end of Clark Street. There was a full moon looming over Norwich, but its brilliant glow held little comfort for him. The night air was stiflingly hot, but it didn't warm him. Nothing had comforted or warmed him for the past eight months except the shred of hope that Helen might still be alive, might still be returned to him.

Boyd had left the defense plant on this, his last day of employment, at about six that evening. Over the long hours since, he had been sitting armed and in uniform in front of a desk at the Norwich Realty office in town, agonizingly closing out the past twenty-four years of his life with a few strokes of a pen. The realtor had given him two certified checks to close the quickly made deal. One check was for twenty thousand dollars and represented only half the equity he would have been able to realize if he could have given the realtor more time to sell the house. The other check was for two thousand dollars, all the realtor could allow him for the household furnishings and the personal articles he had to leave behind. The money would help him finance a few plans he'd made out of desperation. He knew he had to try. If Helen were still alive and would be released by her captors, he might still be able to live out the rest of his years in peace with her.

He got out of the car, checked the mailbox, and took out the phone bill. He unlocked the front door and stepped inside to reach for the switch to turn on the hall lights, when a powerful arm gripped him from behind and squeezed his windpipe. Boyd struggled to free himself. He dropped the phone bill and reached for his service revolver, but his hand found only an empty holster. A tall shadowy figure sprang out from the hall alcove and joined in the skirmish. The pressure on his throat intensified as he felt himself being pulled down to the floor. He gasped for air, his lungs feeling as though they had been set afire.

Mr. A slammed the front door closed, then switched on the hall lights. Seeing that Boyd's face was turning blue, he shouted at Mr. B. "We don't want to kill him. Just restrain him, you fucking animal." Mr. B slackened his grip at once. "I've got his gun. Let him go."

"Okay," Mr. B said as he released Boyd. "But if he tries anything cute, I'm going to rip his fucking head off."

Boyd gasped violently to suck desperately needed air into his burning lungs. He was pulled to his feet. His throat throbbed painfully from the choke hold, but it was nothing like the pain in his eyes when he realized who his two attackers were. He had known them for eight long hate-filled months. "What do you want of me?" he growled.

"Now, that's a very unappreciative way to speak to the guys who are going to return your daughter to you, Rudy," Mr. A said.

"You're going to release Helen? Tonight?"

"Not exactly, Rudy," Mr. A replied. "But very soon. Maybe this coming Monday, if all goes well and you do what you're told."

"I'll do anything you say! Just . . . please let Helen go!"

Mr. A ushered Boyd across the living room to an armchair and gestured for him to seat himself. "Sorry we had to jump you like that, Rudy, but we had to make sure we got your gun before you did something stupid with it. Now, we need some information pertaining to the U.S.S. *Trident*'s involvement with Operation Ghost over the coming weekend. Do you know what Operation Ghost is, Rudy?"

"It's a special Naval exercise designed to test the new submarine's sonar avoidance system."

"That's right, Rudy," Mr. A said. "A number of Navy ships are going to be operating search patterns all along the coast of Long Island over the Labor Day weekend, hoping to detect the U.S.S. *Trident* sneaking back into home waters at some undisclosed time. The *Trident* is supposed to stay overnight at secret holding coordinates before coming into home port. We need you to find out the U.S.S. *Trident*'s precise holding coordinates and when it is due to arrive there. Once you get that bit of information, come back here and wait for a call from us. After that, we'll give you your daughter back."

"Those holding coordinates are very secret. I have no access to . . ."

"Don't try to snow me, Rudy," Mr. A interrupted. "As captain of the defense plant security police, you have a classified clearance card. Your C-card allows you to go anywhere on the submarine base. You'll find the information we need in the Combat Information Center at the base. CIC keeps on its plotting board information pertaining to the movements of the flotilla's submarines. Look on the plotting board for the information that pertains to the *Trident*'s planned overnight stay back in home waters. You'll do that, Rudy, if you ever want to see Helen alive again."

"How do I know for sure that you haven't killed her already?"

Mr. A nodded to Mr. B. "Show Rudy the snapshot we took of Helen this morning, Mr. B."

As Boyd looked at the photo, Mr. A said, "In the snapshot Helen is holding a copy of the *New England Times*. Did you read the *Times* today, Rudy?'' A nod. ''Notice the date on the front page circled in red, Rudy? It's today's date. And the headlines Helen is pointing to. Aren't they the same headlines that appeared in your copy of the *Times*?'' Boyd nodded again. ''Then you have your proof, Rudy. I guarantee you that if you don't do what we ask tomorrow's edition of the *Times* will feature your daughter's mutilated body on the front page.'' He gestured at Mr. B. ''Mr. B is an expert at administering slow and torturous death.''

''You'll get your goddamn coordinates,'' Boyd said bitterly. He knew he had to give in. Helen was alive, or at least she'd been when they'd taken the snapshot. He refused to believe they might have killed her right after that. He decided to tell them one aspect of the plans he implemented to safeguard Helen's release. ''Just in case you're planning to kill Helen and me after this is all over, you should know I've protected myself.''

''How?'' Mr. A asked angrily.

''I've written a letter explaining everything about Helen's abduction, including all I know about you two. It's in trusted hands with instructions to mail it to the authorities if I fail to keep in touch or if anything happens to either me or Helen.''

''That was a real dumb thing to do, Rudy,'' Mr. A said, disturbed by the news. ''You have no idea who Mr. B and I really are—who we're working for, where we're from. What good will your letter do you? All you know is that you were forced to let us in on the defense plant to deliver something. What and why, you don't know. Fuck you and your dumb letter, Rudy.''

Boyd still felt that by revealing that he had written a letter now in safe hands he had placed Helen's abductors in check, though not yet checkmate. He straightened and said, ''I don't care what you say. That letter can hurt you.''

Mr. A controlled his anger and his new feeling of vulnerability. ''Keep your letter if it makes you feel more secure. When we release Helen, you can give it to us.'' He pretended to Boyd the letter didn't bother him but it did. Deeply. He knew it was going to be disturbing to the others involved. He needed time to think. ''It's time for us to leave, Mr. B.'' He walked over to the front door and noticed the phone bill lying on the floor. It gave him an idea. Mr. B was blocking Boyd's view, so Mr. A slipped the phone bill into his pocket. ''We expect you to be home tomorrow night when we call, Rudy.''

Boyd watched the two men leave. When the taillights of their car vanished, he quickly crossed the living room to the telephone and dialed the area code for Berlin, West Germany, then the familiar phone number itself. After several rings, an unsteady, squeaky voice came on the line. In fluent German, Boyd said, "It's me, Uncle Gunther. Sorry to wake you. Just wanted to say that everything is fine here." He paused to listen. "Yes, keep holding the letter." He paused again. "Yes, I will continue to stay in touch. If all goes well, Helen and I should be leaving for Berlin in a few days. If you don't hear from me, you know what to do."

# PART TWO

## Chapter Four

*Friday*

The Colonial Airways airbus from Washington, D.C., came to a stop outside the Hartford, Connecticut, terminal under a gleaming early morning summer sun. Fay Parks squirmed restlessly in her seat by the cabin window in anticipation of deplaning and getting some badly needed breathing room between herself and the persistent male colleague seated next to her.

A very pretty brunette with warm hazel eyes and a sensuous figure, Fay was a reporter in her early thirties who'd left San Diego after finishing college and relocated to D.C. to start her career in journalism. She'd managed to get a job with the *Washington Globe*, a conservative newspaper that routinely hired men but took Fay on after being reminded that job discrimination based on sex was against the law. Despite constant advances from both eligible and ineligible male journalists, she managed to stay single, safe, and happy. She had spent six years with the *Globe* working on meager, low-profile assignments in and around D.C. But she'd gotten restless and had begun preparing herself for the fulfillment of her greatest ambition in life—winning the Pulitzer prize for outstanding journalism.

Fay's trip to Connecticut didn't seem to hold the smallest chance of turning into a Pulitzer-bound assignment, but it was her first assignment out of D.C. and that alone made it exciting. Her managing editor, Tom Hurt, had been given an invitation for one reporter to spend the Labor Day weekend as guest of the Navy at the submarine base in New London. The reporter would cover the *Trident* submarine's return to home port from its maiden voyage. It was a military assignment meant for a man but Fay managed to talk Tom into giving her a chance after agreeing to a stipulation: "Take your cues from Tolbin."

Ray Tolbin, a renowned journalist for the *Washington Chronicle*, was also covering the U.S.S. *Trident*'s return home and commissioning ceremonies. Fay had heard a lot about Tolbin and for a time had regarded him as her idol, right after Walter Cronkite. When she finally got to meet him in person, her idolization of him was shattered at once.

Throughout the flight Ray Tolbin had told her that covering the new submarine was a freebie, a weekend of free food and fun and unlimited good booze, all on the Navy. Tolbin also had other ideas for a good time at the Navy base, which he suggested included her. Fay diplomatically had said she had no interest in his other ideas.

Fay had spent weeks researching Capitol Hill's sentiment toward the new expensive submarine. She knew the President was quite bullish on the Trident program. The Navy was happy about that. But she learned the Army and Air Force upper brass weren't all that keen about placing the major portion of the nation's defenses in the hands of the Navy. Fay's research had armed her with a barrage of tough questions to ask at the admiral's press conference, scheduled for noon. It was not going to be a weekend of fun for her—nor for the Navy brass either, when she got through with them.

Fay filed down the narrow cabin aisle behind Ray Tolbin. After deplaning, they entered the main concourse. "As I told you on the plane, Mr. Tolbin, I—"

"Ray," Tolbin interrupted. "We might as well get onto a first-name basis right off the bat, Fay. We're going to see a lot of each other over the long weekend." He smiled at her hungrily.

Fay looked into the scrawny man's bloodshot eyes, guessing he was in his late forties or early fifties. She had seen his type all around D.C.—a jetsetting boozer, horny and pushy. She could just imagine what the coming weekend was going to be like, stuck on a Navy base with him. "Ray it is," she agreed reluctantly. "As I said on the plane, I have trouble finding my way around by car. Maybe you'd better do the driving."

"Nonsense," Tolbin insisted. "You'll do fine. Besides, I don't have a valid driver's license. I forgot to renew it the last time it was due." He decided to tell her that little white lie rather than the truth, which was that his license had been revoked for driving while under the influence of far too many martinis after leaving a Republican bash in D.C. He saw Fay shrug in indifference. "Okay, then. I'll get our luggage while you pop over to Avis and get the car I reserved."

In a few minutes they were on the road, heading for New London. Fay drove and Tolbin leaned back in the seat and fell asleep.

# Chapter Five

The Marine lance corporal guarding the door of the CIC room, in the basement of the Naval Warfare and Intelligence Center, snapped to attention when he saw Captain Allen A. Kowalski, C.O. of Naval Intelligence. The CIC room, a highly restricted area of the Naval Submarine Base in New London, could be entered only by showing to the guard the correct classified clearance card. Though he knew Captain Kowalski well, the Marine had to issue the regulation challenge.

"May I see your C-card, sir?" he asked with a smile.

Ski, as most of his fellow officers called him, presented the card. "As you can see from the photo, Finch, I haven't changed much since this morning."

Corporal Donald Finch grinned, looked at the card, and nodded. "Okay, sir."

Ski entered the rectangular-shaped CIC room crowded with rows of radar, sonar, and communications modules. He looked around, expecting to find his executive officer, but Lieutenant David Lee was nowhere to be seen. He walked over to a chief petty officer manning a code-ciphering machine and asked, "Chief, do you happen to know where my XO is?"

"He went over to the gedunk to grab some pogie bait, Skipper." *Gedunk* was Navy jargon for *snack bar* and *pogie bait* was a term for *sweets*, especially candy. "He ought to be back any minute."

Pain in the ass, Ski thought. "Fine! He summons me here on something he says is urgent, then he trots off to the PX."

"If you don't mind me saying so, Skipper, your exec seems to think everything that happens around here is urgent. You can count on him to max out whenever he thinks there's a calamity."

"Do you have even a guess as to what it is this time, Chief?"

"Not a hint, Skipper."

"I guess I'll have to wait for him to get back to find out what's wrong," Ski said, then went over to the duty officer's desk and sat down. After glancing at his wristwatch and finding it was near time to secure routine work at the base, he picked up the phone to call his fiancée, Janet Pulvey, the admiral's daughter. Janet answered right away. "It's me, Janet. I'm in a bit of a bind. Your father scheduled me to attend a press conference at the new sea hangar. It was supposed to be for fourteen hundred hours, but an important journalist from Washington is late. He won't be here till about sixteen thirty. That means I'm going to miss our tennis match this afternoon.'' He listened as Janet protested about the short notice. "I couldn't let you know earlier. I only found out myself a little while ago. Just get someone to take my place, or else reschedule the match for tomorrow.'' There was a click on the other end. Pain in the ass, he thought, then hung up the phone.

He hated tennis, and he hated Janet's aristocratic social club friends. At first he'd hated the idea of having to attend the admiral's press conference. But now that it had gotten him out of the tennis match Janet had forced on him, he was glad the Bull was forcing him to attend. On reflecting on Admiral Pulvey and his daughter, he was beginning to realize they were both taking turns bullying him around. If he had his way, he'd spend more of his off-duty time sailing his sloop. But the sloop was out because Janet didn't like sailing and was a fanatic about tennis. A pain in the ass, he thought.

Lieutenant David Lee, a rather short and quite skinny man in his late twenties who possessed an IQ of near genius, hurried into the room carrying a package of Twinkies and a pint container of chocolate milk and nodded to Ski.

Ski watched as Dave sat at his desk and began wolfing down one of his Twinkies, washing it down with great gulps of chocolate milk. No real sailor would dare be caught snacking on Twinkies and chocolate milk, Ski thought. And no real shipmate would snack on anything in front of a buddy who was on a diet.

"You called me," Ski said with a frown, "about another urgency."

"Oh, that! I took care of it myself," Dave said confidently.

"Well, what was it, now that I'm here?"

"Bad Ass Buel radioed in. He said he had a Soviet, Zebra class, reconnaissance sub on sonar. It penetrated our limits and Buel requested permission to roust the bastards.''

"How far inside our limits, Dave? And what did you tell Buel to do?" Ski was apprehensive.

Dave took another bite of the Twinkie before answering, "Twenty miles, Ski. I told him permission granted.''

Ski shot up from his seat, surprising Dave and causing him to spill his milk on the desk. "You did *what*?" he shouted. "How far away is Buel from that sub right now?"

"About ten miles," Dave answered as he cleaned up the milk.

"What destroyer is Buel skippering?"

"The *Dart*." Dave's confidence had diminished.

Ski rushed over to a ship-to-shore radio operator. "Contact the U.S.S. *Dart*. Advise Commander Buel his authority to take action against that Soviet sub is now *rescinded*. He's to belay rousting them and *stand off*. Tell him that sub is just to be kept under surveillance, and have him send you a confirming acknowledgment to my attention."

"Aye, aye, Captain," the radio operator said, then began calling the U.S.S. *Dart*.

Ski returned to the OOD's desk. "Dave, we don't go rousting Soviet reconnaissance subs out of our limits for intelligence reasons. If you'd read some of those intelligence reports you're always signing off, you'd know they are no threat to our national security, and we learn an awful lot about their detection gear just by observing them."

"Sorry, Ski. I didn't think—"

"And," Ski interrupted, "never give that lunatic Buel authority from us to roust any sub. He just loves that. Having our authority takes him off the hook. The last time I gave Buel permission to order a Soviet boat out of our limits he bombarded them with warning depth charges before they had a chance to respond to his order to surface. Then he made a full report to COMSUBOPS, after the Russians formally protested, saying that he was acting under *my* orders, not *his*. That little incident put *me* on the carpet with the admiral, not *him*."

Dave shook his head. "I see what you mean, Ski."

Ski sighed as he seated himself at the desk. That's all he needed to complete the day—an international incident at sea. He picked up the duty roster Dave had prepared for the three-day weekend and felt a sudden pain. It was all fouled up. He shook his head. "Jesus H. Christ, Dave! What in hell did you do to this?"

The desk phone rang and Dave picked it up to avoid answering Ski's question. It was the base Commanding Officer and as he cupped the phone he asked, "It's the 'Bull,' Ski. Are you here?"

Ski nodded and accepted the phone. "Good afternoon, Admiral. This is Ski. What can I do for you, sir?" He listened. "The reporter from Washington has finally arrived," he said, repeating the admiral. "Fine, Admiral. I have a small matter to close out here, then I'll get right over to your office, sir." He returned the receiver to its cradle, then regarded Dave. "Dave, you're going to have to go over the duty roster and get it squared away."

"Come on, Ski. It's time to secure. I'll square it away tomorrow."

"Now, Dave. That's an order." Ski crossed the room to the ship-to-shore radio operator. "Did Commander Buel acknowledge the rescinding order, yet?" he asked. The operator gave him a thumbs-down gesture. "Call the *Dart* again. Tell 'em I want that acknowledgment on the double."

Five minutes after the ship-to-shore operator made his second call to the patrol destroyer, U.S.S. *Dart*, Commander Buel's raspy voice blared into his headset. He listened, then said to Ski, "Sir, Commander Buel reports that your rescinding order was not received in time to abort his challenge of the Soviet sub. He had already fired one warning depth charge when the belay advise was given to him on the bridge. He said the Soviet sub has hightailed it for international waters, and he wants to know if you still require a confirming acknowledgment in writing that you did make an attempt to rescind your prior order to attack."

Pain in the ass, Ski thought. Buel had to get one warning depth charge off. He knew the rescinding order had been received in time, but there was no way he'd be able to prove it. "Tell Commander Buel affirmative. I want it in writing that he received my rescinding order too late to abort his attack. That is all." Ski rejoined Dave at the duty officer's desk. "You heard that, didn't you, Dave?" Dave nodded. "Besides being a tyrant, Buel is also a goddamn liar. You keep that in mind when you deal with him in the future." Another nod. "I'm shoving off to the admiral's office. When you've finished getting the weekend duty roster squared away, you can secure, Dave. See you at oh eight hundred hours tomorrow." He headed toward the door, then stopped. "That's oh eight hundred hours sharp, Dave. Not sometime around that hour, after you've had breakfast." He got a faint nod and left. As he took the steps two at a time enroute to the admiral's office in the Administration Building across the street from the Naval Intelligence Center, he thought, the entire day has been a pain in the ass.

# Chapter Six

Rear Admiral William "Bull" Pulvey paced the carpeted floor of his spacious paneled private office. He was puffing vigorously on one of his Bering cigars. A cloud of blue smoke swirled around his snow-white hair and matching eyebrows. Standing just under six feet tall, he was a husky, thick-necked, broad-shouldered man. At age sixty, he had the vibrance of men much younger than he, an electricity that seemed inexhaustible.

In a stance that was neither at attention nor at ease, Lieutenant Roger Strong nodded his head in a bobbing motion that resembled a just popped jack-in-the-box as Bull Pulvey bombarded him with rhetorical questions in rapid succession. He anticipated most of the admiral's comments, knowing the Bull's memory left a lot to be desired. But rather than remind the admiral he was being redundant, he acted as though he were hearing all for the first time. That had gone on from the first moment he had arrived back at the admiral's office, some ten minutes ago. Now the admiral asked him a straight question.

"Yesterday I dictated a letter that was to go out to Marine Dynamics people no later than today. Where in hell did you put it, Roger?"

"I had the duty driver deliver it to Marine Dynamics yesterday, Admiral. Right after you signed it."

"That's queer!" Pulvey exclaimed. "For the life of me, I can't remember signing it. Oh, well, as long as it went out to them. As for my press conference, I won't need you there, Roger. Ski is going to sit in on it with me. But don't do your usual disappearing act. I may need you after the buffet is over. In fact, I'm expecting to hear from Bentsen aboard the *Trident* sometime this afternoon or evening. What I want you to do is stick around CIC and wait for his communiqué, then get word to me wherever I am at that time. Got that, Roger?"

"Yes, Admiral. How long should I wait for the communiqué, Admiral?" Strong had some pressing business at the Holiday Inn that evening with Betty Worth, one of the new ensigns that had recently arrived for duty at the submarine base. He had paid for a room at the Holiday Inn in advance.

"How in hell should I know, Roger?" Pulvey growled. "Until the *Trident* radios in."

"But . . . that might not be until midnight, Admiral," Strong said with a sigh.

"Whatever," Pulvey said. "Now, make damn sure that BOQ knows enough to assign the female member of the press contingent her own room. The male press people can share rooms at bachelor officer's quarters if we're a little tight for space. Everyone, without exception, is to regard the female member of the media as off limits. If I catch anyone trying to put the make on her, officers and enlisted men alike, I'll cut their balls off. You pass that word around the base, Roger. Especially over at BOQ."

"Whose balls are you going to cut off now, Admiral?" Ski asked, overhearing Pulvey's threat as he stepped into the admiral's office.

Pulvey handed Strong the clipboard. "Ah, Ski. We haven't much time. The press people are waiting for us. I'll have to explain what I want you to do during the press conference on the way over to the new sea hangar. Is my car waiting, Roger?" Strong nodded. Pulvey motioned for Ski to head out of the office, then followed after him, puffing vigorously on his cigar.

As they made their way across the admiral's reception room, Pulvey nodded to his WAVE secretary. "I'll be over at the new sea hangar, Joyce," he said, then returned his attention to Ski as they stepped out into the hall. "One of the members of the press contingent is a female liberal, Ski. She's with the *Washington Globe*." They headed down the highly polished passageway and exited the Administration Building. "Being liberal may not necessarily make her an enemy of the Navy, but she certainly can't be counted upon to be one of the Navy's devout friends. That's where you're going to come in handy, Ski."

"Me?" Ski asked as they got into the rear of the admiral's battleship-gray Ford sedan with a two-star flag affixed to the right front fender. "I've never been any good at handling the media, Admiral," Ski said as the driver pulled away. "In fact, I can't stand press people."

"Perhaps not, Ski. But you are known to have a way with women, as my daughter has pointed out to me on more than one occasion." He saw that Ski was about to say something in defense of his reputation. He waved his hand to stop Ski's rebuttal. "That doesn't matter, Ski. You're an extremely good-looking man. Small wonder you get attention from the females. I'm hoping your good looks will soothe Ms. Liberal Bitch a little. I'm not asking you to get into her pants or anything of the sort. Although if you weren't my future son-in-law and I thought it would help matters . . ." He smiled. "I'm jesting, of course."

Ski returned the admiral's smile. "I rather doubt that Janet will appreciate my charming another woman, Admiral."

"Janet is a Navy man's daughter. She'll understand what you're doing is all in the line of duty. You see, there's bound to be some liberal flak thrown at us about costs and cost overrides, Ski. We all know that prototype *Trident* submarine soared well above estimated construction costs, and the media won't let us forget the fact. We can depend on the members of the media attending today who are profound friends of the Navy. They will be asking questions that will help the program. One reporter in particular that we can rely upon for favorable treatment is Ray Tolbin of the *Washington Chronicle*. There are others. What you will concern yourself with is the obvious enemies of the program. The CNO called me last night and told me my overdue promotion to vice-admiral depends upon the smooth and effective handling of the media over the open-house weekend. His orders came straight from the President. Now, I've mapped out a tactical approach for handling the liberals."

"Which is?" Ski asked.

"As a Naval Intelligence officer, you can declare any questions we don't want to answer a possible breach of national security. When such unwanted questions arise, I'll either nod to you or direct the question to you. All you have to do is invent a believable reason why an answer can't be given at this time for defense security reasons."

"Okay, Admiral. But surely even the liberals agree that we can't have a strong defense posture that would be competitive with the Soviet Union's without spending a little money."

"Don't kid yourself, Ski. These goddamn liberal congressional subcommittees would have us on a military defense budget that wouldn't support the Boy Scouts. They'd have us refitting older subs with new missiles that have increased strike capacities. But do they consider that such existing subs are almost obsolete? Hell, no! 'Use older subs, smaller subs, fewer aircraft carriers, fewer surface ships.' That's what they're advocating. And while they're asking us to flounder, the Russians are quickly becoming the top navy of the world. I don't like lying to the sons of bitches, but I'd rather lie now than pay later because we listened to them."

# Chapter Seven

Ensign Betty Worth, a pretty and voluptuous WAVE officer in her mid-twenties, sighed into the telephone on seeing the two people heading toward her in the new sea hangar. "I've got to get back to work, Roger. Looks like two more reporters," she informed Lieutenant Strong on the other end. "I'll meet you at the Holiday Inn in Groton as soon as I can slip away." Returning the wall phone to its cradle, she smiled at the attractive female and middle-aged male reporter walking toward her. In a thick Southern drawl she sang out, "Good afternoon and welcome to New London. The admiral will be here in a few minutes to begin the press conference. You can join your colleagues over at the refreshment tables by Slip One or, if you prefer, I'd be happy to show you around our new facility while you wait."

Tolbin winked at the sexy redhead. "No tour for me, sweetie. I saw the place when it was being built. Just point the way to the booze. I'm parched from the long ride." He looked at the direction Ensign Worth pointed and noticed his colleagues standing around some buffet tables. "Come on, Fay. I'll introduce you to the guys."

"In a minute, Ray," Fay said. She smiled at Ensign Worth. "I'd like to take advantage of the guided tour first."

"I warn you, it'll be a bore," Tolbin said, then hurried off.

"Let me show you a model of the U.S.S. *Trident* first," Ensign Worth said.

Fay took in the spaciousness of the new sea hangar's interior as they made their way across the concrete floor. At one end there were two large doors that were raised up and tucked into the towering rooftops, affording her a broad view of the Thames River outside. Off to one side was a platformed podium that faced rows of folding chairs. Ensign Worth called this area Slip Two, where the press conference would be held. On the opposite side of the building was Slip One, where Tolbin and his buddies were partaking of the refreshments. Dividing the two submarine slips was a huge crane set atop railroad tracks on the center pier. Ensign Worth explained that was used to load missiles and supplies aboard the submarines and to help perform maintenance.

On reaching the model, Fay was in awe of its detail. It was ten

'eet long, three feet high, and set on a waist-high stand at the
beginning of the center pier. One side of it was made of clear plastic
o that the submarine's numerous compartments could be viewed,
and each compartment was labeled with a brief description of its
function. There were even miniature figures representing crewmen
aboard, meticulously arranged at working stations. Fay was impressed by the hospital aboard, the crew's and officer's mess and
sleeping quarters, the barber shops, ship's laundry, a library, lounging areas, even stores and a movie theater. "It appears the Navy has
gone to great lengths to make the submarine crews quite comfortable," she said.

"The crews go aboard for periods of three months at a time,"
Ensign Worth said. She then noticed a male tour guide trying to get
her attention and gesturing that she had a phone call. "I'm wanted
on the phone, ma'am. Excuse me." Pointing to pamphlets set along
the surface of the submarine model's stand, she added, "Help
yourself to some literature. It tells you all about the technical details
of the new submarine. Unclassified, of course."

"Thank you, I will," Fay said. "May I take some pictures?"

"Affirmative. Just stow your gear anywhere and make yourself at
home." Ensign Worth dashed off for the wall phone, certain it was
Roger Strong calling her back.

Fay set her attaché case down on the model's stand and selected
an assortment of pamphlets, which she stuffed into a divided compartment of the attaché case for easy access during the press conference. She placed the case under the stand, unslung her tote bag from
her shoulder, and took out her Canon AE 35-millimeter camera and
mounted a 135-millimeter lens to take pictures inside the building.
After placing the tote bag under the stand also, she panned the sea
hangar's interior for her first subject and decided on a shot of the
conference area. Then, swinging her camera around, she chose Ray
Tolbin as her next subject and readied herself as he raised a martini
garnished with a small green olive to his lips. Gotcha, she thought,
clicking the shutter as Tolbin sipped from the clear plastic glass.

She took a few shots of the cutaway model of the U.S.S. *Trident*.
Then she made her way along the missile crane's railroad tracks and
stood by the huge object. It towered on its tracks like a monstrous
robot, waiting for someone to bring it to life. Fay decided a photo of
its massiveness would illustrate how tremendous the missiles it put
aboard the submarines were. Aiming her camera, she felt she should
back away from it a little and began a slow march backward,

unaware of the direction she was taking. "Oops!" she called out, realizing she had bumped into someone. She swung around and settled her eyes on the well-tanned, handsome face of a Navy officer who looked to be in his late thirties. She couldn't see his eyes, only her reflection in the metallic-shaded lenses of his sunglasses. "Excuse me," she said, "I didn't mean to bump into you. I was . . ."

"You didn't bump into me," Ski said with a friendly smile. "But you would have dropped into Davy Jones's locker if I hadn't come along to stop you." He eyed her well-tailored outfit, then pointed to the murky river water filling Slip One beneath them. "One more step backward and things would have gotten quite messy for your lovely outfit."

Fay glanced down at the shiny oil slick coating the surface of the river water. "Thanks for rescuing me." She offered her hand. "I'm Fay Parks. I'm with the *Washington Globe*."

"Captain Kowalski of base Naval Intelligence," Ski said as he removed his hat and sunglasses. He shook her hand.

Fay unconsciously continued appraising the Navy captain, taking notice of his chiseled jaw, his narrow lips, and straight white teeth. She noticed next that he had soft gray eyes and short cut jet-black hair that sharply contrasted with his gleaming white Navy uniform. She eyed the gold embroidered peak of his cap next as he returned it to his head, then in suddenly feeling awkward over staring at him, she said, "I was trying to photograph your crane."

"Go ahead and take the picture," Ski said. "I'll make sure you don't fall into the drink."

Fay hesitated, then faced the crane and aimed her camera. She felt the Navy captain's hand resting protectively against her lower back as she snapped the shutter. When she turned around to face him, she caught sight of an older Navy officer coming over to join them. His distinguished look and the gleaming trimmings on his white Navy uniform suggested at once that she was about to meet Rear Admiral "Bull" Pulvey, the tough old seadog Ray Tolbin had bragged about being close friends with.

"Mrs. Parks, may I introduce our base commanding officer, Admiral Pulvey. Admiral, this is Mrs. Parks of the *Washington*, eh . . ."

"*Globe*," Fay finished for him. "And it's *Ms.* Parks."

*Ms.*, Pulvey thought with disapproval. "My pleasure, Ms. Parks. I trust you will enjoy your visit. On behalf of the Navy and myself, welcome to New London."

"Thank you, Admiral. I'm sure I will enjoy my stay. And on behalf of the *Washington Globe* and myself, thank you for your most gracious invitation."

"You're quite welcome," Pulvey said. "Now if you will excuse us, we have to greet your colleagues before getting the press conference under way." He nodded to Ski. "Come along, son."

"Keep clear of the deck edge, Ms. Parks," Ski warned politely, then joined Pulvey in a fast-paced walk toward the buffet area.

Fay nonchalantly glanced over at the buffet area as she returned her camera to her tote bag. She observed the hearty greeting Ray Tolbin paid the admiral, which seemed to suggest good ol' Ray was telling the truth about their being old friends. She decided to head over to the buffet area and say hello to Walt Roland, a casual friend of hers who was with *The New York Times* and who often shared her liberal views.

After being introduced to Tolbin's cronies, Admiral Pulvey asked, "Can you point out the troublemakers to me, Ray?"

"You might get a little flak from Walt Roland of *The New York Times*. He's been known to side with the opposition occasionally. But the rest of 'em are just here to enjoy a weekend off at the Navy base with pay."

Nodding in the direction of Walt Roland and Fay Parks, Pulvey asked, "What about Ms. Parks? Is she going to be a problem?"

"Leave her to me, Admiral," Tolbin said boastfully. "I had a nice long talk with her on the plane. This is her first military assignment, so I took the liberty of offering to tutor her, sort of show her the ropes." His statement drew sighs of envy from his peers, encouraging him to brag on. "She's into suave older men." He winked at his cronies. "I've got her eating out of my hand."

Ski narrowed his eyes, finding the reporter's boasting hard to believe. He glanced over at Fay Parks and studied her as she chatted with *The New York Times* reporter.

Tolbin noticed Ski staring at Fay Parks. "Pretty little thing, isn't she, Captain Kowalski?"

"Not bad."

"Are you married, Captain?" Tolbin pried.

"Engaged."

"Ski is engaged to my daughter Janet," Pulvey interjected proudly.

"Congratulations, Captain," Tolbin said, relieved that Kowalski wasn't in a position to compete with him for Fay Parks.

Pulvey asked, "Can I speak frankly with your friends, Ray?"

"Of course, Admiral," Tolbin said. "I've already suggested to them that you might want their cooperation during the press conference." He winked at his cronies again.

"Good," Pulvey said to all of them. "Now let me brief you on the types of questions I'd prefer that you pose during the conference."

As soon as he was satisfied he had Tolbin and his three friends cued on what to do, Admiral Pulvey invited all the reporters, including the late one who'd finally arrived, over to the conference area, then climbed the steps of the platform along with Ski and took his place at the podium. He adjusted the microphone as Ski seated himself at the adjoining table to his right. When the media members were all seated, he opened the conference with a welcoming speech and a brief rundown of the itinerary he had planned for them over the three-day Labor Day weekend at New London.

A half hour into the admiral's press conference, it had become obvious to Fay that a conspiracy existed among the admiral, Ray Tolbin, and Tolbin's three cronies. Good ol' Ray had begun the session with questions about technical aspects of the new submarine that promoted the new weapon. Once or twice Fay glanced back at Walt Roland, expecting to see him pop out of his seat and pose some meaningful questions. But Roland seemed content to just sit there along with everyone else and take it all in. She had raised her hand numerous times, but the admiral had merely pretended he didn't see her raised, even-waving hand. She wasn't going to win a Pulitzer by sitting idle. Enough was enough.

When Tolbin's raised hand was recognized *again* by the admiral and hers was ignored *again*, she pulled Tolbin back down into his chair by the seat of his pants under the astonished eyes of her colleagues. Jumping up in his place, her voice edged with impatience, she called out, "Admiral! How much is this new submarine going to cost the taxpayers?"

Pulvey's face reddened. He knew discussing cost and cost overrides would incite the borderline liberals into attacking the Trident program. Hoping he could avoid answering her, he shouted back, "I'm sorry, Ms. Parks. I was recognizing Mr. Tolbin." He grew alarmed when Tolbin tried to get up and retake the floor but was pushed back into his seat by Fay, who remained standing.

"He's had a number of turns to ask questions," Fay said. "So has everyone else who wanted to pose questions. Everyone except me!'' Her complaint drew supporting cheers from Walt Roland of *The New York Times* and a few other reporters who had remained aloof until now. Encouraged by their cheers, she added, ''Either you have failed to see my raised hand all this time or you have some reason for deliberately avoiding me. Are you afraid to answer my question, Admiral?''

Pulvey said, ''Not at all, Ms. Parks. I assure you it was an oversight, not deliberate. Please feel free to ask any question you feel you must.''

''I already have, Admiral,'' Fay said with a bite to her voice.

''Again, my apologies, Ms. Parks,'' Pulvey said. ''I seem to have forgotten what it was you asked. Would you repeat your question, please?''

Fay said slowly, ''How much money is this new submarine going to cost the taxpayer?''

Pulvey glanced over at Ski and their eyes met. Looking back at his audience, Pulvey cleared his throat. ''When we attempt to pin an exact price tag on a prototype weapons system as complex as the new Trident submarine, Ms. Parks, a number of extenuating factors must be taken into consideration so that the layman won't be unduly alarmed over the figures. We must first consider engineering and design costs for such an intricate vessel as this. They run extremely high. We must take into account the many technical systems put aboard, which have soaring price tags. Many more hidden cost factors come into play as construction begins, and there are ever-changing factors inherent in economic trends. Matters that are indicative of the desired use of the vessel constantly change right along with technological advances over the course of time it takes to complete a huge ship like the U.S.S. *Trident*. Many points pertain to matters that are guarded for national security reasons. In view of all the finer points, and the fact that figures are still trickling in from the builder and subcontractors, we have nothing by way of an actual price tag to pass on that we could expect to make any sense to the layman.''

What a mouthful of double-talk that was, Fay thought. She wasn't buying any of it. ''Discounting the figures still trickling in, Admiral,'' Fay said, ''I'm for trusting the layman to be intelligent enough to comprehend that a ball park figure is not conclusive. Are you prepared to offer me such a figure? Or should I quote you as saying you don't know and seek an answer from the Defense Department on your recommendation?''

Pulvey was concerned by the outcries of support for Fay. She was gaining allies and alienating him from his. The ball park figure she was seeking was embarrassing. The actual cost far exceeded earlier estimates. It could be explained, and in time it would be. But to be too informative on the subject of cost at a time when approval for additional construction was being sought was to be disadvantaged. Yet he knew he couldn't get away with being evasive with her. She'd seek other sources of information, then expose him as a liar. Even Ski couldn't help him now by throwing in a pitch about risking national security.

"A ball park figure, as you put it, Ms. Parks," Pulvey finally said, "is rather unfair. We are talking about a prototype submarine. The Navy doesn't wish to have the figure misunderstood by people unfamiliar with . . ."

"Trust us, Admiral," Fay interrupted, then looked around at her colleagues, cheering her on. "We'll do our best to understand."

"Approximately two billion dollars for the first Trident submarine," Pulvey forced out, the words leaving a bitter taste in his mouth. "Again, that's for the prototype," he added in hearing cries of alarm from several reporters. "But we . . ."

"And just how many of these expensive supersubmarines does the Navy feel it is going to need to be on a more competitive level with the Soviet Navy, Admiral?" Fay asked.

"Well, ten similar submarines are presently under contract. But construction will be spread over a period of time—"

"Why that comes to twenty billion dollars, Admiral," Fay interrupted coarsely. "Isn't that an awful lot of taxpayers' money to spend on a theory that a gap in naval defense capabilities exists?"

Pulvey was losing patience with her and he responded bitterly, "You can't base the cost of the entire fleet on the cost of the prototype, which is always more expensive. In addition, my statement that a serious gap exists between our Navy and the Soviet Union's isn't a theory. It's a goddamn well-known fact. Having Naval supremacy over the Russians is essential to our nation and its allies, and cost should be of no consequence in closing that gap."

"Admiral, do we have an alternative that would be less costly to the taxpayers?"

"Well, it was suggested that smaller versions of the new submarine be built, but in the opinion of the Navy—which, incidentally, has to put them to use and is therefore the best authority on need—the larger version is what is needed to get the job done. Another proposal was to refit older vintage submarines, such as the Poseidon and Polaris, with longer-range missiles. But those vintage submarines will soon be obsolete, and new submarines will have to be built to take their place anyway. Why not do the job right in the first place? was the Navy's viewpoint.''

"Why not do a little of both? would be mine," Fay said. "Build fewer new supersubmarines and refit some of the older ones."

"That, my dear, is just what we are being forced to do," Pulvey said in exasperation. "It's against our better judgment, but that's politics for you. We'll have to cut the complement of these submarines so that defense spending can be allocated to land-based missile silos and maybe some additional bombers for the Strategic Air Command. I'm not saying we don't need the TRIAD program. SAC and land-based missile silos are vital to our national defense. But no one can dispute with any believability that neither SAC nor land-based missile silos are going to pack the kind of wallop that submarine-launched missiles can. Submarines can be hidden in millions of square miles of ocean. Submarines like the *Trident*, which are virtually undetectable and therefore invincible. In fact, *Ms.* Parks, this new goddamn submarine is equipped with an antisonar detection device which makes it virtually invisible to its goddamn enemies." Pride and anger were in his voice, and this unexpected statement caused his audience to react with astonishment.

An invisible submarine! Walt Roland of *The New York Times* shot out of his seat. "Admiral, would you be a little more specific about this new antisonar detection device?"

Ted Whitney of the *Boston Sun* shouted, "How long has the Navy had an invisible submarine, Admiral? What does it mean?"

"Are the missiles invisible too, Admiral?" shouted another reporter. "Do the Russians have an invisible submarine?"

The room was in an uproar. Ski quickly got up from his seat and crossed the platform to the podium. Covering the microphone, Ski whispered, "Admiral, I was going to pretend that you couldn't answer certain questions because of a potential breach of national security. Well, I'm afraid that now I have to do it in earnest and insist that you refrain from further discussion about the antisonar detection system."

"I understand, Ski," Pulvey said. "I guess I lost my temper and it slipped out." The reporters were still standing, shouting demands for more news about the invisible submarine. "I really blew it, son. What do you suggest I tell them?"

"Why don't you let me handle them, Admiral?" Ski asked.

Pulvey nodded, crossed the platform, and took his seat at the small table. Standing behind the podium, Ski raised his hands to quiet the reporters. Everyone took their seats except Fay, who stared at him as though unaware of anyone else around her. Returning her stare, Ski said, "I'm afraid what the admiral has just told you must be regarded as a potential breach of national security. To elaborate on the device any further would nullify the top secret classification of the device."

The media members released a flood of protests, prompting Ray Tolbin to get up and attempt to defend the Navy's point. "Give the captain a break, guys. If it's top secret information, he can't tell us and that's that."

"Oh, bunk, Ray. Sit down and shut up," Fay said curtly. "Surely there is something about the device that isn't top secret that we could reveal to our readers, Captain," she insisted. Her statement was supported by cheers from most of her colleagues, including Ray Tolbin's three cronies, all of whom demanded the Navy let the people know something about the invisible submarine. She felt elated. She had united the men of her profession and encouraged them to make a stand in the name of freedom of the press.

Ski raised his hands again to stifle the outcries. "As I said, in the interest of safeguarding national security, the finer points of the *Trident*'s new sonar avoidance system are top secret information. We considered it premature to release news about the device because it is still undergoing final stages of testing as part of a special Naval maneuver code-named 'Operation Ghost.' This Naval exercise is to be concluded over the Labor Day weekend, and we expect to pass along then some unclassified information about the device. However, now that Admiral Pulvey has leaked news of the new device by accident, I suppose I'd better satisfy your curiosity as best I can, if we're going to get any favorable PR for the new submarine."

"Now you're talking, Captain," Bill Simms of the *New London Post* shouted from his seat. "This new device will be the best kind of PR the Navy can get."

There was certainly something to that, Admiral Pulvey thought. "Tell 'em something about it, Ski," he called over in a low voice. "Tell the sons of bitches anything, but don't get them soured on the Navy."

Ski nodded to the admiral and to the audience. "Okay. Take notes on this if you want." He gave them a moment to prepare to take notes, then, speaking slowly so they could jot down the information, he began. "The system's technical name is a BSQ dash twenty-five, contact sonar avoidance system. It is augmented into the submarine's active, which is detection sonar, and passive, which is listening sonar. It is an integral part of SAM, the *Trident*'s Systems Aggregate Monitoring computer. How it works I can't reveal. You wouldn't understand all of the technical terms anyway, even if I did tell you. By means of technical advances in antidetection research, the *Trident* can hide from the probing signals of enemy sonar as though it were invisible. Any more information than that would, I'm afraid, be a serious breach of national security."

Pulvey got up and crossed to the podium. Speaking in a near whisper, he said, "I think at this point we'd better wrap things up, son. I've said quite enough already, and so have you. After I close the conference, I'd appreciate it if you'd invite Ms. Parks over to the buffet area for coffee and sort of tone down her animosity for the Navy. As a favor to me, Ski. Soothe her a little." Ski nodded and Pulvey faced his audience. "I must ask all of you not to treat this information as a scoop and to hold off contacting your editors until after Monday. We have the rest of the weekend to cover other points of interest. And Monday, when the *Trident* returns, you'll learn everything. Right now why don't we all partake of more refreshments?"

Tolbin motioned for his cronies to go on over to the buffet area. "I'll join you in a few minutes, guys," he called to them, then he pivoted in his seat to face Fay. "Speaking as an old pro, Fay, I really feel you're missing the point of the admiral's press conference. The submarine is built and is on its way home from its maiden voyage. We're not here to judge its performance or its cost. We've been chosen to help the Navy educate the general public on what this new weapon is all about. We're here to do that . . . and, if possible, to have a partying time while we're here."

"I'm not here to party, Ray," Fay said. "I'm a reporter and it's my responsibility, among other things, to remind my readers how expensive this new weapon is."

"Have it your way, kid," Tolbin said as he got to his feet. He shook his head and walked over to the buffet.

Ski had lingered around on the platform pretending he was gathering his things. He watched Tolbin walk off, then, seeing Fay pick up her tote bag and attaché case to leave, he intercepted her. Reaching out for her tote bag, he said, "Let me give you a hand with your things."

Fay didn't really need a hand, but she accepted the gesture of help, sensing the Navy captain was attempting to be friendly. "Thank you, Captain."

"Would you consider joining me over coffee? I'm not really such a bad guy . . . and Navy coffee is quite good," he said as they slowly headed toward the buffet area. He smiled warmly. "It's the least you could do for my having saved you from Davy Jones's locker."

Fay returned his smile. In the heat of the press conference she had forgotten that the Navy captain had saved her from falling off the pier. "Well, I could use a cup of coffee."

Walking on, Ski said softly, "I apologize on behalf of the Navy if you feel you were treated too harshly."

"No apologies necessary, Captain. Military men must support their views on defense matters, and I, as a reporter, must question them. Let's just say it was all in the line of professionalism and let it go at that."

Ski nodded, then, as they neared the cutaway model of the U.S.S. *Trident*, he said, "Have you seen our pride and joy?"

"Yes, and I'm very impressed. Are all submarines so lavishly equipped?"

"The Navy does everything possible to make life aboard all its submarines as comfortable as space will allow. But the *Trident* is considered the most lavish ship in the fleet. Being such a large submarine, it has more space for comfort."

"With the crews submerged for such long periods of time . . . how do they breathe? I mean . . . ."

"A sufficient supply of spare oxygen is carried aboard in portable cylinders for emergencies," Ski said. "But the normal supply of breathing oxygen is manufactured aboard in this area." He pointed to a compartment in the stern of the model.

"Manufactured?" Fay asked. "How?"

"This compartment is the submarine's environmental control room. The machinery in the compartment extracts oxygen molecules from seawater taken aboard while the sub is submerged. Through a process of electrolysis, the oxygen molecules are captured and passed along to accumulators. Then, as air is used up, the oxygen-manufacturing plant replenishes it with oxygen-rich air. At the same time, a system of purifiers called scrubbers bleed off carbon dioxide, carbon monoxide, and any other form of impurities from the sub's environment, such as cigarette smoke, cooking odors, aerosol sprays. In short, the system works like the gills on a fish.''

"Very interesting," Fay commented as they began walking again. "And very economical, considering you get the oxygen supply for free from the sea.''

"We try our best to be cost conscious whenever and wherever we can," Ski said pointedly. "After all, military men are taxpayers too.''

Pulvey broke off his conversation with Tolbin on seeing Ski pour coffee for the female reporter. Good, he thought. He wasn't sure if Fay was single, but as she sipped her coffee, he noticed she wasn't wearing a wedding band. He decided he'd assign Ski as her chaperon during her stay at the base. He also finally decided he'd treat the press people to a dinner and dance party at his home off the base on Sunday night. It would give him an opportunity to have one last shot at winning them over before they returned to their home offices on Monday to write their articles about the new submarine. He made the announcement at once.

"May I have everyone's attention for a moment, please," Pulvey called out. "You are all invited to my home on Sunday night for a dinner and dance party in your honor. I realize you are traveling light over the weekend, so I'll make the dress informal.''

As the reporters expressed their delight, Ensign Betty Worth hurried across the sea hangar to Pulvey. "Admiral, your aide is on the hook, sir. CIC just got word from side number seven-two-six that it's departing the Mid-Atlantic Ridge and is making knots for home waters.''

"Good," Pulvey said. "Tell Lieutenant Strong that I'll leave for CIC at once. He's to ask Captain Bentsen for an advance maintenance summary.''

"Aye, aye, Admiral." Ensign Worth said.

Pulvey took Ski to one side. "We just received a radio message from Bentsen, Ski. The *Trident*'s under way for home waters at this very moment. I want you to look after my guests until I get back from CIC. Keep the buffet going at least till then.''

"But I was supposed to meet Janet right after the press conference, Admiral.''

"Just call her and tell her it's my fault you can't make it. I've taken the liberty of assigning you to chaperon duty during Ms.

Parks's stay at the base, so let Janet know that she's to include a third party in her Labor Day weekend plans for you.''

"Admiral, you know Janet isn't going to appreciate my disappointing her two days in a row. Because of your press conference, she's already been forced to reschedule today's tennis match for tomorrow. A twosome, she and I. Then there's the small matter of my own plans to go sailing on my sloop Sunday with Dave. You see, we're already pretty booked up for the weekend, so—''

"I'll make this short and simple," Pulvey interrupted. "If you're considering not volunteering to help, then consider it an order. Get my drift, son?" Without waiting for an answer, he added, "One, forget your planned voyage with Dave on Sunday. It would be too risky taking Ms. Parks along. We've already come close to losing her overboard and I don't want to risk tempting fate again. Two, pass the word to Janet that she's to make tomorrow's tennis match a foursome or she's to scrub it entirely for this weekend. If it's to be held, then you can volunteer Dave for duty as Ms. Liberal Bitch's partner and play till you all max out. But it's to be a foursome or nothing. Three, as an officer, a gentleman, and my future son-in-law, you'll be expected to arrive at my home early on Sunday to help me with the arrangements for the party. To disappoint an old admiral would be very unkind." In response to Ski's disappointed look he patted him lightly on the back. "Don't look so glum, son. You'll be making admiral soon, then you'll have your turn at playing God. Now, excuse me while I go and excuse myself to my guests."

The Labor Day weekend, Ski thought. They sure named it right. Reflecting on his life before he was promoted to captain, he decided he'd been happier as a commander, pulling sea duty aboard subs as XO to his close friend Jack Bentsen. The promotion to captain automatically made him CO of the Intelligence Center, but the admiral saw to it that he spent more time serving as his XO than running his own command, and Janet bossed him around even more than her overbearing father. He was beginning to believe getting involved with the Pulveys was deep gumbo, certain to cause him to max out in no time at all. If he was going to marry Janet, sea duty with frequent long patrols would be in order.

Ski returned his attention to Fay. She was deep gumbo, too, he decided. He rejoined Fay and forced a smile on his face. "I've just been informed by the admiral that I'm to be your congenial chaperon during your stay at New London."

Returning his smile with equal insincerity, Fay said, "How very gracious of the admiral. Perhaps we should get on a first-name basis, then. You can call me Fay. And what can I call you besides Captain Kowalski?"

"My first name is Allen, but most people call me Ski."

"I like Ski much better than Allen."

"Fine. Do you play tennis at all?"

"Only a little," Fay said. She was being modest. She actually played expertly.

Ski hoped her game was terrible. His was and he didn't relish making an ass of himself in front of her. "Would nine tomorrow morning be okay?"

"Eleven would be better. I enjoy sleeping late whenever I can."

"Eleven, then" Ski agreed. He hoped she'd sleep right through the entire day. Jotting down his home number on a piece of notepaper, he said, "Call me when you're ready in the morning and I'll pick you up at BOQ."

A thoughtful shipmate's warning from Lieutenant Roger Strong that the admiral was on his way over to CIC saved Marine Private Nathan Lucas from being caught off guard when Pulvey thundered down the stairs to the basement of the Intelligence Center and steamed over to his post. Lucas's better judgment said, Forget challenging the admiral for a C-card and get the door to CIC opened on the double. "Attention on deck! The admiral is coming aboard!" he called into the bustling room, bringing all activity to a halt.

"As you were! Carry on with your work. Pretend I'm not here," Pulvey called out as he hurried over to Strong and Dave Lee. They were standing in front of a huge world map and a large sea chart of the eastern seaboard that occupied one wall of the room. His presence kept all hands a notch more rigid at their stations than normal. "Did you get an advanced maintenance report from Captain Bentsen?" he asked anxiously.

"Aye, aye, Admiral," Strong replied, then handed Pulvey a teletype communiqué received from the *Trident*. As the admiral pulled on his reading glasses, Strong said, "According to Jack Bentsen, the *Trident* had to surface out in the Mid-Atlantic Ridge to deal with a noisy diving plane slaving servo. He also reported being plagued with a massive electrical short circuit in the engine room, and . . ."

"I can read, Roger!" Pulvey said sourly. When he finished, he shifted his eyes from Strong to Lee and asked, "Let's see if you can tell me something I don't know—like the name of the Marine Dynamics tech rep aboard the *Trident*." His question drew blank expressions from them both. Regarding Strong directly, he said, "Well, find out who he is. The man obviously saved the day for Operation Ghost. It would have been most embarrassing if the *Trident*'s final phase of testing had had to be aborted because the quietest submarine in the world was making too much noise to complete its mission."

"I'll get on it right away, Admiral," Strong said, wanting desperately to get away from the admiral so he could keep his date with Ensign Betty Worth.

"You'll get on it first thing tomorrow morning."

"But . . . tomorrow is Saturday, Admiral."

"Haven't you heard, son?" Pulvey snapped. "Due to priorities, holiday routines for Saturday, Sunday, and Labor Day have been canceled for all officers not actually on emergency leave. The three-day weekend is to be considered an extension to the normal work week at the base, and there will be hell to pay if I catch anyone shirking their duties, without exception." Regarding Dave Lee, he said, "I believe Ski has plans for you over the weekend, too, son. Be sure to check with him before you secure for the day." Returning his attention to Strong, he added, "Roger, get out your little notebook and I'll fill you in on my weekend plans for you." But before he could begin, Pulvey's attention was drawn to the door as two uniformed Marine Dynamics Security Police captains entered.

Rudolph Boyd, tucking his C-card back into his wallet, was astonished. He hadn't expected to find Admiral Pulvey in CIC. In fact, he had done all he could to avoid running into the admiral today, the day he was to obtain the new *Trident* submarine's holding coordinates for his daughter's abductors. He and Pulvey had been good friends over the past years. Spying on the Navy right under the admiral's nose was going to make his task even more unnerving. Still, he managed to offer Pulvey his usual warm smile. "Good afternoon, Admiral. I was hoping I'd run into you," he lied. "Now I can personally say good-bye."

"Good-bye?" Pulvey repeated in a puzzled tone as he shook hands with Boyd. He thought for a moment, then remembered Arthur Harrowman, vice-president of plant industrial relations at Marine Dynamics, mentioning that Boyd was planning to retire early. "That's right! You're leaving us, aren't you, Captain Boyd?"

"Yes, Admiral. This being my last day, I thought I'd take my replacement on a familiarization tour of the Navy base." He gestured to the police captain with him. "Admiral, meet Captain Wilbur Brown, the new CO of Marine Dynamics' security police."

Pulvey shook hands heartily with Brown. "Welcome aboard, son. I'm sure we'll get along just fine." He gestured for Strong and Lee to come over and meet the new security police captain. He waited through a round of handshakes, then ushered everyone over to a wall opposing the huge world map and sea chart, where a large detailed map of the base was hung encased. "Now that you're in command of defense plant security, Captain Brown, let me brief you on some safeguards I plan to initiate over the Labor Day weekend."

As Pulvey and Captain Brown went over security measures, Boyd drifted over to the huge sea chart. A look around reassured him that no one was watching. Without delay he scanned the grease-pencil notations neatly printed on the sea chart, then settled his eyes on the references that were titled, "U.S.S. *Trident*, holding coordinates, 2200 hours, 2, September." When he was sure he'd be able to recall every detail, he retraced his steps across the room and rejoined the others, just as Pulvey was summing up his security briefing. Boyd said good-bye to the admiral and walked out of CIC with Captain Brown.

Pulvey gestured toward the sea chart and said to Strong and Lee, "Let's get back to the *Trident*'s return to home waters. Can either of you tell me the classes and names of the patrol ships COMDESOPS has assigned to participate in Operation Ghost?"

Lee had made the pertinent notations on the sea chart. "All Newport could spare for the exercise were three Spruance Class combatant destroyers."

"That's odd," Pulvey said. "I've got a side bet of a hundred bucks with Admiral Abbott of COMDESOPS that the *Trident* is going to sink every patrol ship in its area as a grand finale to Operation Ghost. I'd have thought that old frugal bastard would have put more of his hardware out there to beef up his chances of winning the wager. Which destroyers are they, Dave? What patrol patterns are they using?"

"The U.S.S. *Elliot* and U.S.S. *Spruance* are set up out along the Georges Bank discipline of the continental shelf. Our spy planes from Quonset Point observed them as running defined zigzag search configurations, supplemented with variances of straight leg and grid search patterns, used alternately. The element of surprise is theirs by virtue of changing tactics unpredictably, but—''

Pulvey interrupted. ''I'm not worried about the activities of the *Elliot* and *Spruance*, so long as they remain that far out. If Bentsen can penetrate our submerged ASW towers out along the shelf, he'll have no problem defying the surface patrol ships overhead.'' He looked up at the chart. ''What's the name of the third destroyer?''

''It's the U.S.S. *Dart*, Admiral, and—''

''The *Dart*!'' Pulvey interrupted again. ''Isn't that Bad Ass Buel's ship?''

''Affirmative, Admiral,'' Dave replied. Pointing to a search pattern he had drawn on the chart that ran parallel to the Long Island coastline, he explained, ''The *Trident*'s holding coordinates are fifty miles out from the coast. With Captain Bentsen snuggled on the bottom some ten miles north of where Commander Buel's search pattern is concentrated, the *Dart* will never even pass overhead of the *Trident* once during Operation Ghost. That gives our side a marked advantage over the mere three destroyers COMDESOPS deployed to find Bentsen.'' Seeing he had Pulvey's undivided attention, he added, ''If Buel happens to change his search pattern to include these grids further to the north, things might get a bit more interesting for Bentsen. But, knowing how stubborn Bad Ass Buel is, he'll probably go on chasing his tail ten miles away, confining his efforts overhead of gas hole Beta at grid five-nine-two.''

The gas hole Lee referred to was one of several subterranean valleys that dropped to fathomless depths below the ocean's floor. Many of the gas holes were designated as refuge-dumping zones for waste-transport ships to dispose of garbage and other unwanted material. Certain gas holes that were close to shore were protected against refuge dumping by Maritime ruling, and the Navy knew that the larger of these subterranean valleys were used as hiding places for submarines. One in particular, gas hole Alpha, was to be used by the *Trident* as its holding position during the special Navy exercise.

Pulvey was disturbed that Commander Buel had chosen to confine his search for the *Trident* overhead of gas hole Beta some ten miles south of the *Trident*'s holding coordinates. That meant he would win the wager he'd made with Admiral Abbott of COMDESOPS hands down. Being a true sportsman, he would have preferred to make winning more difficult by giving Admiral Abbott the marked advantage of having Commander Buel precisely overhead of the *Trident* during his search. ''Dave, is gas hole Beta still under the protection of Maritime ruling?'' Pulvey asked, wanting to be sure that the subterranean valley hadn't recently been declared a refuge-dumping zone without his knowledge.

"Affirmative, Admiral," Lee said after he rechecked the zoning classification for that gas hole on the sea chart.

"Get a communiqué off to Captain Bentsen at once," Pulvey said. "Use our COMSUBOPS special coding so no one from COMDESOPS can decipher the message. The *Trident* is to shift its holding coordinates from gas hole *Alpha* to gas hole *Beta*."

## Chapter Eight

Something crawly woke Helen Boyd as she lay on the narrow cot in her one-and-a-half-room prison. She opened her dark-circled eyes and cringed on seeing the ghastly brown cricket dash down her neck to her chest. She leaped from the cot and swatted at the insect, knocking it to the cement floor. With a grunt she brought one of her tennis shoes down on the creature and crushed it to death. Shivering from the spine-chilling feeling the insect had caused, she sat down at the small eating table in the middle of the twelve-foot-square room and sobbed uncontrollably. The insects were everywhere.

When she was first brought to her place of captivity in late December, she'd had only a variety of water bugs and spiders to contend with. Now that it was well into summer the crickets had moved in with her, crawling across her bed, up the bare concrete walls, and over her eating table.

The doorless bathroom that branched off from her small prison cell was the most infested area. The crickets hopped up on the cracked toilet seat and bowl and made themselves comfortable around the water taps, the soap, and her toothbrush and paste. She couldn't trust using a towel or putting on fresh clothes without first shaking them free of crickets and spiders. Nothing was more horrifying to Helen Boyd than insects. Nothing.

Helen complained to her abductors about the insects, had pleaded with them to fumigate her infested prison cell and toilet. But her captors remained insensitive. They made a mockery of her complaints, insisting she was exaggerating her fear.

She knew her captors only by their code names, but she was sure she'd never forget their faces. There was Mr. A, whose large black eyes looked out of meaty sockets with a cold unnerving stare. She sensed that his partner, Mr. B, and his superior, whom they both called Capi, were quite afraid of him. Fortunately for her, Capi listened to Mr. A's logical suggestions. It was Mr. A who'd insisted that she be given an anesthetic when Mr. B hacked off her pinky. Capi had approved. If he hadn't, she was sure Mr. B would have enjoyed performing the heartless amputation that much more.

Mr. B was a vile and despicable man. He was enormous and very strong. He sweated profusely, even in a cold room such as hers, and always stank. His light brown eyes were beady and always gleamed at her hungrily, as though he could see right through her clothes. He was preoccupied with making loathsome sexual suggestions. In return for sex, he said, he'd kill bugs for her. Though Mr. A and Capi both warned him in front of her that there'd be serious reprisals if they ever caught him sexually abusing her, Helen kept a chair wedged tightly against the door at all times. She felt she was on the edge of a nervous breakdown.

During her captivity Helen had had the opportunity to see beyond her locked cell door. Outside was a larger area of the basement, with rows of wine racks, well stocked with bottles. Lunch and dinner were almost always some kind of seafood. Fried fish aromas always seeped down to her room from early morning till late at night. Since winter's end, there had been an increase in activity upstairs. Also arriving with summer were distinct blasts of nearby boat horns. By now she was convinced she was being held prisoner in the basement of a busy seafood restaurant a good distance from New York City by the sea. She had arrived blindfolded, but she remembered hearing sea gulls and smelling salt sea air. There had been a ride from Grand Central by car, then a rather short airplane flight, followed by a second short trip by car.

Helen heard the door to her room unlock. Capi entered with a steaming tray of food that was to be her evening meal. It was on rare occasions that she got to see him. The last time was when he'd photographed her holding that day's newspaper to furnish proof to her father that she was still alive and being treated well.

Tony Capobianco, a small, bald, potbellied man in his early sixties, set the tray of food on Helen's table. "We were in touch with your father a little while ago, Helen. He sends his love, of course. He also gave us some news that should smooth things along. If all goes well, you and your father will be reunited very soon."

"Please don't tease me about something as serious as that," she pleaded.

"Who's kiddin' you? I'm dead serious. We've made arrangements with your father already."

"Please, when will you let me go?"

"Perhaps as early as this Monday night."

"What day is it today?" she asked excitedly.

"Friday!"

Helen sank deep into her seat. "God! Please let it be true."

"It is true, Helen," Capobianco said. "I've got to get back upstairs, so eat your dinner." He crossed the room to the open door, then faced her again. "By the way, you have an Uncle Gunther living in Berlin, West Germany, don't you?"

"Yes . . . I do," she said apprehensively. "Why do you ask?"

"His name sort of popped up along the way to working out your release. What does your Uncle Gunther look like? Where in Berlin does he live?"

Helen became suspicious. "Why do you need to know that?"

"Questions, questions," Capobianco said sourly. "I ask you a question and you answer me with one of your own." He narrowed his eyes. "Look, you want to get the hell out of here, don't you?" Helen nodded. "Then you're going to have to trust me, right?" A faint nod. "I have a lot of details to work out by Monday so I can reunite you and your old man. And I have to protect myself once I do let you go. So either you trust me or you stay here and rot. It's your choice."

"I'll do whatever you say. Just . . . please let me go."

"I'm trying to work that out right now, kid. Just help me so I can help you. Okay?" Helen nodded emphatically. "That's more like it, kid. Now once again, what does your Uncle Gunther look like, and where in Berlin does he live?"

## Chapter Nine

For many monotonous months the *Brighton Explorer* remained at anchor some ten miles south of Martha's Vineyard. It was a two-hundred-eighty-foot oceanographic research ship of U.S. registry licensed to conduct marine biological studies along the coast of Massachusetts and Long Island. High over the western horizon a full summer moon cast its amber glow on the vessel's forty-foot-high superstructure, while the radar antenna that topped the wheelhouse deck spun to monitor the surrounding area. Along her topside decks fore and aft were clusters of booms and winches. Below decks from her heavy bow to her broad-beamed midships were numerous repair shops, large storage holds, ship's galley and mess, and living compartments and heads for its handpicked crew of two dozen officers and men. From midships to her bulky stern, and occupying three full levels from her keel to her topside decks, was the ship's spacious aft hold. A unique design of the ship's owner, Dr. Phillip Grant, the aft hold had been modified into a hangar bay, the deck of which was steeply beveled out to form a basin and serve as an onboard dry dock for the *Scorpion*, a submersible craft that Dr. Grant also had created.

Sitting above the drained basin atop its mechanized launching cradle, the *Scorpion* was eighty feet long from her glass-bubble bow to her fluke-shaped tail. Her rounded cigar-shaped pressure hull stood twenty feet high from keel to topsides and was hatted by a five foot tall dorsal fin-shaped sail. Her body was treated with a thick rubberized dull gray coating, the color and texture of which would have the naked eye or electronic impulses of probing sonar and radar accept its mass as a blubbery substance, a whale rather than a vessel made of steel. On her back, just behind the cockpit hatch, was a blowhole. Inside the cockpit were two bucket seats set close to the deck, which were surrounded by maneuvering controls and electronic apparatus. The seats faced dual steering wheels, banks of indicators and switches, and the submersible's sonar and radar scopes. Three levers were situated on a standing console between the pilot and copilot seats. One operated a pump that spouted water out of the simulated blowhole. The second lever extended dual speakers out of their recesses in the submersible's outer pressure hull. Working in conjunction with a switch-operated reel-to-reel tape recorder, the dual speakers broadcast the repetitious cracking and barking noises of whale echolocations. The third lever engaged two high-speed, low-noise output submerged pumps that would drain the submersible of its cargo of liquid death kept in two back-to-back storage tanks that occupied the inner pressure hull from aft of the cockpit entry hatch to its tapered tail. Set on a pedestal directly in front of both seats were dual sound-sensing meters that would monitor a homing signal being broadcast to the submersible on a megahertz frequency well above the level of human hearing, functioning much like a radio bird dog. It was one of Dr. Grant's backup systems engineered into the *Scorpion*'s design.

Working feverishly in the hangar bay to prepare the *Scorpion* for a trial voyage scheduled for late that night were a dozen crewmen from the ship's engineering department. They serviced the submersible from portable scaffolds rolled lightly against the *Scorpion*'s rounded body and from a network of catwalks that were suspended by girders from the aft hold's forty-foot-high ceiling. A huge air compressor was refilling the *Scorpion*'s breathing oxygen tanks aboard. As an electric-powered boat, the *Scorpion*'s numerous batteries, which supplied power to its dual-propulsion power plants, were being recharged by a ship's electric cable played out to an input receptacle at the submersible's bow. Shadowing her hull above two pressure hull hatches midships and aft was a high-capacity fueling nozzle that would fill the *Scorpion*'s inner tanks with its venomous liquid. Along the submersible's undersides were two high-capacity dumping nozzles. They were the *Scorpion*'s stingers, which would be used for the first and only time late Sunday night when she would rendezvous with her submerged prey.

Favoring starboard amidships and spanning nearly the entire beam of the ship's superstructure on the deck just below the wheelhouse was Dr. Phillip Grant's graciously sized and lavishly decorated stateroom, furnished in French Provincial. There were two glass sliding doors, which afforded a panoramic view of the surrounding sea on that side of the ship and also gave access to Dr. Grant's personal promenade and lounging deck. His private bath included a sunken tub made of ivory, which accommodated two people comfortably and converted into a whirlpool bath with the flick of a switch. The bedroom was situated in a large alcove equipped with draw drapes. The bed was king-size and roofed with an elegant canopy made of light blue satin, which matched the sheets, pillow cases, blankets, and bedcover. Fronting the sleeping area was a spacious dining and sitting salon, delicately arranged around numerous exotic plants to form an indoor garden. Along one wall was a glass-doored cabinet, the shelves of which displayed Dr. Grant's priceless collection of artifacts, which he had gathered from all over the world. Occupying the other walls of the salon were his treasured paintings hung at eye level in gold frames. Set well off in another large alcove that winged the stateroom was Dr. Grant's library and study.

Dr. Grant was seated at his marbletop desk awaiting news of the ship's twenty-eight-foot cabin motor launch, which had been dispatched to make a discreet call to Montauk Point from a public phone on Martha's Vineyard. Grant was a tall, lean man in his mid-fifties. His nails were professionally manicured by the member of the crew who served as his barber and valet. He spoke commandingly and in a Bostonian accent. He possessed a near genius mind and displayed his intelligence with refinement and grace. His nature was exacting, his character meticulous.

The gold-plated French phone on his desk rang and Dr. Grant picked up the receiver at once. "Yes?"

"Captain Horthorne here, sir," the ship's master said. He was calling from the bridge deck, glancing over the shoulder of the ship's radar operator as he spoke. His voice had a distinct British accent. "We've just been in radio contact with the launch. Miss Marlow informs us that all went well and she expects to be back aboard within fifteen minutes."

"That's wonderful news, Brendon," Grant said. "How soon will the *Scorpion* be ready?"

"Within the half hour, Dr. Grant."

"Advise me the moment the *Scorpion* can be launched."

"Straightaway, sir," Horthorne said.

Grant got up and crossed the stateroom to a liquor cabinet and poured a generous splash of Napoleon brandy into a brandy snifter. He seated himself in a nearby armchair and thought nostalgically of all the preparations he'd made for his secret mission. He owed much to Felicia Marlow, the woman he had come to adore, who had in turn come to worship him. She had come to him as the ship's research liaison. During their first meeting, Grant saw immediately how generously gifted with brilliance she was, but also how terribly shortchanged on beauty. She was a fiery redhead who fancied a butch haircut that served to drain an already exhausted femininity. Her eyes were bright blue and slashing. She had thin lips and a milk-white face and used neither makeup nor lipstick. She stood just under five feet six and flaunted an athletic, almost masculine body. Grant appreciated her fine physical condition.

Within two short months as the ship's research liaison, Felicia, who had a Ph.D. in oceanography, had dazzled Grant with her ability to digest, retain, and recall information on marine biology with pronounced speed and accuracy. Within a year the employer–employee arrangement developed into a romance that seemed magi-

cal. Marriage was dispensed with. All that was important had taken
place within. Engraved in their hearts were vows of devout loyalty
and unshakable trust. Her life became his. Dominating her hadn't
been his demand, it was her desire. She would die for him, kill for
him. A few short years after the bond was made a major setback had
tested their vows. But they'd persevered and combined their re-
sources to defeat their enemies.

Grant pulled himself out of his chair when the door to his stateroom suddenly opened and Felicia stepped in exuberantly. He met
her halfway across the room and kissed her affectionately. "How
did your call to Mr. Capobianco go?"

"As expected," Felicia said, handing him a note with her scrib-
bling on it. "Mr. Capobianco said he's quite anxious to finalize
matters with the Boyds."

"He can't be any more anxious than we are," Grant commented.
Handing the note back to her, he said, "Read the *Trident*'s holding
coordinates to me carefully, Felicia." He crossed the room to his
desk and pressed a concealed button on its edge, then faced the wall
behind the desk as a panel lifted up smoothly. It revealed a hidden
sea chart of the Massachusetts and Long Island coastlines. There
were notations concerning the patrol ship movements that were of
particular interest. A large black dot depicted his ship's anchorage.
He took a felt-tipped pen out of his shirt pocket as Felicia began to
recite.

"Seventy degrees, thirty minutes, fourteen seconds, west longi-
tude," Felicia said, then paused to give Grant time to locate that
coordinate on the chart. She went on. "By forty degrees, twenty-
five minutes, eight seconds, north latitude." She drew closer to the
chart to examine Grant's markings. "Well, congratulations, darling!
The Navy picked gas hole Alpha for the *Trident*'s holding coordinates,
just as you guessed they would."

"Yes," Grant said quietly. "Now we have the entire picture. The
U.S.S. *Elliot* and U.S.S. *Spruance* will be of no consequence to our
mission. They're well out over the Georges Bank, some fifty miles
away from the holding coordinates. We will have the U.S.S. *Dart*
ten miles south of our rendezvous with the *Trident,* however."

"The *Dart* shouldn't pose a problem, either," Felicia said. "If its
commanding officer maintains the present search pattern his ship is
on."

"He might elect to change grid concentrations and shift over from gas hole Beta to gas hole Alpha without warning, just when *Scorpion* delivers its sting.''

''Why should he do that?'' Felicia asked.

''The *Dart*'s reaction to the submarine that penetrated home waters earlier today is what's worrying me. I seem to sense something about the *Dart*'s commander. He strikes me as being an alarmist, the way he broke off his patrol pattern and rushed to hound that submarine. Neither of his sister destroyers reacted to the intruder, and both the *Elliot* and *Spruance* were in closer proximity to the sub.''

''What are you getting at, Phillip?''

''I'm not sure, Felicia. But I do have an idea that might ease my apprehension about the *Dart*.'' He looked away from the chart. ''We have to take the *Scorpion* out on a trial run, and we have tonight and Saturday night for that purpose. We should extend the *Scorpion*'s trial voyage limits to include the fringe of that Navy destroyer's search pattern. I want to know how the skipper of the U.S.S. *Dart* will react to the *Scorpion*'s whale impersonations.''

''Won't visiting the rendezvous area ahead of time be risky?''

''Not really,'' Grant replied confidently. Using the nautical slide rule, he drew a straight line across the sea chart from the mother ship's anchorage to the *Trident*'s holding coordinates. ''I plan to introduce a bit of stimulus-reflex conditioning into the crew of the *Dart*. After a couple of nights of broadcasting echolocations to the patrol destroyer's sonar operators, they should become used to sharing the area with a noisy, but harmless whale. If I'm right, then on Sunday night we will be able to concentrate the *Scorpion*'s demonstration on the *Trident* without hindrance from the U.S.S. *Dart*.''

The desk phone rang and Grant moved away from the sea chart to answer it. ''Yes?''

''I've just heard from my number one, sir,'' Horthorne said into the bridge phone. ''All is ready in the hangar bay. The *Scorpion*'s been given a capacity recharging of breathing oxygen and battery power. You and the Missus can get under way at your discretion.''

''We'll be leaving at once, Brendon,'' Grant said. ''However, be advised that we plan to visit gas hole Alpha on the trial voyage— tonight and tomorrow night as well. I've decided we should toy with the *Dart*'s sonar operators to test the *Scorpion*'s tactical systems fully. We still have time to rectify problems with the apparatus if we encounter any.''

Horthorne thought Grant's decision to tease the crew of the *Dart* was a trifle unorthodox. But he knew his superior's behavior could be odd at times. Perhaps overconfident. "Very good, sir," he said. "I'll have ship's sonar and radar keep a sharp watch in the area. We'll be standing by smartly for a coded distress signal from the *Scorpion*, should you encounter any difficulties."

"Do that, Brendon." Grant returned the phone to its cradle. "Let's get into our jump suits, Felicia. The *Scorpion* awaits us."

## Chapter Ten

It was a balmy Saturday afternoon at the submarine base in New London, and with the grand tour of the Naval shore installation scheduled for Sunday, followed by the admiral's dinner and dance party at Pulvey's home, most of the media members were free to meditate on yesterday's exciting press conference or nurse the hangovers they had from last night's booze bash at the BOQ officers' club. Ray Tolbin, still in hot pursuit of Fay Parks, had volunteered to referee the tennis match between Fay and Dave and Ski and Janet Pulvey on one of the six courts in officers' country behind BOQ.

Two of the sets were already over, and the scores had left an air of heated competition hanging over the court during the third and final set. The first set had gone to Fay and Dave, six to one over their dazzled and somewhat dismayed opponents, a win that Fay had secured for her side almost single-handedly. With little help from Ski, Janet managed to pull the second set to her side by a score of six to four. Now, with a game score of love–thirty in the final set in favor of Fay and Dave at five games to three, Tolbin sensed that Janet was becoming alarmed.

"Time out," Janet shouted after losing the last point on Ski's serve. She moved to the rear of the court and regarded Ski. "Ski, I was about to take Fay's service return down the middle with a backhand. Why did you crowd me?"

"I didn't. You were on my side of the court."

"Ski, if you'd pay attention to the game, you'd notice that Fay keeps playing the ball to you, to deliberately avoid me. What I'm trying to do is keep some of the pressure off you."

"All I've noticed is that you keep ridiculing me." Looking down court at his opponents Ski saw a smirk on Fay's face. "I'm not one of your damn tennis students, Janet."

"Play like you're not, then. I intend to win this match," Janet said, and resumed her position at the net.

"Play ball!" Tolbin called out from the bench on the sideline. He felt a chuckle coming on as he watched Ski take his position for his serve. Poor Kowalski, he thought. Tennis just wasn't his cup of tea. But he could easily see it was Janet Pulvey's game. She not only played like Chris Evert Lloyd but she also looked like the famous tennis pro—from her blond hair down to her sexy figure. He took out the flask he brought along and helped himself to a hearty swig "Play ball!" he shouted again after the swig.

Ski bounced the ball, cocked his arm, tossed the ball up, went into his wind up, and swung.

"Net ball!" Tolbin called out through a hearty laugh as the ball rolled over to Janet's shoes.

Janet faced Tolbin with an exasperated look. "Mr. Tolbin. If you're going to call the damn match, please use the proper terminology. It wasn't a net ball. It was a fault." She picked up the ball and tossed it to Ski, commenting, "You're still putting far too much power into your serve, Ski. Try serving with a little less brawn and a lot more brain."

Ski looked across the court at Fay's grin. Envisioning the ball going right into Fay's big mouth, he tossed the ball up into the air and smashed it with a powerful swing.

"Double net ball!" Tolbin called out with authority.

After slamming into the net, the ball rolled past Janet, but she paid it no attention. Instead, she looked over at Tolbin with fiery eyes. "Double fault!"

"Right," Tolbin said with a nod. "Double fault. Wasn't that what I said?"

"You're impossible," Janet said. "Ski is impossible. This *match* is impossible. This entire *day* is impossible. Time out!" She picked up the ball and handed it to Ski. "This isn't like you at all, Ski. You lack control. You're giving them point after point. This is your last chance. You give them this point and that's the match." She skipped back to the net before Ski could unleash his fury at her.

Without hesitation Ski tossed the ball up and smashed it with his racket high above his head. It sailed over the net and for a time he feared it was going to be too long. Instead, to his sheer delight, the ball hit the service line, taking Fay by surprise. She was unable to get her racket on the ball.

"Point," Tolbin called out.

"*Ace*, Mr. Tolbin!" Ski shouted with a wide grin.

"Forty–fifteen, Mr. Tolbin," Janet added, then faced Ski. "That's more like it."

Fay glanced over at her partner. "Sorry, Dave. I just couldn't get it."

"That's okay, Fay. All we need is one more point and the match is ours."

Ski served to Dave, who returned easily. Janet poached the net to send the ball back sharply to Dave's side of the court. Fay moved over and drove the ball back toward Ski. Again Janet intervened and used a forehand stroke to drive the ball at Dave. Again Fay drove it back, and Janet intercepted the shot. In no time Fay and Janet were engaged in a heated singles rally with Dave and Ski standing idly by.

Enough was enough, Fay finally decided. She drew Janet into the net one last time, then sent a perfect forehand lob deep to the corner opposite Ski.

Janet tried to recover. She leaped in the air and swung her racket high. The ball soared a good foot above her racket. "Ski!" she shouted when she missed the shot. But Ski was too hypnotized by the action to reach the ball as it bounced good in the far corner. "Long!" Janet called out anyway.

"Wrong!" Tolbin called back. He'd had the ball in sight and had seen exactly where it had come down. "Fair ball! It's inside the boundary line!" he shouted happily.

Fay called out teasingly to mimic Janet, "It's not called a fair ball, Ray. It's called . . . end of match."

Janet looked at Ski. "You must have seen I was too far out of position to play that shot. Why didn't you go after it?"

Ski simply shook his head.

"You really didn't want to win, did you, Ski?" Janet said bitterly.

"You have it wrong as usual, Janet. I really didn't want to *play*."

"I'll remember this, Ski."

"I'm sure you will."

# Chapter Eleven

*Sunday evening*

Faint humming sounds seeped up to the main decks from the aft hold of the *Brighton Explorer*, poised at her anchorage in the calm sea. On the bridge Captain Horthorne stood silently, overseeing the ship's sonar and radar operators as they scrutinized the surface and subsurface of the surrounding sea. For the third day in a row the engineering crewmen labored in the hangar bay over the *Scorpion*, checking the submersible from stem to stern, filling the breathing oxygen tanks and recharging its numerous wet cell batteries. For the third day in a row the submersible would slide out the stern of her mother ship and dive beneath the forbidding depths. But this time the submersible's tankerlike holds would be filled to capacity with her cargo of liquid death. The *Scorpion* would keep her long-awaited rendezvous with her submerged prey and deliver her venomous sting.

Mitchel Spragg, the *Scorpion*'s crew chief, stood at his launch control position outside the *Scorpion*'s glass-bubble bow. Spragg was a short and rather stocky man in his early sixties. Ever since the *Scorpion*'s conception, Spragg had been privileged to work side by side with Grant and Felicia Marlow as they designed and installed all the technical systems that had been created for just this day. He shared Grant's and Felicia's determination to have the mission succeed.

On seeing Grant and Felicia descend a long staircase leading down to the hangar bay, Spragg moved over to the boarding ladder to greet them. He rendered Grant a laxed-hand salute. "We are ready to launch, sir," he announced. He shook Grant's and Felicia's hands vigorously. "Good luck and safe return home." He watched them climb the boarding ladder, then descend through the cockpit hatch. In another moment the cockpit hatch was pulled closed and dogged shut, and he returned to his launch control position at the *Scorpion*'s bow.

Grant took the pilot's seat across the narrow aisle from Felicia's copilot position. With the cockpit located in the undersides of the bow, almost forming a mammal's mouth with its wraparound glass-bubble enclosure, the seats had to be arranged so close to the floor that they needed to place their legs straight out in front of them, well under the instrument panels they both faced. Rows of indicators and multicolored monitoring lights were already vibrant with life from the external power being supplied to the *Scorpion* by her mother ship. "Proceed with a radio check," he said to Felicia, then joined her in slipping on their headsets.

Felicia switched on the *Scorpion*'s ship-to-ship radio and selected the mother ship's closed-channel band. Using the special call signs, she keyed her radio mike. "Kangaroo from Cub. Radio check. How do you copy, over?"

"Cub, this is Kangaroo. I copy loud and clear," the *Brighton Explorer*'s radio operator replied.

"Kangaroo from Cub. Testing coded distress signal on IFF, over." She depressed a button on the *Scorpion*'s Interrogator, Friend or Foe, transponder, sending a radio frequency signal that would be monitored only by the mother ship's radio operator.

In the radio shack on the bridge, the operator heard the established coded signal for distress. "Cub from Kangaroo, I copy on IFF, over."

"Kangaroo, radio check and IFF testing is completed. Cub, out." She keyed her intercom mike button next. "Launch control from Cub. How do you copy, over?"

Standing outside the glass-bubble bow, Spragg said, "Cub, this is launch control. I copy loud and clear, over."

"Launch control, standby, we're ready to start engines."

Grant keyed his intercom mike. "Clear astern?"

Under the submersible's fluke-shaped tail, the stern watch replied, "All clear astern, sir."

"Starting port," Grant said and engaged the port magneto. In a surge of current that dimmed the cockpit white lights, the port power drive motor released an electric-sounding howl as it began to turn. When it reached idling revolutions, Grant keyed his mike. "Turning starboard." Two mike clicks came over his headset to indicate the stern watch was clearing him to do so. His eyes were now on the starboard engine RPM indicator as he advanced that throttle to meet the position the port throttle was in. "Synchronizing engines," he called into his headset. The action caused both drive motors to hum in unison. The needles of the sync meters danced together, prompting him to engage a crossbar that spanned the dual throttles and would have them operate as one. "We have the power plant synchronized. Switching to internal power." He flicked the battery power-supply switch and again the submersible's current surged. "Pull external power cable," he called out to the crew chief over his mike.

Outside the cockpit Spragg nodded to a crewman manning the external power cable. The man yanked the ship's electric cable out of the *Scorpion*'s power input receptacle on the port bow. "External power cable is away," he reported.

"Standby for launching commands," Grant said, then regarded Felicia. "Proceed with prelaunch checklist."

It took Felicia five minutes to recite the checklist to Grant, who checked each system. Felicia verified each item on her control console, then joined Grant in functional testing the race car-size steering wheels set before each of them and the rudder control pedals and other maneuvering levers. "Prelaunch checklist completed," she announced to Grant.

Grant said to Spragg, "We are ready to be backed out. Open stern doors and acknowledge when they are fully extended. Order side handlers to standby for dry-dock flooding."

"Away stern doors," Spragg ordered, then watched as the huge doors parted like clamshells and opened to the sea. Instantly, a wave of seawater rushed in and splashed against the dry-dock basin's concrete sides. The water foamed and bubbled as it quickly climbed the steel girders of the launching cradle, swallowing it as the cradle sat motionless atop its traverse tracks. Within moments the cradle was completely submerged in the basin and the seawater rushed up the *Scorpion*'s sides. The flow of seawater neutralized with the surface of the sea outside the open stern doors and Spragg keyed his headset mike. "Stern doors fully away. Dry dock is flooded. We are ready to launch."

"Back us out," Grant ordered. In a moment he felt the backward motion of the *Scorpion* as the launching cradle's towing cable was slowly played out. Beneath the flooded dry-dock basin the launching cradle's trainlike back wheels reached their stops. The *Scorpion* was now hanging halfway out of the stern doors.

Mitchel Spragg keyed his mike. "Ready to release the launching cradle's locking grips. You are in the slot for launching."

"Roger," Grant replied. "Pull your headset cord, then release us."

Spragg detached his headset cord from its jack, closed the water-tight jack cover, and signaled the winch operator to actuate the remote-control locking mechanism. The jawlike grips of the launching cradle shot away from the *Scorpion*'s sides. For an instant, the

submersible stayed motionless, unrestrained; then it plunged backward off its cradle and splashed into the sea outside. A wave of
foamy water washed over its rounded back as the *Scorpion*
sank beneath the surface of the sea. In a moment it plunged up and
settled on the surface in neutral buoyancy.

"Switching to red lights," Grant said into his headset.

Spragg gazed at the submersible's wraparound glass-bubble bow
as it suddenly turned crimson, taking the shape of an awesome
creature's growling mouth. When the *Scorpion* began to power away
from the rear of the mother ship, he ordered, "Close stern doors."

Grant used a low power setting as he maneuvered the *Scorpion*
around to the mother ship's starboard side. He glided to a stop
abreast of the *Brighton Explorer*'s cabin motor launch.

"Kangaroo from Cub, are we clear to dive, over?"

Captain Horthorne took the headset and mike from the radio
operator. "Cub from Kangaroo. Roger that. Bon voyage and a safe
round trip. Kangaroo, out. Care to join me out on the catwalk,
gentlemen?" he said to his first and second officers. They followed
him out of the wheelhouse and joined him off starboard, where they
faced a western horizon, tinted scarlet by a setting sun.

Horthorne and his two senior officers watched as *Scorpion*'s
crimson cockpit sank under an onrushing swell. The sea around the
submersible's body foamed wildly as it climbed *Scorpion*'s back. A
second later, *Scorpion* was gone.

Fay Parks sat alone at an umbrella-topped patio table on the rear
grounds of Admiral Pulvey's home. She was mulling over her mixed
emotions about attending the admiral's press party. If she hadn't
come, she'd have missed seeing the twenty-one-acre Pulvey estate,
the fourteen-room vintage Colonial mansion set on a hilltop that
overlooked Block Island Sound, and the crescent-shaped terrazzo
terrace that afforded a panoramic view of the Sound. She wouldn't
have seen the servants' house, where the admiral's butler, up and
downstairs maids, gardener, cook, and Mrs. Pulvey's personal chauf-
feur were quartered or the four-car garage that sheltered Mrs. Pulvey's
Mercedes-Benz limousine, the admiral's Jaguar sedan, Janet Pulvey's
Porsche sports coupe, and Ski's dreamy Corvette.

Fay would have missed the sunken living room and the formal
dining room, both of which had full-size fireplaces and French doors
that opened on the terrazzo terrace, and the room-size front hall and
marble staircase that curved its way up to guest rooms, Janet's

oversized bedroom, and Admiral and Mrs. Pulvey's master bedroom—all of which had individual bathrooms. She wouldn't have seen the den where the family watched TV and video movies on a twenty-inch screen. She'd have missed the admiral's wood-paneled study, which also had a fireplace and French doors that gave access to the rear grounds. And she wouldn't have been sitting starry-eyed on the rear grounds, gaping at Mrs. Pulvey's screen-enclosed gazebo, Janet's private tennis court, the admiral's personal helicopter landing pad, and the in-ground Olympic-size family swimming pool with its submerged rainbow-colored floodlights gleaming in her face.

Fay pulled herself out of her trance and took in the party setting. It was obvious that the admiral had thought of everything from the four-piece combo to the dozen WAVE officers in gleaming dress white Navy uniforms on hand to dance with and flatter the male media members. There were also a half dozen male Navy officers neatly groomed and well informed about the Navy, the submarine base, and the Trident submarine program especially.

Fay noticed that Ski's executive officer, Lieutenant David Lee, was circling about, supervising the male officers, while his WAVE officer friend, Lieutenant J.G. Gloria Snow, encouraged the WAVE officers to perform their hostess duties. Janet and Mrs. Pulvey were overseeing the caterers and waiters, making sure that the admiral's guests were well wined and dined, and Ski and the admiral kept an eye on everything.

After a few minutes of watching Janet and Ray Tolbin dancing, Fay sensed someone standing over her. It was Ski, holding two drinks.

"A penny for your thoughts," Ski said in a friendly tone.

"I was just sort of taking in the surroundings. The admiral's home is gorgeous."

"Yes, it is." He gestured to the empty chair across from her. "Mind if I sit down?"

"Not at all." As Ski sat down, Fay eyed the two drinks he was holding. "Do you always drink your cocktails two at a time?"

Ski laughed. "No. I fetched this drink for Janet, but she went off to dance with Ray Tolbin. Do you by any chance like martinis?"

"They'll do in a pinch," Fay said, and accepted a glass. "Thank you." Fay looked around. "Everything is so breathtaking. The admiral has quite a lovely home. I had no idea the Navy paid its admirals so well."

"The Navy doesn't. Admiral Pulvey inherited all this. His great grandfather was a cannon and munitions manufacturer during the Revolutionary War. When the war was over, he managed to get licensed to sell cannons and munitions worldwide. Before long he was worth millions. He bought this spread and named it Woodcrest Hills. The estate and the munitions business was passed down to the admiral's father, who sold the business right after World War I. The money from the sale has been more than enough to keep the Pulveys financially secure. For Admiral Pulvey the Navy is not a financial necessity but a way of life."

"And what does the Navy mean to you, Ski?"

"It's both my living and the way I prefer to live my life."

"And sailing is your hobby," Fay said.

"How did you know that?"

"Janet mentioned it after our tennis match yesterday."

"I have a sloop. I call it *The Smile* because I'm in a smiling mood whenever I'm aboard her. Would you care to see her?"

"I'd love to," Fay replied, wanting to leave the boring party anyway.

"Grab your drink and follow me." He ushered her around the swimming pool. "Have you seen the admiral's terrazzo terrace yet?"

"Yes. Why?"

"At the bottom of the estate on that side of the house is our yacht club harbor. The admiral has a telescope mounted on a viewing pedestal out on the terrace." He took her arm to help Fay up the marble terrace steps, then brought her to the terrace's waist-high marble wall. The estate property was cleared of woods on that side of the mansion, and the side grounds sloped down steeply to a harbor and pavilion that was illuminated by floodlights, allowing Fay to make out a number of boats at docks along the yacht club piers and moored out in the harbor.

Ski unzipped the leather protective cover, removed it from around the telescope, and peered through the eyepiece. "You should be focused right on her cabin," he said to her as she stepped up to the telescope.

Fay felt Ski's muscular frame against her back. His arms were steadying her, just as they had at the admiral's press conference to prevent her from falling off the pier. It was a reassuring and sensual feeling to her, and she did nothing to make him feel uncomfortable, certain he wasn't aware of the physical contact. Her nostrils filled with the masculine fragrance of the cologne he was wearing. She felt as though she should say something about the sloop she was gazing at, but she was experiencing a breathtaking feeling that conversation would have spoiled.

"Do you see it? Is the telescope focused on an all-white sloop with a dark blue stripe climbing the side of her cabin?" Ski asked after a few moments of silence.

"Yes . . . I see it," Fay finally said. She turned and faced him, her eyes staring into his.

Ski returned her gaze for a long silent moment. He experienced an urge to kiss her rose-colored lips but didn't. He found her perfume very appealing, arousing. He cleared his throat and took a step backward. "Shall we get our drinks?" he said, his voice husky.

Fay smiled at him, sensing his embarrassment, which she thought was cute. She stood beside him at the terrace wall and sipped her drink, making no effort to leave the enchanting view of the Sound and return to the party. She was pleased that Ski didn't seem anxious to do so either.

For what seemed an eternity, the *Scorpion* hung in neutral buoyancy some three hundred feet beneath the sea's surface with less than ten feet of water between her keel and the ocean's floor. Her glass-bubble cockpit faced at the black void that was gas hole Alpha's craterlike walls, making a circumference of nearly a mile before descending to seemingly fathomless depths.

Dr. Phillip Grant listened carefully as a faint beeping sound suddenly became audible, and the dual megahertz indicator needles began to flicker simultaneously. The movement was being caused by a signal from a source known to the *Scorpion*, transmitted on a megahertz radio wave frequency well above the level of human hearing and beyond the detection range of a ship's passive sonar. To enable Dr. Grant to listen to as well as see the effect of the source of the signal on the megahertz indicators, a beeping device was electronically linked to function in unison with the needles. With this device he could tell when the source was moving toward or away from him.

The *Scorpion* was at the U.S.S. *Trident*'s overnight holding coordinates, and Grant knew the relative course the new submarine would strike to arrive at that rendezvous. The bird-dog signal grew stronger and Dr. Grant speculated on the *Trident*'s proximity as the submarine's movements indicated that it was heading straight for the *Scorpion*. So that the *Scorpion*'s presence at the holding coordinates would go unnoticed until it was time for her whale impersonations, only the quietest and most essential equipment was turned on.

Turning to Felicia, Grant said happily, "Our visitor is home and enroute to us. What are things like on the surface?"

Through her earphones, Felicia heard and noted the surface engine sounds that correlated with the displays on her passive sonar oscilloscope. The *Elliot* and *Spruance* are still over the Georges Bank region of the continental shelf. The *Dart* is on a westerly course about ten miles south of us. I don't detect any other activity in the direction of the Georges Bank."

Grant settled back in the pilot's seat and listened as he continued to plot the *Trident*'s progress visually along the line he had drawn on the active sonar scope to mark her expected course. He was envisioning the *Trident*'s position to be within ten miles of the *Scorpion* when suddenly the needles flickered and leveled off along with the beeping sound, indicating the submarine had altered its course. He became tense behind his controls. "Something's gone wrong," he said.

"What is it?"

"I'm about to find out right now," Grant replied, then reached between the left side of his seat and the cockpit wall where his sea charts were stowed in their protective container. He removed one chart and opened it fully, then folded it in sections until the immediate area around the *Scorpion* was displayed. Studying the chart, he said, "Mr. Nelson Hobart's little installation aboard the U.S.S. *Trident* is about to prove to be indispensable. The coordinates Rudolph Boyd gave us are wrong. According to our bird-dog signal the *Trident* is passing by gas hole Alpha at this very moment."

"Do you think Boyd deliberately lied to us?"

"I doubt he would have risked his daughter's life to do so. He might have inadvertently gotten the wrong information, or perhaps the Navy made a change in plans after he obtained the coordinates for gas hole Alpha."

"Can we use the bird dog to follow the *Trident*?"

"Yes. But we needn't do so. According to this sea chart, there's only one other area deep enough and vast enough to accommodate a submarine the size of the *Trident*." Using a pen, he scribbled lines on the sea chart that plotted a course for the *Scorpion*. "We'll get under way at once. I think we'll arrive at gas hole Beta at the same time the *Trident* does."

\*　　\*　　\*

". . . And you're absolutely sure of those calculations, Roger?" Admiral Pulvey said into the phone as he gazed out of the double French doors of his study at his guests. He listened as his aide, Lieutenant Strong, repeated the information being relayed to him by CIC personnel at the base. "Very well, Roger. You can secure for the day. I'll see you at the base bright and early tomorrow morning." He hurried out to the patio to find his wife. He located Elizabeth Pulvey standing near the barbeque pit. "Elizabeth! The news has come and it's all good. I want you to have all the waiters bring champagne and glasses out to my guests. I'll be over by the band shell, waiting for your cue to stop the music when the waiters are in position." He walked over to the center of the patio and interrupted Janet's dance with Ray Tolbin. "Janet! I just got word from the base! It's time to make my announcement. See to it that everyone stays within hearing distance of the band's drumroll."

Ski released a hearty laugh as he and Fay continued gazing out at the Sound from the terrace. He was more relaxed than he had been in months and was enjoying their conversation. He had learned that Fay was a native of San Diego, of the Mission Beach area, while he had been born and raised in nearby Chula Vista. He'd been delighted to learn that Fay shared his enthusiasm for sailing.

Fay's eyes shone with the brilliant light of the moon. "It's beautiful here, Ski."

So are you, Ski thought, admiring her face and silky hair. He wished Janet were like Fay.

"Am I interrupting anything?"

Ski spun around to see Janet climbing the last step to the terrace. "We were just looking through your father's telescope."

"How interesting," Janet said, and added drily, "Might I suggest, though, that you can see a great deal more if you actually put your eye up to the telescope."

Ski smiled grimly. "What do you want, Janet?"

"Come inside. Dad's about to make an announcement. He's heard good news from the base."

"You and Fay go on. I'll be along as soon as I've covered up the telescope."

"Don't be long," Janet said, then headed down the terrace steps with Fay.

Ski replaced the protective cover on the telescope and zippered it closed, then went to the terrace wall and resumed gazing at the

Block Island Sound. He knew what the admiral's announcement would be and wasn't interested in hearing all the details again.

Admiral Pulvey lifted a glass filled with champagne from a waiter's silver serving tray, then climbed the one step to the band shell and accepted the microphone from the band leader, who signaled the drummer. The drumroll stopped the dancing and drew everyone's attention to the band shell. "Everyone! Get a glass of champagne, but don't drink a drop of the bubbly until I give you the cue!"

When everyone had their champagne, he spoke again. "As I mentioned rather prematurely at the press conference on Friday, we are in the process of putting the U.S.S. *Trident* submarine's new sonar avoidance system through the most grueling tests our own air-sea warning systems can give it. Also, out in her home waters and searching relentlessly to detect her arrival are three Spruance Class combatant patrol destroyers. I am pleased to announce that I received a telephone call from base. Based on calculations our CIC personnel have made about the *Trident*'s plotted course progress, we can safely assume that the new submarine is now at its planned overnight holding coordinates, that it arrived there in total defiance of our ASW system and the three destroyers poised to catch her sneaking home." He raised his glass. "You reporters will be given more detailed information about the new system tomorrow, when the *Trident* gets back into port. Information, I might add, that you will be allowed to release to the public. In celebration of this momentous accomplishment, please join me in a toast."

On hearing faintly the admiral's announcement, Ski reflected on how he would have been aboard the *Trident* with his close friend and former shipmate Jack Bentsen as Jack's executive officer, if it hadn't been for a reassignment to shore duty. He watched the navigation lights of a ship passing out on the Sound, wishing he could have gone on the U.S.S. *Trident*'s maiden voyage, wishing he could somehow return to sea duty and get away from the Pulveys for a while.

## Chapter Twelve

Fifty miles out at sea on a patrol course that paralleled the coast of Long Island, the clipper bow of the U.S.S. *Dart*, a modern antisubmarine combatant destroyer, sliced westward through the slow rolling sea under the moon's silver glow. The *Dart*'s radar antenna spun continually to search the surface of the sea and the night sky above her quiet decks, while her active and passive sonar probes scrutinized the surface and the depths below her broad-beamed five-hundred-thirty-foot hull. On her forward deck, facing the night sky and unmanned, was the *Dart*'s four-tubed computer fire-controlled antisubmarine rocket launcher, the ship's nuclear air-to-sea defense system, which had a complement of sixteen ASROCS. Also un-manned and looking skyward on her aft deck was the ship's computer fire-controlled surface-to-air multirocket launcher, the *Dart*'s nuclear antiaircraft defense arsenal. Mounted on her bow and stern were five-inch, fifty-four-caliber deck guns, which were the *Dart*'s nonnuclear surface defense weaponry. Amidships, port and starboard, were twin depth-charge launchers that fired live or warning charges into the sea to encourage an unyielding submarine from hiding. Towering above the depth charges amidship was the *Dart*'s bulky superstructure, which housed the bridge deck topside and the CIC room below the bridge. Connected to the superstructure on her aft deck was the flight deck that accommodated the ship's HH-2D Seasprite helicopter, the *Dart*'s aerial flyaway extension of her search-and-defense system, which also served as a rescue arm of the fleet.

The *Dart*'s bridge windows were aglow with red night-vision lights as the hour neared 11:00 P.M. Standing the twenty hundred to double-zip bridge OOD watch was Ensign Karl Schmidt, a wiry man in his twenties and a new junior officer in the destroyer squadron, who was constantly uneasy in the presence of his commanding officer.

Commander Brewster Arnold "Bad Ass" Buel released a loud belch that turned all heads on the bridge in his direction. "Send my compliments to sick bay, Mr. Schmidt," he said in a sour, throaty voice. "It took three goddamn doses, but their bicarb finally worked."

He massaged his potbelly. "Christ! I've been waiting for that one all night. Now I feel another burp in the making."

Buel shifted his hefty frame in his captain's swivel armchair, then regarded the digital display clock on his command console in front of him. The evening meal the ship's cook had conjured up was depriving him of sleep. So was the spook submarine. He sensed the new submarine's presence, knew it was somewhere under his ship, hidden in the depths. Its skipper and crew were probably laughing at him right now. He removed his baseball cap with the gold embroidered peak and the matching *CO* letters on the front of it, then ran his hand through his thinning silver-gray hair. Just over fifty, with over twenty years of destroyer duty under his belt, half of which he'd spent as a veteran tin can skipper, he had participated in more war maneuvers than he could count. Each war game was real to him, a welcome challenge to his professionalism. As a destroyer skipper he had a reflexiveness about submarines. He was the hunter, conditioned to stalk the seas for the submerged fox.

For Buel Operation Ghost was a special kind of war game. It was a match of man against machine. At stake was Buel's precious E-flag, an efficiency award bestowed upon the *Dart* and her crew by Admiral Abbott. The E-flag had been flying on the *Dart*'s mast for two full years, with every destroyer in her squadron itching to take it away from her. His crew had hated every drop of sweat poured into getting the E-flag and had since hated every drop of sweat spent on keeping it. But if the flag were ever lost to a sister ship, Buel would see them hate themselves far more than they hated him for driving them to win the E-flag.

A radioman third class stepped out of the radio shack and crossed the bridge to Schmidt. "We got the royal shaft, sir," he said in a low voice. He handed Schmidt the radio message he had just received from the *Dart*'s home base in Newport, Rhode Island.

Schmidt quickly read the message, then sheepishly brought it over to Buel. "Bummer news from the base, Skipper."

Buel looked at him. "You just tell me, Schmidt. Maybe it'll be easier to take that way."

"Per COMDESOPS, the *Dart* is not to return to base upon conclusion of Operation Ghost. Admiral Abbott is extending our patrol for another week. We won't see liberty until a week from tomorrow."

"Why are we being extended?" Buel asked acidly. "Why not the *Elliot* or *Spruance*?"

"Word has it the *Elliot* and *Spruance* are shipping out to the Med after Operation Ghost. They're being deployed to beef up COMSIX operations along with the *Foster* and *Kinkaid*."

"Hell, the *Beach*, *Drexell*, *Hewitt*, and *Radford* are out with the sixth fleet now. What in hell is going on over in the Med that requires that much of our squadron's complement?"

"It seems like things are flaring up there again, Skipper."

"It *seems* like that, does it?" Buel barked. "I'll tell you what it *seems* like to me! It seems we're always getting screwed! Goddamn bastards. My wife and kids are counting on our getting back in tomorrow. We're having a Labor Day backyard bash."

"COMDESOPS wants you to acknowledge receipt of the extension advise personally, Skipper."

"Goddamn bastards!" Buel growled again. He knew Admiral Abbott was making sure he didn't ignore the message by demanding a confirmation. "Send it! Message received! Wilco! B. A. Buel."

"Aye, aye, Skipper," Schmidt said, then hurried off to the radio shack.

In CIC beneath the bridge deck, Ensign Sheldon Lichenberg was just turning the last page of the paperback novel he was reading, anxiously anticipating the climactic unfolding of the mystery thriller, when the *Dart*'s active sonarman called over to him. He slapped an angry fist on the arm of his chair, then threw the novel across the desk and got up to see what was disturbing the sonar operator. "One more minute, Dawson! That's all I needed to know who killed Mrs. Greene!"

"Want me to tell you who did it, sir?" Sonarman Dawson asked. "I read the book last week."

"No, I don't, Dawson. I want you to tell me why you had to disturb me. If it's anything less than the U.S.S. *Trident*, I'm going to kill you."

"I'm picking up a return that's about the same strength as the whale we chased after the last two nights. Should I forget about it, sir?"

"Believe me, Dawson, I wish we could. But Bad Ass wants us to report everything we detect in the area. I'd be the one to get murdered if he ever found out I failed to obey that order." He turned to the passive sonarman. "Are you monitoring whale echolocations, by any chance, Otis?"

"Sorry, I can't help you out, sir," Sonarman Otis replied sympathetically. "Right now everything's quiet."

Lichenberg nodded. "Then it's going to be GQ time once again in the middle of the night." He picked up the phone and pressed the call button for the bridge.

Ensign Schmidt picked up the bridge phone on the first ring, hoping to prevent the call from waking up Bad Ass, who was just starting to doze off in his captain's chair. He watched Buel stir and waited until the skipper settled down again, then answered in a near whisper, "Bridge, Schmidt."

"Karl, it's me," Lichenberg said at the other end. "We have a contact on active. Dawson thinks it's that goddamn whale again."

"Does passive have anything to back that up, Shelly?" Schmidt asked anxiously.

"Not a goddamn peep," Lichenberg replied.

"Crap! Bad Ass was just dozing off, too."

"Sorry about that, Karl. It's your baby now. Want me to hold on while you tell Bad Ass or shall I let the GQ alarm tell me his reaction?"

"Standby, Shelly," Schmidt said in a disgruntled tone, then crossed the bridge to Buel. He shook his commanding officer gently. "Skipper. CIC has a contact on active sonar. Sonarman Dawson thinks it's that nuisance whale again."

Buel opened his eyes at once. "He does, does he?" he bellowed, then slipped his headset over his baseball cap and keyed the mike button. "Active sonar from bridge!"

Dawson gestured to an earphone of his headset to let Lichenberg know he was talking to Bad Ass. "Active, aye!"

"What makes you so damn sure you have a whale on sonar? Did it introduce itself? Did it say, 'Hello! My name is Moby Dick?' "

"No, sir. I assumed it was a whale by the kind of return I'm getting from it, Skipper," Dawson explained.

"Rule number one aboard this ship is never assume anything," Buel snapped back. "Now, where is it?"

"Subsurface contact is bearing zero-four-five. Range, five thousand yards. Heading, two-two-zero. Speed, ten knots. Depth, three hundred feet."

Buel played his long headset cord out behind him as he moved across the bridge to the plotting table. "Get off that phone, mister," he said to Schmidt. "I want your fanny over here." He bent over a sea chart of his patrol area and noted in pencil the bearing and heading, then drew a connecting line between the two notations. "Pay attention, Mr. Schmidt, you're about to learn something." Using the pencil as a pointer, he explained. "Last night and Friday night we chased a contact hanging out between these two gas holes. When we gave chase, the contact began making loud clicking and barking noises. Right?'' Schmidt nodded. ''So we assumed we were chasing a whale and broke off the pursuit. Right?''

"Some of those gas holes are pretty deep, Skipper. Whales like to sound in 'em,'' Schmidt offered.

"You're missing my point, Mr. Schmidt. I know whales like to sound in 'em. Submarines like to hide in 'em, too. Especially big submarines . . . like our ghost boat. What if by assuming those cracking and barking noises were whale echolocations we've played right into the hands of the spook? What if the spook has been having a high ol' time running us around?''

"But those whale echolocations sounded authentic to passive sonar. And active was getting the kind of return from the contact that a mammal would cause,'' Schmidt said defensively.

"There are more things we don't know about the ghost sub than there are things we do know. That's why I'm always chewing you people out for assuming things.''

"Yes, sir.''

"Sound GQ. Order flank speed.'' Buel glanced at the sea chart. "Come about on an interception course of zero-nine-zero. Load port and starboard launchers with warning depth charges.'' He regarded Schmidt. "We'll go and have a look-see this time. Either lightning can strike three times in the same place or it isn't lightning at all.''

"Skipper,'' Schmidt said in a troubled tone, "are you planning to kill the whale?''

"Rule number two aboard the U.S.S. *Dart*, Mr. Schmidt, is never respond to an order with a question. That's one sure way to wind up on my shit list. Sound GQ, please, Mr. Schmidt,'' Buel repeated, then keyed his headset mike. "Active sonar from bridge.'' He was acknowledged by Dawson. "You keep that contact of yours in check. We're heading after it.'' Holding his mike button down, he added, "Passive, keep listening. I think you'll be hearing something very soon.'' He crossed the bridge to his captain's chair as the General Quarters alarm bell and shrilling horn sounded. Smiling devilishly he picked up the PA-system microphone and keyed on. "Yes, gentlemen! It's GQ time once again. Sorry to disturb your sleep, but war is hell—even when it's a game. You have two minutes to report manned and ready, so get the lead out of those fannies. Pretend you're heading down the gangway to pull liberty.''

The U.S.S. *Dart* leaned hard to starboard as the ship was brought about to port for her interception course. Out of compartments and passageways below decks officers and enlisted men scrambled, half asleep, to get to their battle stations.

Lieutenant Commander George Carwell, the *Dart*'s executive officer, arrived on the bridge as the last few GQ stations were reporting in, manned and ready. In a near whisper he asked Ensign Schmidt, "What's the GQ for?" He was one rank below Buel, next in command aboard the *Dart*, with five years less service time in destroyer duty than his superior.

"Active sonar thinks we've got a whale in our area again. Bad Ass thinks it's the spook, screwin' around with us," Schmidt whispered back.

"What does passive have?"

"Not a goddamn thing, George. But I'll bet passive will be reporting whale echolocations very soon now that we're barreling after the whale. The poor creature's gonna have a goddamn cardiac arrest if it sticks around this ship much longer." He leaned closer to Carwell's ear. "He ordered the launchers loaded with warning depth charges."

Carwell nodded, then made his way over to Buel. He glanced at the captain's digital clock. It was displaying 11:49 P.M. "Good morning, Brewster!" he said sarcastically.

Buel glanced at the clock too. "Yes, I guess you could call it morning." He regarded his XO and took note of Carwell's disgruntled expression. "I suppose you're going to give me your little speech about how the crew needs their sleep. How midnight GQ drills foul up things for ship's work the next day. How the men are bound to become overwrought if we keep interrupting their beauty rest night after night."

"You forgot one, Brewster. How GQ drills should be spread out over daylight hours when and where possible, so as not to create unnecessary morale problems for me."

"Morale problems!" Buel grunted. "I could wake the bastards up every night at midnight and never hear a bitch from them if it was for liberty call. They'd be willing to swim back to Newport from here if the boatswain piped commencement of liberty right this minute. You wouldn't see one of 'em too tired to haul ass for shore."

"All I'm saying, as the man responsible for the morale aboard ship, is this midnight GQ crap for the third night in a row seems an undue harassment of the crew. It's bound to lead to inefficiency. That could cost you your precious E-flag."

"And you tell every goddamn one of 'em that I'd better not catch 'em dragging their ass deliberately. You can also tell 'em there's gonna be another week of the same harassment coming up. We've had our patrol extended till next Monday by COMDESOPS. Now, why don't you get Admiral Abbott on the horn and ball him out for screwing up ship's morale and let me do my job in peace?" Buel heard someone's voice in the headset. "What was that? Who just called to the bridge?" he bellowed into his mike.

"Passive sonar, Skipper. I'm monitoring whale echolocations."

"You're picking up clicking and barking noises that sound like whale echolocations, you mean," Buel said.

The U.S.S. *Trident* had just arrived overhead of gas hole Beta and was about to settle to the bottom of its overnight holding coordinates when passive sonarman Rudges pulled his earphones away from his head in response to loud and repetitive cracking and barking noises he suddenly began monitoring nearby. "Skipper, I believe we have a visitor heading toward us. I'm monitoring defined mammal echo-locations, and by the sound of them, I'd say it's a whale with a hell of a hangover." He returned the earphones to his head, then cupped his hands over them. "Wait . . ." He listened more intently to something accompanying the whale noises. "The whale isn't the only visitor we have, Skipper. That surface patrol ship I reported fading when we were coming in has just reversed course. It's bearing two-seven-zero at about three thousand yards. But it's now heading zero-nine-zero. Right for us, sir."

"Belay that order to descend!" Bentsen called to the ballast station. "All stop!"

Lieutenant Commander Harris broke off his conversation with Nelson Hobart and left the engineering tech rep standing by himself at the plotting table. Looking anxious, he crossed the control room and joined Bentsen at the captain's command console. "Do you suppose that surface patrol ship detected our arrival somehow, Jack?"

"Either us . . . or the whale Rudges is also monitoring," Bentsen replied. "We'd better sit tight and see what happens next." He keyed the PA-system mike. "All hands! This is the captain speaking. Maintain quiet about the ship!"

"It's still coming right toward us, Phillip," Felicia Marlow said as she listened to the approaching engine noises on the surface some distance away.

"The *Trident* has stopped," Grant commented. "It appears the skipper of the *Dart* wants us to do a repeat performance of our whale skit. We'll lure the surface patrol ship away from the *Trident*, then come back after we've convinced the *Dart* we're nothing for her to be concerned with."

"Bridge from active," the *Dart*'s active sonarman called into his headset mike.

"Bridge, aye," Buel answered before Schmidt or Carwell could.

"Contact is changing course to zero-zero-zero. Range, three thousand. Speed, still ten knots. Depth, still three hundred feet."

"Passive! Do you confirm?" Buel asked into his mike.

"Roger that! Cracking and barking sounds still intense and repetitious, Skipper."

"Come about to port!" Buel called to the helmsman. "Steer zero-two-zero. We'll cut the bastard off at the pass." He regarded Schmidt. "Are depth-charge launchers loaded with warning shots?"

"Aye, aye, Skipper. Loaded port and starboard."

"Arm them! Standby for my order to fire!"

Felicia banged a closed fist on her control panel. "The *Dart* has turned! Her skipper intends to hound us."

"Remain calm. The destroyer skipper is doing exactly what I want him to."

"What if he keeps running us down? He doesn't seem satisfied with hearing the *Scorpion*'s whale echolocations. He's forcing us to waste precious time and power."

Grant knew he couldn't allow the pursuit to go on indefinitely. There was still much to be done. "You're right, of course. We'll allow the *Dart* to get a little closer, then perform our spouting act."

Aboard the *Dart*, active sonarman Dawson quickly keyed his mike. "Bridge from active. Contact is changing depth." He paused, then added, "It's heading for the surface, Skipper."

"Are you sure of that, mister?" Buel barked.

"Damn sure, sir," Dawson replied.

"Do you confirm that, passive?"

"Roger that, Skipper. Contact is surfacing ahead of our bow."

"Get the bow floodlights switched on," Buel ordered, then grabbed his night-vision binoculars and hurried out to the forward-bridge catwalk. "Bow watch! Do you see anything?" he called into his mike as he checked the sea off starboard bow.

"I see a fin, Skipper," the bow watch replied, his binoculars trained on the sea ahead as well. "It's at one o'clock, sir."

Buel aimed his binoculars slightly to the right of starboard bow, then settled them on the dorsal fin knifing through the sea.

"It's a whale, Skipper," the bow watch reported firmly. "It's clearing its blowhole, sir."

Buel eyed the water spouting up from the sea, then played his binoculars on what was a trace of a rounded body. He lowered his binoculars when the dorsal fin slipped back under the surface. "You're a lucky bastard," he muttered as he headed back into the bridge.

"Contact is sounding," active sonarman Dawson reported, still leery of naming the contact a whale.

"Disarm and unload depth-charge launchers port and starboard," Buel ordered. "Secure from General Quarters. Come hard to port. Ahead half speed on course two-seven-zero." He regarded Carwell, noticing a smirk on his XO's face. "At least we didn't assume. We found out," he said softly.

"Engine sounds fading rapidly, Skipper," passive sonarman Rudges reported, ending the silence in the *Trident*'s control room. "It was that damn whale the surface patrol ship was chasing after, not us." He looked across the room at Bentsen. "Still monitoring those whale echolocations. They seem to be getting louder now, sir."

Bentsen nodded and erased the display on SAM's viewing screen that identified the surface patrol ship.

"I'll note in the ship's log the course changes the destroyer made while chasing after that whale," Harris said. "Just in case her skipper claims he had detected us instead of the mammal." Looking into Bentsen's eyes, he added, "You know, it's a scary feeling penetrating our own ASW systems and sailing right under the keels of our own patrol ships without being detected."

"Let's just hope the Russians never attain that capability." Bentsen turned to the ballast station. "We can resume our descent to the bottom now. Set us down nice and easy." He joined Harris at the navigations plotting table and stared down at the three-dimensional display that was simulating the *Trident*'s descent down the center of gas hole Beta's steep walled subterranean canyon.

"Whale echolocations intensifying, Skipper," Rudges reported.

He was becoming annoyed by the repetitious clacking and barking sounds. "The contact is bearing zero-zero-zero. Range, one thousand yards. Heading, one-eight-zero. Speed, ten knots. Depth, three hundred feet." He looked across the control room at Bentsen and Harris. "The damn thing is coming straight for us, yelping away."

Nelson Hobart was standing on the opposite side of the plotting table from Bentsen and Harris. Seeing Bentsen raise a concerned eyebrow, he said, "Congratulations on a safe and unobserved return to home waters, Captain."

Bentsen smiled. "Thank you, Mr. Hobart. In all probability the silent-running repair you made on our diving plane servo insured that we would arrive unobserved."

The needles on Grant's megahertz indicators reached optimum range as he brought the *Scorpion* overhead of gas hole Beta. After circling the subterranean canyon, he put the submersible into a steep dive and began his descent. "Standby to switch on the dumping pumps, Felicia. The *Scorpion*'s sting of justice is but moments away." He raised the volume on the whale echolocations to the highest setting so the continuous clacking and barking sounds would compensate for what little noise the dumping pumps would make. The whale echolocations would also compensate for whatever noise was made when the payload being dumped was replaced by seawater needed to maintain ballast during the delivery.

"Neutral buoyancy," the *Trident*'s ballastman called across the control room. "We're on the bottom, Skipper."

"Secure ballast," Bentsen replied. "Set overnight watches," he said to Harris.

"Damn!" passive sonarman Rudges shouted as he pulled his earphones away from his head.

"What's wrong, Johnny Reb?" Bentsen asked as he crossed the room to Rudges.

"It's that damn whale, sir. It's right overhead and it's making so much noise I can't hear anything else." He offered his earphones to Bentsen. "Just listen to that dang yelping, sir."

Bentsen slipped the passive sonar earphones over his baseball cap and listened for a moment. Then, looking puzzled, he turned up the volume and listened more intently. "Isn't that peculiar?" he said.

Nelson Hobart watched with concern as Bentsen listened to the whale echolocations. Bentsen's extreme interest in what he was hearing disturbed him. As the captain reached for the passive sonar module's sound-detection separation switch, Hobart grew frantic. The SDS switch would link the passive sonar with a series of mix-down sound channels that would enable Bentsen to isolate the noises being detected. With the aid of the Systems Aggregate Monitoring computer each separate source of noise could be referenced in SAM's memory bank for an identification. Hobart couldn't allow that scrutiny to take place. He crossed the room at once and shook Bentsen's arm to get his attention. "Excuse me, Captain Bentsen!"

Bentsen's hand stopped short of flicking the SDS switch. He turned to face Hobart and removed the earphones. "Yes, Mr. Hobart?"

"Captain, I detected a problem with the ship's annunciator module that I'd like to look into further with your permission." It was a fabricated problem that he hoped sounded convincing.

"When did you detect that, Mr. Hobart?"

"When you called for all stop before," Hobart said. "It may be just a small thing. There are a number of plastic tumblers that can wear down and cause the annunciator to respond to bells sluggishly. I'd hate to let it go unchecked. You might experience a sluggish response as you're maneuvering into the new sea hangar tomorrow and that could result in ramming into the dock."

"What does looking into the problem entail?" Bentsen asked, sounding exasperated.

"Dismantling the telegraphic annunciator module in the engine room, so the plastic tumblers can be inspected and replaced if necessary."

"Well, I'd hate to risk ramming into the slip walls of the new sea hangar right under the Bull's nose. We won't be moving out of here till morning, so go ahead. Just be sure you don't delay our return to port."

"Thank you, Captain. I'll get on it at once."

Still feeling disturbed by what he had been listening to, Bentsen slipped the passive sonar earphones back on, but the whale echolocations had stopped. He took them off and handed them back to Rudges. "It seems your whale friend has gone, Johnny Reb." He crossed the control room to Harris. "Take the night watch here in the control room, George. I'll be up bright and early to relieve you." He thought to have a bite to eat in realizing he hadn't eaten all day, but passed on doing so and went right to his cabin.

*     *     *

"Problems!" the engineering chief growled at Hobart as they stood at the annunciator in the engine room. "Problems right up till the last damn minute! I had all my tools packed and ready for offloading when we got into port tomorrow. Now you want me to dismantle the goddamn TA. You sure this can't wait till we get into port?"

"I'm afraid not, Chief. We can't risk a maneuvering accident."

"Then I might as well get started on it and get it over with."

"All you need do is inspect the annunciator's engaging tumblers and replace any that seem worn. If you need me for anything, I'll be in my cabin." The chief nodded and Hobart headed forward to his private cabin. He let himself in and locked the door after him. Without delay he slipped a portable breathing oxygen tank onto his back and strapped it in place, then covered his mouth and nose with an oxygen mask and turned the tank's air valve on. To make sure he'd leave his cabin precisely at the planned time, he set his Seiko wristwatch alarm. Now the waiting began.

Grant settled the *Scorpion* on the bottom, just aft of where the U.S.S. *Trident* was situated. He shut down his bird-dog apparatus, then gestured for Felicia to hand him the submersible's passive sonar earphones. "We'll know when it's time to make our ascent to the surface by what I hear through these, Felicia. No need for both of us to stay awake. You rest. We'll have to accomplish things very quickly when we do surface. The more rested you are, the better."

"Will you be all right, Phillip? You look quite tired yourself."

"I'll be fine." He raised the volume on the passive sonar to a high setting, then, as Felicia closed her eyes, he settled back in his seat for the long wait.

## Chapter Thirteen

Lieutenant Commander George Harris stopped making notations in the ship's log. He felt a sharp pain in his chest, which seemed to radiate to his arms and was accompanied by a shortness of breath. The symptoms were those of a heart attack. He dropped his pen and gripped his chest with both hands as the pain intensified, and was about to call across the control room for help when the pain subsided as quickly as it had come on. He took a deep breath, then picked up his pen and continued making notations.

Passive sonarman Rudges brought his right hand up to his chest as he, too, felt a sharp pain and experienced restricted breathing. He was about to tap active sonarman Peterson on the shoulder when the pain stopped. What the hell was that all about? he wondered. He shook his head and returned his attention to the silence he was monitoring outside the submarine with his earphones.

Active sonarman Peterson had his station shut down while the sonar avoidance system was turned on. He had been fighting an urge to doze off when suddenly a knifing pain stabbed him in the chest. He called out immediately to Rudges, seated next to him, "Johnny Reb!"

Rudges saw at once that Peterson's face was pale. "You all right?"

"I am now," Peterson replied as the pain and shortness of breath vanished.

"What was it?"

"Nothing. Just a muscle spasm, I guess."

Rudges thought of telling Peterson he just had something like a muscle spasm, too, but decided not to. "We're overworked and underpaid. That's all it is."

Harris suddenly felt nauseous. He gagged, then, feeling embarrassed when some of his men turned and faced him, he pointed to the cup of coffee he had been sipping. "Ship's coffee is gettin' worse and worse." Feeling better he returned his attention to the ship's log.

Radarman Randy Chase had just finished the novel he was reading when he suddenly began to feel sick to his stomach. The nausea was momentary but was immediately replaced by chest pains and shortness of breath. He had taken a couple of ups before coming on duty to ensure he wouldn't doze off and be put on report for sleeping on watch. Certain the ill feeling was an adverse reaction to the speed, and fearful of an overdose, he got up from his station, crossed the control room toward Harris, and began to gag.

Harris got up from his desk to assist Chase, but found himself experiencing a little weakness in his legs. "Were you drinking ship's coffee, too, Randy?"

"It's not the coffee, sir," Chase managed between gasps. "I took speed. An overdose." His eyes were becoming blurry.

Harris shook his head disdainfully. "Think you can make it to sick bay with some help?'' Chase nodded. ''I'm going to have to put you on report, kid.'' Another nod. Harris looked around the room for someone to take Chase to sick bay. With the active sonar station secured, he could spare Peterson. ''Peterson! Take Randy down to sick bay. Tell the corpsman on duty about the speed, so he'll know how to treat him.''

''Aye, aye, sir. I'll get looked at while I'm there, too. I don't feel so hot, either,'' Peterson complained. He looked into Harris's eyes. ''I know what you're thinking, but I didn't take speed. I think I'm coming down with the flu or something.''

''I don't feel too good, either, sir!'' Rudges called out.

''Well, we can't all go to sick bay at once, damn it!'' Harris said curtly, then paused. ''I don't feel up to par myself. Let's . . . just try to stick it out if we can. We'll be getting relieved soon.'' He returned to his desk as Chase was helped out of the control room by Peterson. He forced himself to return to updating the ship's log, but he was finding it difficult to concentrate on his work. There was one final entry he needed to make, yet he couldn't recall what it was. As he glanced around the control room, searching for something that would help remind him, the desk phone rang. *Damn*, he thought. Every time he attempted to finish up his logbook work, he was interrupted. He yanked the phone off its receiver. ''Control room, Harris speaking,'' he said angrily.

''George, this is Burt,'' Dr. Post, the ship's medical officer, said on the other end. ''Is Bentsen there?''

''Negative, Doc. He went to bed hours ago. What's up?''

''I was summoned to sick bay half an hour ago. It seems we have a number of crewmen reporting here from all over the ship with complaints of chest pains, muscle soreness, shortness of breath, and nausea.''

''As a matter of fact, Doc, I've been experiencing those symptoms, too.''

''So have I. So have my corpsmen. It seems we have some ailment that's quickly reaching epidemic proportion.''

''What should we do, Doc?'' Harris asked, alarmed.

''I don't know yet. I'm trying to come up with a diagnosis, but some of the symptoms don't make sense in a controlled environment like ours. I'm going to wake Bentsen now and let him know. In the meantime, I'd like you to see about getting some food and water samples from evening meal down to sick bay for lab tests.''

''So you suspect food poisoning.''

"At the moment, yes. I'll be able to tell more precisely once you get those samples to me. I've got to go, George. More men just came in for help. I'll call you back after I talk to Bentsen."

Harris felt compelled to cross the room to the command console and check on the submarine's environmental vitals. Checking the ranks and rows of monitoring indicators and lights, he found all of them reading normal. He returned to the desk and sat down to finish his log entries, then remembered Dr. Post had requested food and water samples be sent to sick bay. He dismissed his lapse of memory as mere fatigue and picked up the desk phone to call crew's mess.

It took Bentsen several moments to get his heavy eyes open, several more to raise himself in his bunk, and several more still to find and switch on his bedside lamp. Pains were shooting through every part of his body and he was experiencing shortness of breath. His eyes were blurry. His throat felt as though it were on fire. The ringing phone echoed in his head several more times before he finally managed to reach out and lift it off its cradle. He made throaty noises. "Yes?"

"Jack! It's me!" Dr. Post said excitedly on the other end.

"Who?" Bentsen asked, unable to recognize the caller's voice. It seemed distant.

"It's me, Burt," Dr. Post said loudly. "We have a crisis on our hands!"

"Crisis!" Bentsen repeated. He made more throaty noises to clear his windpipe of phlegm. "What kind of crisis?" He heard a commotion in the background. "Where are you?"

"I'm in sick bay. So is half the damn crew. It seems we have a widespread ailment that's hitting everyone with chest pains, muscle soreness, restricted breathing, and nausea. A few men have vomited. One is convulsing. I tell you I'm going out of my mind down here! It's like a front-line MASH unit."

Bentsen took inventory of his own ill feeling. "Whatever it is, Doc, I've got it too." He got to his feet, then had to steady himself by holding onto the edge of his bunk to keep from falling forward. His legs were refusing to support his body. He tucked the phone between his head and shoulder and struggled to get dressed. "What's your diagnosis?"

"I'm still not sure, Jack. The symptoms point to a virus or influenza infection, except for the lack of high body temperatures. I can't imagine how a flu or virus strain could have been aboard without infecting the crew long before this. Not unless it's some strain unfamiliar to us with the capability of remaining dormant all this time, then manifesting as suddenly as it did.''

Bentsen felt short of patience. "Are you or are you not telling me it's a flu or virus?''

"Most likely, it's food poisoning. I've asked your XO to get me some food and water samples so I can . . .''

There was an uproar at the other end and Dr. Post left the phone. When he came back, he shouted, "A man is convulsing, Jack! I've got to go! Get me some help down here! Hurry!''

The line went dead at the other end and Bentsen headed for the cabin door. He was about to step into the passageway when he stopped. Food poisoning? he thought. He hadn't eaten in the past eighteen hours, yet he was inflicted by all the symptoms Dr. Post had based his diagnosis on. He hurried back to the phone and pressed the button to connect him with sick bay. The phone rang without end. Dammit! he thought, then pressed the button to connect him with the control room. His chest felt as though it were about to explode as he waited for an answer.

A ringing noise reverberated in Harris's ears until it finally got him to open his eyes. He found himself slumped over the ship's logbook. He moaned as he raised his aching head and glanced around the control room. The ballastman, planesman, and helmsman were all slumped over the controls at their stations. "Hey! Let's stay awake, gentlemen!'' he called out before he answered the phone. "Control room, Harris speaking.'' His throat felt raw.

"George, it's me,'' Bentsen said hurriedly. His chest pain was intensifying and he was experiencing more difficulty in breathing. "I want you to take a reading on our environmental vitals.''

"Didn't Doc Post get through to you, Jack? He seems to think we're all suffering from a case of food poisoning.''

"He mentioned that, but . . .''

"Hell, we're all getting sicker by the minute here.''

"The vitals, George!'' Bentsen said. "We have no time to lose. Read them off to me!''

"Hold on, Jack. I have to go over to the command console.'' His legs felt as though they were made of Jell-O as he crossed the control room. He had to stop halfway to the command console to fight off a violent urge to vomit, then staggered the rest of the way and picked up the phone at the command console. "I'm on again, Jack.''

"Hurry, George. How's our air supply first of all?''

Harris checked the ship's oxygen-flow meter. "We're in the green . . . with our air reading. Nothing wrong there, Jack."

It was obvious to Bentsen that Harris was close to being out on his feet. So was he. "Carbon monoxide and carbon dioxide levels?"

Harris rubbed the bleariness from his eyes. "They're both registering safe levels."

Bentsen forced himself to think, finding it hard to envision the vital monitors he wanted checked. "Radiation level, George?"

Harris had to draw close to the Roentgen meter to read it. "We're reading safe."

"Make a press-to-test check on the Detection and Warning system next, George."

Harris depressed the green-colored light that monitored that system. Immediately a warning bell rang to indicate the system was functioning. "I got a response . . . on the D and W system, Jack. No problem there either."

Bentsen thought for a moment. "One final check. Ask SAM if all of his environmental sensors are on line."

"SAM would have told us if they weren't."

"George, something is fouled up along the line," Bentsen said firmly.

"Yeah! The chow we were served for supper!"

"It can't be the chow, George! I haven't eaten anything in eighteen hours and I'm just as sick as everyone else. I think the computer may have fouled up."

"SAM?" Harris glanced up at the viewing screen accusingly.

"Use mask twenty, George. It's a program that will have SAM count all the sensors he's presently monitoring, then correlate the count to the total number of sensors that are supposed to be operating. SAM will display the location of any sensors that fail to be counted because they are not functioning."

Harris struggled at the computer keyboard to type the mask into SAM's input, then looked up at the viewing screen bleary-eyed.

ATTENTION: . . . . . . . . . . . . . . . . . . . . . . . . . . . . . . . . . . . . . . . . . . . . .
ALL SENSORS ACCOUNTED FOR . . . . . . . . . . . . . . . . . . . . . . . . . . . .

"Jack," Harris said into the phone, gasping for breath. "SAM claims all sensors are accounted for. You think SAM is lying to us? Could it be . . . ." He noticed blood dripping on the program selector keyboard, then felt a tingling sensation in his nose. He raised his hand to his nose, wiped it, brought his hand down, and stared at it. "Oh, my God! I'm bleeding!" A buzzing sound grew louder and louder. He looked up at the viewing screen for an announcement, but it wasn't SAM that was causing the buzzing—it was his own brain, slipping into unconsciousness. His body began to tremble violently.

Bentsen heard Harris's phone bang against something, then there was no sound at all. "George! Are you there? George! Get us up! Crash surface!" There was no reply. He felt a surge of hot flashes bolt through his body and there were dots swarming in front of his eyes. The phone slipped out of his hand. Bentsen staggered out of his cabin and headed for the control room.

Heading down the passageway, he passed officers and enlisted men lying in pools of vomit and blood. He knew he could be of no help to them and continued on. When he stepped into the control room, he saw Harris's body lying in a twisted heap on the floor beneath the command console. With his last surge of strength, he staggered across the control room to the emergency crash-surface lever. The ballastman was slumped over it and Bentsen was too weak to move the body. His only alternative was the emergency distress buoy. Its lever would be easy to pull down and would send a distress buoy crashing up to the surface to broadcast that the submarine was trapped on the bottom. He managed to work his way over to the buoy lever, but as he reached for it, someone grabbed and held his arm. He looked up and saw a man wearing an oxygen mask. "Help!" Bentsen gasped. "Help me!" He frowned when he recognized Nelson Hobart, shaking his head. "Why?" he asked as he collapsed to the floor with a groan of agony.

Hobart stared at Bentsen's lifeless body for a moment, then moved over to the sonar stations and slipped on the passive sonar-man's earphones. He listened for the engine sounds of the surface patrol ships. They were faint drumming noises way off in the distance. He took the earphones off and moved along to the ballast station, jerking the ballastman out of his seat and lowering him to the deck. There was an unlocking mechanism inside a glass door on the ballast panel, which he flicked upon with an index finger and thumb. He squeezed and turned the key inside, then faced the viewing screen on the command console across the room as SAM's beeping sound clamored.

ATTENTION:................................................
EMERGENCY CRASH SURFACE ARMING MECHANISM ACTIVATED

Hobart pulled down the emergency crash surface lever. The action engaged valves and pumps, and changed SAM's beeping tone to a higher, urgent sound.

ATTENTION:................................................
EMERGENCY CRASH SURFACE LEVER ACTUATED ............

Hobart felt the submarine tear loose from the bottom of the sea and begin to rise toward the surface. The lifting sensation seemed slight inside the submarine. He lifted the ballastman and placed him in his seat, then slumped him over the controls with one hand grasping the emergency crash-surface lever. He crossed the control room to the periscope deck and climbed up the steps, then moved along to the spiral staircase and began his ascent toward the bridge deck.

The hissing noises outside the *Scorpion* brought Grant to an upright position in the pilot's seat. He shook Felicia. "The behemoth is climbing to the surface." He handed her the passive sonar earphones. "I doubt you'll hear anything but her belching ascent, which will cover the noise of ours." He turned on the power and awakened the *Scorpion*. "You know exactly what to do?" Felicia nodded firmly. "We have little time. Blow ballast."

The quiet sea erupted as the U.S.S. *Trident* rose tumultuously to the surface. Foamy waves crashed down on the sea in all directions as a deluge of seawater rushed down the *Trident*'s conning tower walls to her topside decks and drained off her broad back. With the first traces of dawn climbing the horizon, the submarine settled on the surface and drifted.

Nelson Hobart felt the conning deck steady under his feet and released his grip on the bridge ladder. He undogged the hatch and climbed out, removed his oxygen mask, and slipped the portable oxygen pack off his back. He was wearing a safety belt, with a lifeline attached. He unraveled the line as he moved over to the port bridge wall and connected the free end to a cleat. He climbed over the bridge wall and descended, using the handgrips, to the diving plane wing. He made his way across the wet surface of the wing to the diving plane slaving servo's watertight access hatch. With a hard crank he undogged the hatch, pulled it open, and reached inside the access compartment. He disconnected the electric feed lines from the compartment light switch and switched the light off, then tugged on the device he had installed on the compartment floor until it finally broke its adhesive seal. After tucking it into a zippered pocket of his jump suit and dogging the access compartment hatch shut, he retraced his steps over to the handgrips and scurried back up to the bridge deck.

Hissing and splashing sounds caught his attention and he watched as the *Scorpion* rose portside from the depths in a bath of bubbly foam. The giant submarine dwarfed the creaturelike submersible. *Scorpion*'s familiar shape was a sight for Hobart's sore eyes. It was his ride away from the submarine he had spent the past few anxious months aboard, the submarine that was now a floating graveyard. He swung over the forward bridge wall, descended to the bow deck, and stood ready to catch a heaving line.

Dr. Phillip Grant had switched to the copilot's seat to judge better his maneuvering alongside the giant submarine. He relied upon the submersible's rubberized pressure hull coating to cushion the *Scorpion*'s starboard side as he negotiated the submersible within inches of the submarine's port amidships. When he had the *Scorpion* stopped in the sea, he listened to the passive sonar for possible intrusions from the sea's surface and below, and he watched the *Scorpion*'s amber radar scope for warning of an interruption from the surface and above.

Standing on the *Scorpion*'s back between the cockpit hatch and the fin, Felicia Marlow had a lightweight portable oxygen tank strapped to her back, the mask of which was hooked securely to one collar of her jump suit. Slung from her neck was a walkie-talkie that would keep her in communication with the *Scorpion*. In her hand was a nylon heaving line with a grapnel hook attached to the throwing end. The hook had spring-loaded flukes that were operated by a mechanical linkage cable that ran the length of the line. Pulling the linkage cable from aboard the *Scorpion* would cause the grapnel's flukes to collapse and free the line from its anchoring aboard the submarine. Seeing Hobart in position to catch the line, Felicia cast the line with the grapnel flukes collapsed.

Hobart caught the heaving line and spread the grapnel flukes open, then hooked one of the flukes to a forward conning wall handgrip at eye level. He tugged the rope a few times, then gave Felicia a thumbs-up gesture.

Felicia brought the heaving line taut, then attached it to an eye pad on the *Scorpion*'s sail at a level lower than the attachment on the *Trident*. Her crossing to the submarine would be hard, but the pitch of the line would allow her to slide back aboard the *Scorpion* on the return crossing when speed might be of the essence. She slipped her hands into a pair of tight-fitting leather gloves, then curled her hands around the line. With the bounce of a gymnast she brought her legs up and curled them around the line, then began the crossing hand over hand, dragging her legs after her. Halfway across she glanced down at the slight gap between the two vessels. To fall from the line would mean being crushed to death between their hulls. She brought her eyes up to the dawning sky and continued across without looking down again.

Hobart reached out, assisted Felicia aboard, and hugged her. "I thought this day would never arrive," he said happily.

"The months of pretense must have been a dreadful experience," Felicia said. "Have you removed the sending unit?"

"I have it right here," Hobart said as he tapped the pocket he'd put it in.

Felicia made a mental note of the indicated pocket. "We'd better get started with the staging. We can't expect to go unnoticed by those patrol ships for very long."

"We can use a block and tackle to hoist some of the bodies to the topside decks," he said. He had prepared for the placing of bodies topside, which was to suggest to investigators that some attempts were made to abandon ship. When he was found missing, the investigators would presume he'd made it to the topside decks and then been lost overboard. One of the bodies was to be dumped into the sea in an inflated lifejacket to reinforce that thinking.

"Let's begin our work in the control room, then work our way aft so we can finish up here on the bow deck," Felicia suggested. Hobart nodded and climbed the conning wall, followed by Felicia. When they arrived on the bridge deck, she helped him to return his oxygen pack to his back, then they both slipped on their oxygen masks. She gestured for him to lead the way below, then hurried down the bridge ladder after him. As he began his descent down the spiral staircase to the control room, she unzipped a pocket of her jump suit. The move went unnoticed behind Hobart's back. She waited for him to step down from the periscope deck, then, with his back still to her, she brandished a blackjack and struck him on the back of the head with all the strength she had. The blow sent him wobbling across the room.

Hobart felt as though an explosion had taken place inside his head. His arms and legs were suddenly growing numb, and his eyes were blinking wildly without seeing. He gasped for air as his legs folded.

Felicia stepped down from the periscope deck and noticed the dead bodies in the control room. She rushed over to Hobart, removed a long needle and syringe from her pocket, and took off the hypodermic needle's protective sleeve. She knelt beside Hobart and opened the front of his jump suit, and inserted the needle, sending its long fine shank deep into one lung. She squeezed half the liquid out of the syringe, extracted the needle, and repeated the injection into his other lung, emptying the syringe. She closed the front of his jump suit, placed her fingers against his jugular vein, and felt his weak pulse. She waited a few anxious moments for the hypodermic solution to travel through his veins to his heart and was rewarded when his body began to convulse. It took just moments more for his nervous system to fail entirely. She replaced her hand on his jugular. This time there was no pulse.

Working feverishly, Felicia rolled Hobart's body over, removed his oxygen pack, dragged him feet first over to the periscope deck steps, and put him in a position that would suggest he had fallen backward from the elevated platform and struck his head on the control room floor. She returned the safety belt and line he'd used on the bridge to the stowage cabin Hobart had been heading for when she'd struck him. It was open and inside was the block and tackle he'd mentioned. There was no longer any need for bodies on the *Trident*'s surface deck, since there would be no one missing, so she closed the stowage compartment. She removed the sending unit from Hobart's jump suit pocket and slipped it into her pocket along with the blackjack and spent hypodermic needle and syringe. She was breathing heavily from the activity, but the pure oxygen she was breathing bolstered her energy and kept her head clear. She picked up Hobart's oxygen mask and backpack, slung them over her shoulder, and retraced her steps to the bridge deck.

Felicia was exhausted from the climb as she dogged the bridge hatch shut. She removed her oxygen mask and took several breaths of fresh sea air. Then, after her breathing settled down, she climbed over the forward bridge wall and quickly descended to the bow deck. Working quickly, she removed a line clip from her hip pocket and attached one end of it to Hobart's oxygen backpack straps. She grunted as she lifted the pack and connected the other end of the clip to the nylon line. When she gave it a good shove, the oxygen pack traveled down the line swiftly and came to an abrupt stop against the *Scorpion*'s fin. Removing a second line clip from her hip pocket, she brought the shoulder straps of her backpack together in front of her and hooked the line clip to them to form a sling. Then, using the handgrips to elevate her, she snapped the other end of the clip onto the nylon line and shoved herself away from the submarine. Her body swung wildly as she slid down the line toward the *Scorpion*'s waiting back. As she neared the submersible's sail, she extended her feet to cushion her arrival. Anxiously, she unhooked herself and Hobart's pack from the line, then pulled on the mechanical linkage cable. The grapnel flukes collapsed, and Felicia quickly reeled in the line. In a few seconds she'd brought everything over to the submersible's cockpit hatch, undogged the hatch, and dropped it all inside. She followed the gear and dogged the hatch shut.

Grant removed the passive sonar earphones as Felicia slid into the pilot's seat beside him. "No problems?" he asked anxiously.

"None," Felicia said, still winded.

"The sending unit?" He glanced at the pocket she was tapping. "And Mr. Hobart?" He got a nod that signified he was dead. "Let's waste no time in getting below." He quickly maneuvered the *Scorpion* away from the *Trident*'s side and turned toward the east to head back to the mother ship. A variety of dead fish floated up to pepper the surface of the sea surrounding the U.S.S. *Trident* as he dipped the *Scorpion*'s glass-bubble bow under the waves.

## Chapter Fourteen

Dawn came and colored the *Dart*'s dimly lit bridge windows raspberry red as the destroyer turned through a one-hundred-eighty-degree arc to take up the easterly leg of its patrol pattern parallel to the Long Island coastline. Ahead of the *Dart*'s clipper bow, the flat surface of the sea was tinted an eerie crimson. Astern, the last shadows of night were descending behind the silhouetted New Jersey shores. It was Labor Day, just five o'clock, and the morning held an early promise of turning into the hottest day of summer.

With Commander Buel still asleep in his captain's chair, where he had dozed off hours ago, Ensign Schmidt was keeping everyone on duty on the bridge as quiet as a mouse. He had told Ensign Lichenberg that if he absolutely had to call the bridge to use a headset instead of the phone. Seeing one of the men on watch with him making a gesture to his headset, then to the deck below the bridge, Schmidt knew the peace and quiet that had prevailed was about to end. He slipped on his headset and keyed his mike. "Yes, Sheldon?" he asked in a whisper.

"We have a little strange activity taking place about fifty miles south off Montauk Point lighthouse," Lichenberg reported. "Passive sonar heard a subsurface commotion a little while ago and . . ."

"Was the subsurface commotion whale echolocations, Sheldon?" Schmidt pried, expecting it was.

"No whale noises this time, Karl. Passive said it sounded more like a volcano erupting. Shortly after that we began monitoring a rather large surface blip on radar in that area. We've been waiting to see what it was up to, but all it seems to be doing is moving north, northwest in a slow drift."

"Any engine sounds?" Schmidt asked.

"None."

"Does active confirm it?"

"That's the mysterious part of it, Karl. Active has nothing in that area at all."

"You have nothing on active sonar and no engine sounds on passive sonar. Just a blip on radar."

"Not just a blip, Karl. A blip as big as one of my testicles."

"And your testicle-size blip is just slowly drifting along out there?"

"Barely moving toward shore."

"Maybe it's a fishing yacht trolling for bluefish."

"Sure. It came up from the bottom and started trolling," Lichenberg snapped.

"Well, what the hell do you think it is?"

"Either passive did hear a volcano erupt and we now have a new island drifting around in the sea off Montauk Point or . . ."

"Or what, Sheldon?"

"Or passive heard a sub coming up in a big hurry and we're now tracking it surfaced on radar. A *big* sub at that."

"I suppose you think it's the spook?"

"The spook is the only sub I know of that can defy active sonar detection, Karl."

"Why in hell would the spook make a bunch of noise and come to the surface with only an hour left before we all secure from Operation Ghost?"

"I haven't a clue. I have it on radar, not on the phone. All I know is you'd better let Bad Ass know about it, just in case it is the spook."

"I hate this fucking detail," Schmidt said as he glanced over at Buel, making bear grunts in his sleep. "Better give me the stats on that blip, Sheldon."

"Contact is bearing zero-nine-zero. Range is seventy miles. Heading is three-one-five degrees. It's barely moving in the direction of the Long Island coastline."

"Keep your headset on. I think Bad Ass will want to chat with you when I wake him up," Schmidt said, and crossed the bridge to Buel. "Skipper! Skipper! Wake up," he said as he shook Buel.

Buel grunted, then rubbed the sleep from his eyes. "What is it, Schmidt?"

"Sir, passive monitored an undersea commotion off Montauk. Now radar has a large blip on the surface in that area, but active sonar doesn't detect anything, and neither does passive. There are no engine sounds. It seems the blip is heaved to and taking up a slow drift toward shore."

Buel shot up out of his seat. "Toward shore!" he bellowed. "Or maybe toward the gateway to the Long Island Sound! What time is it?"

"Just a little after oh five hundred, Skipper."

"Interesting," Buel said with a devilish grin. "We've still about an hour left of Operation Ghost and radar is monitoring a blip off Montauk. I'd say that blip has all the characteristics of a submarine playing possum on the surface." He gazed out the bridge window at dawn growing well ahead of the *Dart*'s bow. "The spook just may be up."

"But why would her skipper bring her out of hiding with the exercise still not quite over, Skipper?" Schmidt asked.

"He could be testing us to see how alert we are. Perhaps he's trying to make the *Dart* the laughingstock of the destroyer squadron." He rubbed his chin as he thought for a moment, then added, "Admiral Abbott warned us the spook might pull some sort of surprise maneuver at the tail end of Operation Ghost. In fact, our

COMDESOPS orders for the exercise advised us to be prepared for a bag of tricks from this submarine. Well, this tin can skipper has a few tricks of his own to pull. Where exactly are we, Schmidt?''

"We're just putting the New Jersey coast astern, Skipper.''

"No, you ninny!'' Buel barked. "Where are we in relation to the radar blip?''

"The surface blip is bearing zero-nine-zero. Range, seventy miles. Heading is three-one-five. Heaved to and in a slow drift about fifty miles south, off Montauk Point.''

Buel slipped on his headset. "CIC from bridge!''

"CIC,'' Lichenberg replied.

"I want an ETA to that blip at flank speed. Get it fast.''

"CIC, aye,'' Lichenberg said and glanced at the radarman. The radarman had heard Buel's request over his headset and was working out the calculations as Lichenberg peered over his shoulder. He read the Estimated Time of Arrival the radarman jotted down, then keyed his headset mike. "Bridge from CIC. Our ETA is one hour and twenty minutes at flank, Skipper.''

Buel looked out the bridge windows at the eastern horizon, brightening dead ahead of the *Dart*. The sun was a ball of fire rising out of the flat sea. "Hold this course!''

"Maintain course zero-nine-zero,'' Schmidt relayed to the helmsman.

"Steering zero-nine-zero, aye,'' the helmsman acknowledged.

"All ahead flank!'' Buel ordered.

"All ahead flank,'' Schmidt relayed to the annunciator operator.

"All ahead flank, aye,'' the annunciator operator repeated, then rang up flank speed.

Buel faced Schmidt. "I want General Quarters! And I want Flight Quarters, too. Tell our flight deck officer I want our Seasprite readied to get airborne in five minutes. Also tell 'em I want to personally brief our chopper crew on their mission before they leave the ship.''

"Aye, aye, Skipper,'' Schmidt replied, then crossed the bridge and pressed the GQ alarm button. Instantly the *Dart*'s shrilling whistle sounded in unison with the alarm bell. "General Quarters! General Quarters! All hands man your battle stations!'' Schmidt recited into the PA mike. "Flight Quarters! Flight Quarters! This is a scramble!'' With the GQ alarm still reverberating around the ship, Schmidt called aft to the *Dart*'s flight deck to relay Buel's orders to the flight deck officer.

Buel picked up his phone from the captain's command console and pressed the automatic dial button that would ring the officers' ward room. The phone was answered by a sleepy voice at the other end. "This is the captain. Send some coffee up to me on the bridge, on the double." He returned the phone to the console and lifted his PA mike. "Two minutes, gentlemen!" he bellowed. "Manned and ready in two minutes!"

As men scurried fore and aft to get to their battle stations, the Seasprite pilot and copilot emerged on the *Dart*'s flight deck, and were met at their helicopter by Lieutenant Fuller, the flight deck officer. "Before you lift off, radio the bridge. Bad Ass has some special orders for you." They nodded and Fuller took his position to clear them to start their engines.

Back on the bridge, a steward hurried over to Buel with a steaming coffee server and a cup and saucer. He poured the black liquid into the cup, then handed it to Buel. "Anything else, Skipper?"

Buel saw his XO arrive on the bridge. As Carwell was heading over to him, he said to the steward, "Pour my XO a cup of that stuff. He looks like he's going to need it." The steward dashed off to fetch another cup. "Good morning, George! Did you sleep well?"

"Brewster, this constant call to GQ is becoming ridiculous," Carwell complained.

"I'm not interested in your tale of woe right now, George. We are about to catch the spook taking in the sunrise off Montauk. It seems the skipper of the U.S.S. *Trident* has come up to the surface to play a little game of possum." He gestured for Schmidt to shut off the GQ alarm just as the Seasprite flight crew called into his headset. He keyed his mike. "Navy one-one-nine, this is the bridge! Over!"

"We are fired up and ready to get airborne, Skipper! Over!"

"Navy one-one-nine, your course is zero-nine-zero. You should come upon a rather large submarine sitting in the sea about seventy miles from us. It's heaved to and drifting in the general direction of shore, some fifty miles south, off Montauk Point. What I want you to do is go in as low as you possibly can to avoid being detected on radar. Then, if you can surprise the spook on the surface, drop a die marker on her before she can dive. Got that?"

"Bridge, Navy one-one-nine. Affirmative, sir," the pilot replied. "We'll go in so low we'll make a wake."

"That's the idea! Now, get airborne and get after that radar blip."

The flight deck officer watched as the Seasprite rose high above the flight deck, then banked and moved out over the sea on the *Dart*'s portside. The down draft from its rotor blades churned up the sea as the helicopter pitched forward, then streaked out toward the rising sun.

On the bridge, Buel keyed his headset mike. "CIC from bridge. Is there any indication that the *Elliot* and *Spruance* are also responding to the radar blip you're holding?"

"Standby," Ensign Lichenberg said, then got a consensus from passive and active sonar and radar. He keyed his mike. "Bridge from CIC, negative that, sir. The *Elliot* and *Spruance* are still maintaining search patterns out over the continental shelf."

"Keep tabs on 'em," Buel ordered. "We can't let our competition find the ghost submarine before we do."

Within twenty minutes after leaving the flight deck, the *Dart*'s helicopter and copilot had visual sighting of a large dull black mass sitting on the surface. As they drew closer the object was identifiable as a submarine. At an altitude of fifty feet the pilot and copilot stared down in astonishment at the countless dead fish surrounding the giant submarine.

"What the hell do you make of it?" the copilot asked over his intercom.

"The way the sub is just drifting along like that with the fish is scary," the pilot replied. "It's definitely the *Trident*. Side number seven-two-six," he said, reading the bold numbers on the submarine's sail.

"They must know we're overhead," the copilot said. "Why aren't they making an attempt to dive and evade us?"

"I don't know," the pilot said. "That's scary, too."

"Should we drop the die marker on her?"

The pilot thought for a moment as he maneuvered the Seasprite in a tight arc over the *Trident*'s lifeless surface decks. "I'm going to call in first. If she makes a move to dive, we'll be able to drop the die marker on her before she can get away." He keyed his radio mike. "Base from Navy one-one-nine! Base from Navy one-one-nine! Over!"

Buel heard the Seasprite pilot's voice blaring over the bridge loudspeaker and hurried into the radio shack, followed by Carwell. He took the earphones and mike from the radio operator. "Go ahead, Navy one-one-nine! Over!"

"We are over the U.S.S. *Trident*. She's making no attempt to dive. Over."

"Did you drop a die marker on her decks, over?" Buel asked anxiously.

"Negative, Skipper. Something seems wrong down there," the pilot replied.

"What do you mean something's wrong?"

"Sir, the sea is full of dead fish. All kinds and sizes. They're just floating along on the surface along with the sub."

"And the sub?"

"She's all buttoned up. No sign of life on deck. No radar scanner or satellite visible. No radio antenna either. Sir . . . I think I should try to raise someone aboard. Over?"

Buel didn't like the sound of things. "Navy one-one-nine. We will try to get the sub to break radio silence over ship's radio. Over."

"Roger, base," the pilot said as he lowered the Seasprite to within twenty feet of the *Trident*'s quiet decks.

Buel returned the earphones and mike to the radio operator. "Call the U.S.S. *Trident*. Try 'em on every frequency. Tell 'em we have a chopper overhead and are concerned they might be in some kind of trouble. Tell 'em it is imperative they break radio silence and acknowledge by giving us their status."

The Seasprite pilot continued circling overhead for a full five minutes, then grew restless and keyed his radio mike again. "Base from Navy one-one-nine, over!"

Buel went over to the radio operator. "No response?" The radioman shook his head. "Give me those," Buel said, and slipped the earphones on. "Navy one-one-nine, this is base. Go ahead, over."

"Any luck getting through to the sub, Skipper?" the pilot asked.

"Negative that," Buel returned.

"Request permission to try and raise someone aboard with a megaphone, over."

"Permission granted. Navy one-one-nine. Advise me if you have any luck, over."

The pilot nodded to his copilot and kept the Seasprite low and close to the sub. The copilot took a bullhorn from its storage bag under his seat, opened his cockpit side window, and pointed the bullhorn at the decks of the submarine. "Ahoy aboard the sub! This is Navy helicopter one-one-nine overhead. We request that you acknowledge us at once." He paused to listen for a response. There

was none. "Ahoy aboard the U.S.S. *Trident*! Are you in trouble?"
He listened.

"They had to hear you!" the pilot insisted. He keyed his radio
mike. "Base from Navy one-one-nine. No response to our hailing
aboard the sub. Request permission to lower copilot aboard and
investigate. Over."

"Navy one-one-nine from base, permission denied! Repeat, do
not go aboard that sub!" Buel said firmly. "You have a nuke boat
out there and she may be hot. Acknowledge, over."

"Base, Navy one-one-nine. Roger that," the pilot replied.

"Remain overhead and keep trying to raise someone aboard with
your bullhorn, Navy one-one-nine. Base, over and out."

"Wilco, base. Navy one-one-nine, out."

Buel returned the earphones and mike to the radioman.

"Shall I radio New London, Skipper?" the radioman asked.

"No. If something's seriously wrong aboard the sub, COMSUBOPS
is going to want to handle the problem delicately, with as little
publicity as possible. We'd better send them a coded communiqué."

"Brewster, maybe we should alert the *Elliot* and *Spruance* about
what's going on out there," Carwell said. "They can scramble their
Seasprites out to join up with Navy one-one-nine, just in case our
chopper gets into trouble."

"Agreed, George. You take care of that. I'll notify New London," Buel said, then moved over to the ship's Teletype operator.
"Send the following communiqué to COMSUBOPS, and send it in
priority-one code. . . ."

# PART THREE

### Chapter Fifteen

Tony Capobianco joined Mr. A and Mr. B on the terrace for breakfast. Except for an occasional ripple caused by a fish jumping, Lake Montauk, outside his restaurant and marina, was mirror still. Tony poured himself a cup of coffee. "Sleep well, gentlemen?"

"You kidding!" Mr. B grumbled. "Not with that band playing till two in the morning."

You'll be getting plenty of sleep soon, Capobianco thought as he stared across the table at the huge man. He sipped his coffee, then glanced up, hearing a slapping sound in the distance. The resounding thunder drew closer quickly. Within moments two all-white banana-shaped Navy helicopters rumbled overhead. Capobianco glanced at Mr. A and Mr. B as the two helicopters continued south toward the blue-gray vastness that was the Atlantic Ocean. "Now I just wonder where they're rushing to!" he said sarcastically. The slapping noise began to fade away as the waiter came out with his breakfast. "Is the extra breakfast ready?" he asked the waiter, who nodded. Tony looked at Mr. A. "Take Helen Boyd's breakfast to her while it's still hot."

The vibrating cabin of the helicopter rocked Admiral Pulvey as he sat shoulder to shoulder on the bench seat next to his aide, Lieutenant Roger Strong. Sharing the cabin with them were metal stretchers, body bags, and other emergency equipment. Before leaving the New London submarine base, Pulvey had managed to mechanically recite orders to Lieutenant David Lee, who had stayed behind at the base to carry those orders out. The slapping sound of the helicopter's rotor blades biting at the air outside the cabin drummed in Pulvey's ears, but he didn't hear the noise. The sum of his awareness as the helicopter streaked out over the ocean toward the U.S.S. *Trident* was a painful throbbing knot in his esophagus. He looked at the body bags uncomfortably, then out the cabin window at Ski's banana-shaped helicopter flying in close formation with his. Knowing Ski and Bentsen were close friends, Pulvey hadn't wanted Ski to join the boarding party. But Ski had insisted on doing so, and there'd been no time to argue.

There was a gnawing ache in Ski's head, caused by the unrelenting questions in his mind. He knew no painkiller could relieve that ache. Only answers would. He glanced down at the decoded version of the *Dart*'s communiqué he held:

0530 HOURS, 3-SEPTEMBER

B.A. BUEL, CDR-USN. C.O.

U.S.S. DART, DD-978, DESSQD-6, 3-NAVDST, R.I. PATDET-4, PATQAD-ROMEO, TANGO, 2.

TO: W. PULVEY, ADM-USN, COMSUBOPS, 3-NAVDST, N.L.

CC: ABBOTT, ADM-USN, COMDESOPS, 3-NAVDST, R.I. PRIORITY ONE: SEASPRITE NAVY 119, SCRAMBLED IN RESPONSE TO RADAR BLIP AT LON. 71°, 31', 14", WEST. LAT. 40°, 25', 08", NORTH. FOUND SSBN-726 SURFACED, HEAVED TO, AND DRIFTING NORTH, NORTHWEST APPROX. 50 MILES SOUTH OFF MONTAUK POINT LIGHT.

ALL HATCHES DOGGED SHUT, NO SIGN OF LIFE ON TOPSIDE DECKS, SUB SURROUNDED BY DEAD FISH. NO DISTRESS BUOY IN SEA. NO MAYDAY BROADCAST. NO DISTRESS FLARES JETTISONED. NO RESPONSE TO EMERGENCY REQUEST THAT SSBN-726 BREAK RADIO SILENCE AND REPORT DISPOSITION IN SEA. NAVY 119 OVERHEAD UNABLE TO HAIL ANYONE ABOARD WITH BULLHORN AFTER SEVERAL ATTEMPTS.

SEA DISASTER INDICATED BY SILENCE ABOARD. POSSIBLE RADIATION LEAK ASSUMED BECAUSE OF DEAD FISH. THEREFORE, DENIED NAVY 119 PERMISSION TO BOARD AND SEARCH FOR POSSIBLE SURVIVORS. NAVY 119 REMAINING OVERHEAD SSBN-726. PROCEEDING FLANK SPEED TO RENDEZVOUS AT COORDINATES. HAVE ALERTED DD-963 AND DD-967 OF PATDET-4. SPRUANCE AND ELLIOT LEAVING PATQAD-SIERRA, JULIETT 5, PROCEEDING FLANK SPEED TO JOIN UP WITH DD-978. SISTER DESTROYERS HAVE SCRAMBLED SEASPRITES NAVY 351 AND NAVY 274 TO BACK UP NAVY 119 ON STANDBY WITH SSBN-726. REQUEST FURTHER ORDERS FOR ALL VESSELS AND AIRCRAFT INVOLVED.

B.A. BUEL, CDR-USN.

C.O. USS DART, DD-978.

Pulvey's reply, dictated by Ski, was that all vessels and aircraft involved should stand off and await the arrival of the special boarding team being airlifted out to the U.S.S. *Trident*. The specialists knew what to touch and not touch.

Ski studied the faces of the specialists accompanying him on the helicopter. He and they were wearing silver protective suits, the hoods of which were held on their laps or placed on the cabin floor in front of them. They were medical personnel and crack submarine engineering technicians, specially trained as rescue teams to handle a sea disaster aboard a submarine. Most of their duty time was spent practicing their techniques.

"Ski, we have the *Trident* visually," the pilot called back.

Ski got up stuffed the communiqué into an inside pocket of his protective suit and joined the pilot and copilot. The *Trident* was just a short distance off the *Dart*'s starboard side. Above its sealed hatches were three hovering Seasprites. Coming over the horizon, their stacks billowing smoke, were two more destroyers speeding to the area. He could see the fish lying lifeless in the surrounding sea.

"DD nine-seven-eight from Navy two, over," the pilot called into his radio mike.

"Navy two, this is DD nine-seven-eight, over," the *Dart*'s radioman replied.

"DD nine-seven-eight, Navy one and two on approach a mile north of you at angles one. Navy two will be boarding SSBN seven-two-six. Handing Navy one over to you with COMSUBOPS aboard. Navy two, out."

In the cockpit of Admiral Pulvey's helicopter the pilot took his cue from the accompanying land-sea chopper and keyed his radio mike. "DD nine-seven-eight from Navy one. Flag requests clearance to land aboard, over." He watched the Seasprite helicopter already on the *Dart*'s flight deck as he waited for a reply.

Buel charged out to the flight deck with Carwell right behind him. He made shooing gestures at the *Dart*'s Seasprite as he growled at the flight deck officer. "Get that chopper airborne on the double. We have a rear admiral waiting to land aboard."

The flight deck officer made a slicing hand gesture across the front of his neck that immediately stopped a crewman who was refueling the chopper. "He's got enough fuel aboard for now. Clear the deck for takeoff.'' He waited for the crewman to withdraw with his fueling hose, then gave the pilot a thumbs-up signal and the Seasprite's rotor blades began to swirl.

Buel gripped the gold-embroidered peak of his baseball cap as the Seasprite's rotors created a windstorm on the *Dart*'s flight deck. He raised his binoculars in the direction of the approaching helicopter.

As the large banana-shaped land-sea helicopter approached the *Dart* from astern and lowered out of the sky, a boatswain's mate stationed on the flight deck raised his whistle to a PA mike. As soon as the shrieking faded, he announced, "COMSUBOPS arriving!" The announcement cued a signal man on a catwalk of the bridge to begin hoisting a two-star flag up the *Dart*'s mast in precision timing with the descending helicopter.

Another windstorm whipped across the deck as the land-sea helicopter settled down. As the rotors slowed, then stopped, one of Buel's crewmen slid the long cargo door open, while another stood by at the doorway to assist the helicopter's distinguished passenger. This was to be Buel's first face-to-face meeting with the boss of submarine operations and he looked on with interest. The admiral disembarked, and Buel found Bull Pulvey to be exactly how he had always imagined him: short and plump, unmistakably nearing full retirement age, an old salt of a man with the Navy written all over his meaty red face. "Attention on deck," he called out, halting all activity on the flight deck.

Admiral Pulvey joined Lieutenant Strong in rendering the customary hand salute to the national ensign flapping in the gentle breeze from the *Dart*'s fantail mast, then he led the way over to Buel. "Permission to come aboard!"

"Permission granted, Admiral," Buel said. "Welcome aboard the U.S.S. *Dart*. I'm Brewster Buel."

Pulvey shook hands with the man he had come to know over the years as Bad Ass Buel. "I've heard a lot of impressive things about you, Commander Buel. It's unfortunate our first meeting is under these circumstances."

"Likewise, Admiral," Buel said, then regarded Carwell. "This is George Carwell, my XO."

Pulvey shook hands with Carwell, and introduced his aide, Roger Strong, to the *Dart*'s senior officers. As they exchanged greetings, Pulvey watched Ski's helicopter lower a man down to the *Trident* by winch, who then guided the helicopter down from the sky.

"Will you be going aboard the sub, Admiral?" Buel asked, seeing him watching the *Trident*.

"Yes, later. When I get the word it's clear to do so."

At the sealed aft hatch, Ski conferred with Commander Hilderbrand, the chief medical officer at the submarine base hospital, and the rest of the boarding party. "We'll split into two main groups. Doc, you take one half of the boarding party and work your way forward. I'll take the rest of the men up to the forward hatch and we'll work our way aft. We'll join up in the control room."

"Right, Ski," Dr. Hilderbrand said.

"Everyone keep the protective gear on until I give clearance to unsuit," Lieutenant Troy Hanley, the officer in charge of the submarine engineering technicians called out, then knelt down at the aft hatch to undog it. His immediate interest below was the reactor room.

Ski led his party of men along the *Trident*'s topside deck to the bow hatch. He crouched down, undogged it, and pulled it open. Peering through the plastic window of his protective hood, he pressed the radio mike button protruding from under the oxygen mask of the hood. "Everyone divide into subgroups of two. Any survivors that are found are to be brought topside at once and handed over to medical personnel." He descended the bow ladder to officers' country, and quickly headed forward to captains' country and peered in Bentsen's cabin through the open door. Bentsen's bedside phone was off its cradle, dangling by its cord. A haunting picture on Bentsen's cabin desk caught his eye. It was of Bentsen, his wife, Donna, and their two teenage sons. Ski himself had taken the picture just before his former CO had left on the maiden voyage.

With tears burning the corners of his eyes, Ski left the cabin and headed aft toward the control room, certain he'd find Bentsen there. Bodies were lying in twisted heaps in pools of blood and vomit all along the passageway leading through officers' country. He recognized all the faces.

As Ski arrived at the control room, he felt a tremor in his legs. He saw Bentsen lying face up, staring lifelessly at the ceiling. A look of agony had replaced the warm smile he had never failed to see on Bentsen in all the years he had known him. Ski knelt down and gently closed Bentsen's eyes. He got up as two corpsmen arrived with a body bag and stretched it out on the deck beside Bentsen.

After crossing the control room to the captain's command console, Ski took out his note pad and pen. He drew a rough sketch of the positions of each of the casualties, carefully labeling each one by name. Next he checked the monitoring indicators along the command console. The Roentgen meter showed no indication that a high level of radiation was being monitored. And all other meters registering oxygen flow, air quality, and carbon monoxide and carbon dioxide registered normal readings. The climate-control setting was a comfortable seventy degrees. There was nothing but silence coming from the Detection and Warning alarm system designed to alert the crew that environmental conditions were at a dangerous level, but to make sure it was properly working Ski depressed the green lighted press-to-test buttons. The siren bell shrilled loudly for an instant, jarring the two corpsmen who were at that moment sliding Bentsen's corpse into the body bag. "Ignore that alarm," Ski shouted to them.

Shifting his eyes to the display on the viewing screen, Ski noted that SAM announced the emergency crash-surface lever had been pulled, and that no one had erased the display. He typed a request on the keyboard and pressed the input key. SAM's announcement gong sounded, and new lines of information sped across and down the viewing screen.

```
ATTENTION:. . . . . . . . . . . . . . . . . . . . . . . . . . . . . . . . . . . . . . . . . . . . . .
ALL D & W SENSORS FUNCTIONING NORMAL . . . . . . . . . . . . . . . . .
ALL MONITORING SENSORS FUNCTIONING NORMAL . . . . . . . . . . .
ROENTGEN READINGS REGISTERING SAFE LEVEL . . . . . . . . . . . . .
OXYGEN FLOW NORMAL . . . . . . . . . . . . . . . . . . . . . . . . . . . . . . . . . . .
CLIMATE CONTROL 70° . . . . . . . . . . . . . . . . . . . . . . . . . . . . . . . . . . . .
AIR QUALITY NORMAL . . . . . . . . . . . . . . . . . . . . . . . . . . . . . . . . . . . .
NO TRACE OF CARBON MONOXIDE . . . . . . . . . . . . . . . . . . . . . . . . .
NO TRACE OF CARBON DIOXIDE . . . . . . . . . . . . . . . . . . . . . . . . . . . .
OXYGEN ANALYZER FUNCTIONING NORMAL . . . . . . . . . . . . . . . . .
SCRUBBERS FUNCTIONING NORMAL . . . . . . . . . . . . . . . . . . . . . . . .
END EVALUATION OF VITALS . . . . . . . . . . . . . . . . . . . . . . . . . . . . . . .
```

Ski was joined at the command console by Dr. Hilderbrand and Lieutenant Troy Hanley, the engineering tech officer. They both had their protective hoods off. Ski slipped his hood off at once. "I gather we don't have a 'hot' sub."

"Every Roentgen meter on the sub reads safe," Hanley said. "So do our hand-carried Geiger counters. Also, the sub's been venting ever since she crash-surfaced, so there's plenty of fresh topside air circulating through the ship." He looked at the viewing screen display. "I see SAM verifies there's nothing wrong with the sub's environment."

"We found no survivors anywhere, Ski," Dr. Hilderbrand said sadly. "I stopped at sick bay and found some notations Dr. Post had managed to record into the medical log. It seems mass hysteria broke out in the middle of the night. Crewmen were coming to sick bay from all over the sub with complaints of chest pains, restricted breathing, and nausea. Dr. Post had diagnosed the patients as possibly suffering from water or food poisoning. There was mention that some men were vomiting, and that a couple were convulsing."

"What's your diagnosis, Doc?" Ski asked.

"I think it was some sort of poisoning or suffocation. Perhaps both. I'm going to airlift some cadavers from various parts of the sub back for autopsies. I'll also take back what fresh water and food samples I can gather."

"Doc, I think testing the sub's fresh water and food supplies for contamination will prove to be a waste of time," Ski offered.

"How so, Ski?" Hilderbrand challenged.

"We've a dead crew sealed aboard a submerged sub, and dead fish locked outside it. Both died from the same thing, is what I deduce. Now I'm sure the crew didn't risk watertight integrity to feed the fish what they drank or ate. And with only one day to go before the sub got back into home port, I'm confident garbage or waste water wasn't dumped into the sea, either. Now we have also ruled out a reactor leak, and knowing there's nothing else deadly aboard the sub that could have leaked out, I think we can safely conclude that nothing from the sub killed the fish. That means something present in the sea surrounding the sub did. And whatever that was, it also managed to get aboard the sub and kill the crew. In my opinion, there's only one thing that could get aboard a submerged sub with all its hatches dogged tightly shut, and that's seawater being drawn aboard through . . ."

"Through the oxygen-manufacturing plant," Hanley said excitedly, "where life-supporting oxygen molecules are extracted to replenish the crew's exhausted breathing oxygen supply."

"Exactly," Ski said. "Doc, I suggest you take back some dead fish to dissect and some samples of the seawater surrounding the sub." Ski turned to Hanley. "Troy, you get started on *how* that something got aboard. Tear into the scrubbers and examine them carefully. If you don't find a malfunction there, disassemble the oxygen analyzer.''

"Ski, I'm going to have to wait till we get the sub back to the new sea hangar before I can disassemble the analyzer. It's no easy task,'' Hanley complained.

"Just do it, Troy,'' Ski said. "We can accept there might have been some sort of existing contamination out in the sea, but those scrubbers and that oxygen analyzer should never have allowed it aboard—not without a warning to the crew. Check the D and W linkup with the oxygen-manufacturing plant, and also go over the gripe sheets in the ship's log. Maybe some repair work was attempted on the oxygen-manufacturing plant that might shed some light on a malfunction. I'll call the admiral now. Then I'm going back to the base on the airlift with you, Doc. I want to get the *Trident*'s voyage recorder and sonar tapes back to the sound lab ASAP. Maybe they will explain how in hell the D and W system never warned the crew of danger.''

"Jesus, Mary, and Joseph. I can't believe this happened,'' Admiral Pulvey said. He had been summoned to the *Dart*'s bridge in response to the ship-to-ship call from the *Trident* submarine. "You did the right thing, Ski. I'll be coming aboard directly. When you get back to the base, check on Dave's handling of the press. I told Dave to tell them that the *Trident* had been delayed enroute to participate in a special Navy red alert exercise involving the third Naval district. He was to cancel the open-house ceremonies, giving the public the same excuse. The press were to be told to go back to their newspapers, that the delay was of indefinite duration. All but Ray Tolbin, that is. I want him to stick around. We may need a friend of the Navy to help us gently break the bad news to the public when the time comes.''

"I'll check on that, Admiral,'' Ski promised.

"I'm going to get the CNO on the patch phone now and break the news to him. He's going to shit. So are the SECNAV and the President. I'll get them to initiate the phony red alert for our district right away. Where will you be in case I need to contact you, Ski?''

"In the sound lab, reviewing the voyage recorder and sonar tapes, Admiral.''

"Very well. Expect me back at the sea hangar with the *Trident* sometime after dark. Let's hope no one sees us sneaking it back into port.''

"Are you going to offload the rest of the casualties back at the base, Admiral?"

"No, Ski. I've instructed the base port officer to get a sub tender and hospital ship underway. We'll close the area out here to commercial and private sea and air traffic and remove the crew while we're at sea. We're not going to release the news about the casualties until we know the cause of death."

"Not even, Donna Bentsen, Admiral?"

"I know this isn't easy for you, Ski. It isn't for me either. Donna and my wife are close friends, but we can't breathe a word of this till we get the okay from Washington. It's to remain a military matter."

"Very well, Admiral. I'm going to shove off now. See you later tonight."

Pulvey handed the radioman the earphones and mike, then regarded Buel. "I'm ready for that patch phone hookup now, Commander Buel."

Admiral Pulvey saw Ski's helicopter streak off just as the patch phone call went directly to the Oval Office.

"Admiral, I hope you appreciate the gravity of all this," the President said grimly. "What's at stake is the contribution the fleet of Trident submarines will make to our nation's overall defense. We also have a global market to consider, friends of this nation who are interested in purchasing the submarine itself, the Trident missiles, and sonar and other systems.

"Yes, Mr. President," Pulvey said. "I understand fully."

"I'm, of course, not suggesting that you alter the truth. What I am suggesting, however, is that if this nation intends to maintain its global supremacy over the Soviet Union in the arms race as well as in the highly competitive weapons market, this *Trident* tragedy has to come to a speedy and satisfactory resolution."

"Yes, Mr. President."

"Get to the bottom of all this, Admiral, then get back to me personally. I need answers for Congress. And I need explanations for our global friends."

Pulvey returned the patch phone to Buel. "I'm ready to go aboard the submarine now, Commander Buel." He glanced out the bridge window at the U.S.S. *Trident*. "Ready as I can make myself for a nightmare like that."

## Chapter Sixteen

Fay Parks was furious as she started up the Thames River Bridge ramp in her rented car on her way to Hartford Airport to catch an afternoon flight back to Washington. She had been ordered out of bed at the BOQ and told by Lieutenant David Lee that there was some sort of red alert going on. At eight o'clock in the damn morning—after getting to bed at 4:00 A.M. She was steaming mad, and she was going to write about the discourteous treatment she and her male colleagues had received—all but good ol' Ray Tolbin, that is. He was still back in his bed at BOQ, sleeping through all the ruckus. Why hadn't Dave kicked him off the base, too? she wondered.

So what if the ceremonies were cancelled? So what if the new submarine's return home was now indefinitely delayed? All she wanted to do before leaving the Navy base was to take a few pictures of some submarines to accompany her article. She'd been given permission to do it today. She had pictures of just about every other damn thing on the Navy base. The pictures didn't even have to be of the new submarine—any damn submarine would do. Now she was going to have to write a full-page story without one picture of a submarine.

Fay slowed down as she got to the middle of the bridge. She saw some submarines parked around the Marine Dynamics construction piers, and more were tied side by side to a submarine tender ship. She knew she wouldn't be allowed near the defense plant or the area across the river that was the plant's warranty work yards. She couldn't stop on the damn bridge to take pictures, either. There had to be another way. She could see a public road running along the river's edge on the opposite side of the Thames from the Navy base. All she had to do was get on that road and ride along it till she was directly across the river from the submarine base, then she could take all the pictures she wanted.

Fay was getting honked at from behind. With horn blasts unnerving her, Fay looked over the bridge railing, barely able to keep from bumping into the curb, then caught sight of a side street that led down to the road paralleling the Thames River's west bank. She could also see railroad tracks running along the river's edge.

Today was not her day, Fay thought as she circled around blindly after leaving the bridge exit ramp looking for the side street. All she seemed to be turning onto were dead-end streets. She made a U-turn on the street she was on, then got back on Route 32, heading north toward Norwich. She made a right at the next side street, which took her down a steep hill. At the bottom of the hill she released a sigh. There she found the railroad tracks and the Thames River's sandy west bank. She made a left and followed the road alongside the railroad tracks, watching the east bank's landmarks for a sign of the Navy base. She was just about to where the submarine base's main gate was when the road abruptly met a cemetery. "Crap!" she said.

Certain she was but a short walk through the cemetery away from the submarines parked across the river, Fay got out and retrieved her camera, loaded with black and white film, telephoto zoom lens, and tripod from the trunk. She climbed the sloped landscape and made her way past the rows of tombstones and crypts. The places a journalist's work takes her, she thought. When she spotted the dull black submarines sitting low in the water across the river, she made her way down to the railroad tracks and then to the river's edge.

The bright sun was climbing the morning sky behind the submarine base. The day was promising to be a scorcher. Her forehead was already damp with perspiration by the time she had the tripod's three pointy legs into the hard sand. After screwing the camera to the swivel seat of the tripod, she looked through the telephoto lens and panned the east bank of the Thames.

Fay focused on the huge structure further upriver at the extreme rear of the Navy base. Its raised hangarlike doors told her it was the new sea hangar, where she had attended the press conference. She panned slightly downriver and aimed the camera at the BOQ building. She settled the telephoto lens on the submarines next, then zoomed in on the aft deck of one of them. There were sailors washing down the submarine's rounded back with a garden hose and long-handled scrub brushes. Using the sailors as the subject, she snapped her first picture, then took a half-dozen shots of the submarines tied alongside. When she panned back to the sailors for another shot, she noticed they were looking up at the sky and she heard a popping sound coming from downriver.

As the popping noise changed to a thunderous slapping sound, Fay saw a banana-shaped helicopter lowering over the river. It suddenly banked to the right and arced down to the ground near a group of flashing red lights. Fay returned to the camera and zoomed in on the activity. She saw a procession of Navy ambulances approach the chopper, accompanied by military police jeeps. The helicopter's side cargo door slid open and the ambulances backed up to it. The attendants riding in the front jumped out and removed wheeled stretchers, then converged around the open helicopter door as two Navy officers deplaned.

Fay trained the telephoto lens on the face of one of the officers. She didn't recognize him, but noticed a medical insignia attached to the collars of his uniform shirt. Training the lens on the other face, her jaw dropped. It was Ski. She held the lens steady on him as he began issuing orders to the ambulance attendants. Then, in astonishment, she saw the attendants begin unloading body bags from the helicopter's cabin and her curiosity went into high gear. The bulgy shapes of the body bags and the strained faces of the ambulance attendants loading them onto the waiting stretchers convinced her the body bags weren't empty. What puzzled her was, where had the bodies come from, and why was Navy Intelligence involved?

Operating on her professional reflex, Fay flicked the rapid-fire lever on the side of the camera, getting shots of everything. Interesting, she thought as she noticed Ski carrying a round metal case that looked to her like a motion picture film transport can, only considerably larger. He had another, smaller cylindrical-shaped metal container gripped by its handle with his other hand. Ski was gesturing to some plastic containers just inside the helicopter door, which two armed Marine MP's unloaded and carried over to one of the jeeps. Then, after all the body bags were unloaded, Ski and the medical officer hopped into a jeep and led the long procession of a dozen ambulances. She took a final snapshot of the helicopter as it lifted off.

Fay packed up her equipment, dashed across the railroad tracks, and trekked through the cemetery, feeling puzzled and uneasy. Her journalist's intuition told her that this was a scoop. She returned her camera equipment to the trunk, then slipped in behind the steering wheel and lit a cigarette. She had to sort things out.

She remembered that Dave had seemed frenzied about getting her and her colleagues off the base and on their way back to their newspapers. When she'd asked Dave why good ol' Ray Tolbin wasn't going back to Washington with her, Ski's XO had told her Admiral Pulvey had some unfinished personal business with the twerp. When she'd asked him to let her take the pictures she needed of the submarines, he'd threatened to throw her off the base bodily.

What worked up her curiosity was that the red alert could have been handled with far more tact and diplomacy. Adding all that mysterious conduct to the mysterious activity she had on film totaled trouble. She was sure that something terrible had happened, and she and her colleagues were being outscooped by good ol' Ray, the admiral's friend. The thought of Ray Tolbin hogging the story about whatever the Navy was so excited about really steamed her.

What a fool she would have been if she had quietly gone back to Washington, just as the Navy had told her to, Fay thought as she threw the spent cigarette out the window and started up the car. She was going to find out exactly what it was that was plaguing the Navy. She had proof that *something* had taken place. The shots of the body bags merited an explanation. But she had to work fast. She couldn't afford the time it would take to have her prints developed for her. She was going to have to develop them herself. Then, once she did, she could wave the prints under Ray Tolbin's nose and demand to be cut in on the scoop. If good ol' Ray refused to share the news with her, then she could show the prints to the Navy. If the Navy was trying to hide something from the public, her prints would hit a nerve. Then maybe she would get special treatment, too, just like the twerp was obviously getting. She'd force the issue, demand an explanation—and a scoop, or at least a share in one.

## Chapter Seventeen

Lance Corporal Finch was on guard duty again outside the base CIC room when he saw Ski hustling down the basement stairs carrying two metal cases. He quickly moved over to open the door to the Intelligence Center. "Good morning, Captain Kowalski."

"Thanks, Finch, but I'm on my way to the sound lab, not CIC," Ski said. He had radioed ahead from aboard the helicopter and left instructions for Dave to prepare a sound laboratory room for him to use.

Finch withdrew his hand from the doorknob. "Okay, sir." He paused. "I'd like to ask you a question, sir."

"Go ahead."

"Are we at war or something?"

"What do you mean?"

"Everyone seems very concerned in there," Finch said as he

gestured toward the CIC room. "Did all hell break loose again over in the Med?"

"The last I heard everything was status quo with our Mediterranean operations, Finch. I'm sure what you're referring to is just a response to the red alert."

"That isn't what I heard, sir," Finch said, thinking he might know more about the strange mood hanging over the base than the Navy captain.

"What *did* you hear, Finch?" Ski asked, just in case there had been a breach of security about the submarine mishap.

"Scuttlebutt has it that the Bull is furious because the new sub is involved in something top secret and dangerous, sir."

"Did scuttlebutt say what that was, Finch?"

"The word from the troops turning away civilians at the main gate is that the U.S.S. *Trident* was ordered into action. The way I see it, that action would have to be something bigger than a red alert."

Ski felt relieved. There had been no security leak. Finch just had a misinterpretation of the story deliberately rumored to cover up the *Trident*'s delay to home port. "As usual, scuttlebutt is wrong, Finch. The word I got was the *Trident* is participating in a red alert exercise."

"That's all, sir?"

Ski sensed Finch's doubt. He wondered how many others on the base saw through the rumor. "Carry on, Finch," he said, then turned and headed down the hall.

The reception area of the sound laboratory was a spacious rectangular room with a long counter that fronted rows of floor-to-ceiling library shelves stocked with metal cases just like the ones Ski was carrying. Each submarine in the fleet was allocated shelf space for voyage recorder discs and sonar tapes stored in chronological order. Adjoining the reception counter and library area on both sides were four sound laboratory rooms. Opposing each other from behind closed soundproof doors, laboratory rooms one and two were like classrooms, with rows of desks that faced a recording studio-type sound control booth. Each desk had individual earphones and electronically operated computer training aids. Rooms three and four, also situated across the reception area from each other, had six comfortable armchairs each, set side by side facing the control booth viewing window. Each chair was also equipped with individual earphones and individual controls.

Ski walked across the reception area and entered sound lab three.

He joined Dave in the control booth, set down the voyage recorder disc, and placed the metal cylinder containing the *Trident*'s sonar tape next to the disc. Dave had read the *Dart*'s communiqué before Ski and Admiral Pulvey left the base. What he'd read told him to expect some bad news when Ski got back. But as he appraised the drawn look on Ski's face now, he was sure the news was going to be worse than anything he imagined. "What's going on out at the *Trident*, Ski?"

"There were no survivors aboard the sub," Ski said quietly.

"My God!" The color drained from Dave's face and he slumped down in his chair. "A hundred and sixty guys!" He knew all of the *Trident*'s officers and many of the enlisted crew. One name in particular brought his eyes up to Ski. "Bentsen?"

"No survivors at all, Dave," Ski muttered as he removed the voyage recorder disc from its case.

"Oh, Ski! I'm so sorry," he said. "The Bull! Does he know?"

"Yes. I told him before I left the sub."

"My God! This is going to be an ordeal for a man his age."

"At the moment he seems to be in sort of a state of shock. Roger Strong is with him. He'll keep an eye on him."

"I don't suppose Donna Bentsen knows yet?"

"No, Dave. We're to keep this confidential till we get the word from the CNO that it's okay to let the truth out. The subject is off limits to all hands not already involved. That includes Janet and the admiral's wife."

"Was it a reactor leak, Ski?"

"No. All we've been able to surmise thus far is that whatever it was didn't originate aboard the *Trident*. The sea is full of dead fish. We'll know more about it after Troy Hanley looks into the scrubbers and oxygen analyzer."

"Why didn't the crew abandon ship when the danger became apparent?"

"It seems it never was apparent to them until it was too late. The D and W alarm never sounded to warn them. There were no indications that a life-support-system peril existed. Doc Hilderbrand is over at base hospital performing autopsies now. He's going to call me here as soon as he establishes the cause of death."

"Ski, this is like having a bad dream that still hangs in there after you're awake. Worse."

"I know, Dave. Finch mentioned that civilian visitors were being turned away at the main gate. Did you carry out the rest of the Bull's orders?''

"Affirmative, Ski. I told the Marine Dynamics warranty people that the *Trident* is delayed indefinitely and that we'd advise them when we needed them. I told the press the same story and they all seemed to accept the red alert explanation.''

"What about Mr. Tolbin? Where is he right now?''

"He's over at BOQ drafting the story the Bull wants him to release to the local papers.''

"Let's get down to the business at hand, Dave. Right now I want to review the voyage recorder disc, particularly the dialogue in the control room just before the *Dart* picked up the submarine on radar when it crash-surfaced.''

"As I recall, the time was o five-thirty this morning,'' Dave said as he selected the digital display, his moves commanding a host of switches, dials, indicators, levers, and lights. He inserted the voyage recorder disc into the huge playback element, depressed the rewind lever, and engaged the computer search mode. Automatically the disc was rewound to the time of day selected on the counter.

The first hour of playback proved to be an emotional drain and offered very little. Ski was disappointed but not shocked to learn one of the crew had taken an amphetamine before coming on duty. He heard Harris's brief conversation with Bentsen, heard the XO become hysterical over his own bleeding, heard cries of anguish followed by a thud, then by silence, eventually broken by Bentsen's voice in the control room, shouting for help. Bentsen's last word recorded on the disc was, *"Why?"* After a brief pause, there was the unmistakable sound of pumps and valves responding to the crash-surface lever, and of SAM's urgent beeping. He was sure there were other faint noises soon after, but they were unrecognizable to him. A long pause broken by the *Dart*'s radioman trying to raise someone aboard, and later, the sounds of a helicopter and someone with a megaphone. There was no more.

"Well, what did you make of it all, Dave?''

"It's the saddest thing I've listened to in my life, Ski.''

Feeling his theory was right about the fish dying in the sea around gas hole Beta before the *Trident* arrived at its holding coordinates, Ski decided to review that segment of the disc. "Dave, get the disc rewound to twenty-three hundred hours last night. That's the ETA we had for the *Trident*'s return to home waters. We'll play the disc back from there through to the point we just listened to."

Dave glanced up at the clock. Its digital display read: 11:00 HOURS. "You're talking about maybe six hours of playback time, Ski. That'll keep us here till seventeen hundred hours this afternoon."

"I have nothing to do until I hear from Doc Hilderbrand about the autopsy findings, Dave. And nothing to do after that until the admiral and Troy Hanley get back in with the *Trident*. We're going to be listening to the voyage recorder disc, then maybe the sonar tape after that, until either we come up with something interesting or someone else does."

## Chapter Eighteen

"That's right—body bags!" Fay said over the phone in her Holiday Inn motel room as she thumbed through the pictures she had developed. She was talking to Tom Hurt, her managing editor. The bathroom across the room was still cluttered with an assortment of developing equipment. "And Captain Kowalski of Naval Intelligence was supervising the job of removing the body bags from the Navy helicopter and transporting them in a procession of Navy ambulances to some other part of the base—I guess to the base hospital."

"That might explain the activity here in Washington, Fay. One of our people stationed at the White House advised us the Presidential barometer fell early this morning, which is an indication there's a storm somewhere in the world. Then we got a call from our Pentagon man, who said the Navy barometer took a steep drop at about the same time. We questioned the President's press secretary, but we were told nothing was going on except a red alert involving the third Naval district."

"That's what we were told here in New London, and I would have believed them if I hadn't seen those body bags. Now I'm sure either a military action involving fatalities took place somewhere or there's been a disaster of some kind—perhaps a disaster directly related to the new supersubmarine."

"You just might be on to something there, Fay."

"I'm sure I am. We were told we had to leave the submarine base because civilians weren't permitted on a military installation during a red alert. Yet the Navy let Ray Tolbin stay on. Now I know for a fact that Ray and Admiral Pulvey are good friends. Maybe Ray talked the admiral into letting the *Chronicle* have an exclusive on whatever is going on."

"Well, it wouldn't be the first time, Fay."

"I tried to call Ray at the BOQ building on the base and some Navy officer flatly told me he wasn't available. Then I called again to talk to Admiral Pulvey and I was told the admiral wasn't available either. It seems everyone at the submarine base wants to stay incommunicado."

"We have to be careful, Fay. You just might be on to something that is regarded as a national security matter. Now, I'd love to see you put pressure on the *Chronicle* or the Navy for a share in the exclusive, but not at the risk of having the *Globe* blackballed around Washington for breaching national security."

"Then what do you suggest we do, Tom?"

"Have you confronted Kowalski with your photos, Fay?"

"Not yet. I wanted to check in with you first."

"Good girl." Tom thought a moment. "Kowalski's the logical next step, Fay. Ask him to explain the photos you have and tell him the *Globe* is willing to cooperate with the Navy as long as we can share the exclusive with the *Chronicle*. Handle the body bag incident carefully. Keep things light and loose. If there is a scoop, things will happen fast enough."

"I promise, Tom."

"Keep me informed on everything you find out, Fay. You have my home phone number. In the meantime, I'll keep the *Globe*'s people probing the White House, the Pentagon, and Capitol Hill."

## Chapter Nineteen

Ski, seated next to Dave, looked across the desk cluttered with medical journals and medical encyclopedias at Dr. Hilderbrand. The base chief surgeon had summoned them to his office just as they had finished the six-hour playback of the *Trident*'s voyage recorder disc. Ski digested Dr. Hilderbrand's autopsy and fish dissection findings, then asked, "Exactly what is this . . . methyl mercury, Doc?"

"According to these medical journals, it is a composition of mercury commonly found in low and high concentrations in seawater that comes in contact with organic waste materials," Hilderbrand said matter-of-factly. "The mercury and organic waste materials fuse together in the ideal seawater environment to form methyl mercury, which is quite lethal."

"Doesn't it occur only rarely in the sea?" Ski asked.

Hilderbrand nodded. "Rarely indeed, Ski. Nevertheless, both sources of information I've probed today document that methyl mercury has proven to be fatal for man and fish alike. The cases cited were in places around the globe such as Minamata Bay in Japan, Guatemala and the Agamo River area. These reports reveal that fish inhalated the methyl mercury, while the humans who consumed the contaminated fish died of ingestion. Out of a hundred and sixty humans feeding on the fish poisoned with methyl mercury, sixty-five died, and the rest never fully recovered."

"But, in the case of the *Trident* submarine crew, no one aboard ate the methyl mercury contaminated fish outside the vessel, did they, Doc?" Dave asked.

"No," Hilderbrand shot back. "But they did depend upon the same source of oxygen supplied by the sea outside the submarine, Dave. In essence, we can readily deduce that both the fish and the submarine crew were exposed to the methyl mercury poisoning by inhalation, rather than ingestion. The fish took it into their bloodstreams and respiratory systems through their gills. The *Trident*'s crew, as Troy Hanley will undoubtedly learn, got their fatal dose of the contaminant through the submarine's life-support oxygen manufacturing plant."

Ski looked puzzled. "I thought our submarine fleet's life-support systems were safeguarded against any toxic mercury compositions and any toxic organic waste materials. How in hell could this methyl mercury invade the *Trident*'s environment?"

"I'm afraid you'll have to wait for the findings of Troy Hanley and his crew of engineering technicians to learn how it did," Hilderbrand replied firmly. "But I can tell you that methyl mercury has some unusual qualities. It is an odorless, colorless, and highly soluble substance that can readily attach itself to oxygen molecules present in fresh water and seawater. Also, its toxicity increases under pressure. That is, the deeper it manifests in the sea, the more potent it is. It can move with sea currents like a killer on the prowl or it can linger indefinitely in stagnant waters, such as subterranean valleys or gas holes like the one the *Trident* submarine spent overnight in. Attached to oxygen molecules, it is extracted from the seawater through the gills of unsuspecting fish. In minutes the blood-stream is infected and they die soon after."

"How soon after initial contact does death occur in humans?" Ski asked.

"Based on the evidence of the autopsies, I'd say a number of hours. You should know, though, that both the men and the fish had present in their lungs and gills, respectively, and commonly in their bloodstreams levels of methyl mercury that were more than ten times the strength needed to be fatal."

"My God! That's horrible!" Dave said.

"Why is it we've never experienced a similar disaster in the past, Doc?" Ski protested. "Hell, we have submarines operating in waters all over the world."

"I'm not sure, Ski. Maybe we've just been lucky. There are stringent laws now that regulate the dumping of mercury and organic waste materials. Disposal is permitted well out to sea in natural or man-made subterranean gas holes designated as industrial waste-disposal sites."

"Doc, are you telling me that the gas hole we picked for the *Trident*'s overnight holding coordinates is one of these designated industrial waste-disposal sites?" Ski asked in disbelief.

"On the contrary. I've already checked out that possibility and learned that the gas holes we commonly use for submarine maneuvers are closed to waste disposal because they're too close to shore, and as such are designated safe waters to fish in."

"That's right, Ski," Dave said. "Admiral Pulvey had me verify that gas hole Beta was not a commercial waste-disposal site when he decided to change the *Trident*'s holding coordinates from gas hole Alpha to Beta. The nearest waste-disposal site was gas hole Yoke, which is about two hundred miles out from the Long Island coastline and a good hundred and fifty miles further out to sea than Alpha and Beta."

"What I'm trying to tell you, Ski," Hilderbrand said, "is that I suspect an illegal use of gas hole Beta took place, perhaps well before the *Trident* arrived there. I theorize that some waste transport tanker captain might have referred to his sea charts for possible short cuts, say a gas hole closer to shore, considered the savings in time and fuel, and dumped his load in a prohibited gas hole."

"What a tragic coincidence that he picked the *Trident*'s holding coordinates for his dumping," Ski said sadly and paused. "I wonder if the tanker was already gone when the *Trident* arrived."

"Hard to know, Ski," Hilderbrand said. "Why?"

"Well, as we were talking, I remembered something. The only thing I found a little unusual on the *Trident*'s voyage recorder disc was Bentsen's attention being called to some whale echolocations upon arrival at gas hole Beta. The sonarman had described them as extremely loud and excessive. We assume Bentsen listened to the whale echolocations, and upon doing so his reaction was, quote, 'Isn't that peculiar?,' unquote."

"Well, whale echolocations can be disturbing to sonarmen at times," Hilderbrand said. "Especially at critical times such as defying ASW detection."

"Disturbing to a sonarman, but not to a sonar expert like Bentsen. His tone was one of questioning rather than commenting."

"How can you be sure of that, Ski?"

"I spent a lot of years aboard subs with Bentsen. I knew his every quirk, mood, and tone of voice. I'm sure he was questioning what he was hearing."

"Why should he have? Whales do appear in the area," Hilderbrand said.

"Perhaps he heard something the sonarman didn't hear, or didn't recognize about the whale echolocations. Perhaps it wasn't the whale echolocations Bentsen was referring to at all. He might have heard background propeller sounds, such as the screw noise a waste-disposal tanker might make." Ski got up from his seat. "Perhaps Bentsen heard the dumping taking place at that very moment." Ski turned to Dave. "Let's get back to the sound lab, Dave. We'll stop off at CIC and raise the *Dart* on ship-to-shore radio. Maybe Commander Buel has some knowledge of a waste-transport tanker being around gas hole Beta."

When Ski stepped into the CIC room, Lieutenant J. G. Miles Reynolds, the OOD, summoned him over to the duty officer's desk. "A woman by the name of Fay Parks just called here for you. It sounds like trouble."

"What kind of trouble?" Ski asked.

"She claims she has pictures of you arriving back at the base in the chopper, Ski."

"Where is she now, Miles?"

"At the Holiday Inn in Groton," Miles said.

"Well, I'd better call her and find out what these pictures are all about," Ski said, exasperated. "We don't need any more trouble than we already have.'' He gestured to the radio operator. ''Call out to the *Dart* and ask Bad Ass Buel if there were any other ships in the *Trident*'s area. Tell him we're especially interested in knowing if a seagoing tanker happened along at any time since the *Dart* was on patrol out there.''

Fay was looking smug when her room phone rang. She picked it up at once, certain of who the caller was. ''Yes?''

''Fay, this is Ski. I . . .''

''How nice of you to return my call, Ski.''

''I got word that you took some pictures of me this morning.''

''That's right,'' Fay said with a devilish grin as she studied one of the pictures. ''Have 'em right here, along with a few other interesting subjects. I must say, you're very photogenic.''

''Did you take these photos while you were on the base, Fay?''

''Where I took them is not the important thing. But *what* I took them of should prove interesting to you. I suggest you come here and take a look at them.''

''You know, you could be arrested and I could confiscate your pictures,'' Ski said. ''It's against the law to photograph a military installation without authorization.''

''You try it and you'll be sued for false arrest. People ride up and down the Thames River in private and excursion boats every day, taking all the pictures they want of the Navy base and your submarines.''

Ski knew she had a valid point, so he moved on. ''What do you plan to do with those pictures you claim you took of me?''

''Come now, Ski. I'm a journalist, remember? What do you think I'm going to do with them?''

''If you plan to put them in your newspaper, why are you calling me?''

''I'm offering you a chance to be fair. I know something big is going on at the base, and I know Ray Tolbin is using his influence with the admiral to hog the story for his newspaper. Now, I've discussed this with my managing editor, and I'm authorized by him to cooperate with the Navy in any way possible. All the Navy has to promise in return is that the *Globe* gets its share of whatever action there is.'' There was silence on the other end that suggested she'd hit a nerve. ''It's up to you, Ski. Do you want the *Globe* to cooperate with the Navy, or shall I go ahead with my story and the photos?''

"All that's going on here is a red alert," Ski said defensively.

"My photos tell me differently, Ski. I strongly urge you to come and take a look at them."

There was silence, then, finally, Ski said, "I'll meet you in the cocktail lounge there in about half an hour."

Ski returned the phone to its cradle, then regarded Dave, who had just gotten off the ship-to-shore radio with the *Dart*. "I'm going to have to run over to the Holiday Inn and see her, Dave. She's threatened to put whatever photos she took in her newspaper. Somehow I've got to con her out of doing that."

"I should have thrown her in the damn brig, Ski," Dave said bitterly. "She's a real chop buster."

"What did Bad Ass Buel have to say?" Ski asked anxiously.

"The last thing in his patrol area since he got on station was that Soviet submarine he reported to us on Friday."

"And that sub definitely left our waters?"

"Affirmative, Ski. There were no other subs, no other surface ships, especially no tanker ships within a hundred miles of gas hole Beta all week long. Outside of the Soviet submarine, all Bad Ass said he found out there was a noisy whale. He said he chased it three times over this past weekend thinking it might be the *Trident* playing tricks on him. The last time he gave chase he saw the whale come to the surface and show its fin as it cleared its blowhole. The next thing he encountered after the whale left the area was the *Trident*, crash-surfaced."

"Was there any word from the *Dart* on when the admiral expects to get back to the base with the *Trident*, Dave?"

"The Bull's latest ETA back into port is twenty-three hundred hours."

Ski glanced at his wristwatch. It was going on 7:00 P.M. He had a good four hours to deal with Fay and listen to the *Trident*'s sonar tapes before going over to the sea hangar to meet Admiral Pulvey when the admiral got back to the base. "Set up the sonar tape for playback. This thing with Fay shouldn't take long."

Seeing Ski was about to leave, Reynolds jumped up from his seat at the desk. "Ski! I almost forgot to tell you that Janet called. She's at . . ."

"Later, Miles," Ski said. Whatever Janet had to say couldn't be more important than his trip to the Holiday Inn.

"Right, Ski," Reynolds said as he watched his CO leave CIC.

He'd been about to tell Ski that Janet had called from the Holiday Inn and wanted him to meet her there. Thinking they might bump into each other anyway, he crumbled up the note he'd made to himself.

## Chapter Twenty

When he arrived, Ski found the Holiday Inn, in nearby Groton, to be emptying of Labor Day weekend travelers. He crossed the lobby to the adjoining cocktail lounge and noticed that the base red alert had voided the long bar, round cocktail tables, and leather-cushioned booths of the usual crowd of Navy and Marine personnel. Fay waved from a booth in the rear of the lounge to get his attention and he walked over to her. He seated himself across from Fay and placed his gold-embroidered uniform cap on the seat next to him. "I wish I could say it's nice to see you again, Fay. We ended the admiral's party on fairly nice terms, but your threat has soured me."

"I don't like having to do this." She gestured in the direction of the service bar and a cocktail waitress came right over. "I'll have another whiskey sour, please." She regarded Ski. "You may as well have a drink, Ski. It might help to cool you down a little."

"Scotch and soda," Ski said to the waitress, then looked across the table at Fay as the waitress left. "What is it you want of me?"

Fay removed a dozen 8 x 10 photographs from her purse and handed them across the table. "All the Navy has to do is promise to make Ray Tolbin share the story with the *Globe*. In return the *Globe* will agree not to release the story until the Navy authorizes us to print it."

Ski pondered Fay's offer as he thumbed through her photos. The photos were very disturbing. They were quite good and would expose the *Trident* submarine tragedy to the public prematurely if she printed them in her newspaper. He accepted that eventually the public would have to know what had happened aboard the new submarine. But it was in the best interest of all concerned if the news could continue to be kept quiet until the investigation was completed.

Ski was tempted to agree to Fay's offer. It seemed reasonable and within the framework of what the Navy wanted Ray Tolbin of the *Washington Chronicle* to do. But there was a troubling air of distrust that seemed built in to Fay's offer. He decided the rivalry between the two Washington-based newspapers was too strong for her to be trusted in such a serious situation. He shook his head. "Well, I hate to bust your bubble, Fay, but all you have on film is a rehearsal of a disaster, not an actual one."

"Bullshit, Ski," Fay commented sourly.

"How do you see it then?"

"Those body bags contain dead sailors or Marines, flown in from some sort of disaster. Maybe even from the new supersubmarine. Why else would the Navy be in such a damn hurry to throw the media off the submarine base?"

"You were not thrown off, Fay. You were asked to leave."

"Your executive officer would have thrown me off bodily if I hadn't gone, Ski."

"The Navy *is* a branch of the armed forces. As such we are required to follow orders. Those orders are, above all, to keep the Navy combat ready at all times. Playing host to the media or the public comes second to that responsibility. Regulations require that we be called upon to practice combat readiness on surprise notice, just the way a real military action would come. The practice drill orders come from either the White House or the Pentagon in the form of red alert exercises. I'm sure you've seen them taking place in and around Washington from time to time. When a red alert is called, we sometimes don't know if it's the real thing or just a practice alert. Therefore, as a precaution, we are required to evacuate all civilian personnel from military installations."

"Then why didn't you evacuate Ray Tolbin?"

"Mr. Tolbin is an old friend of the admiral's, as I think you know. Admirals have a lot of horsepower in the Navy. They usually get what they want. As a special favor to Mr. Tolbin, Admiral Pulvey allowed him to remain on the base as a red alert correspondent, to cover the activities of the exercise. Tomorrow Mr. Tolbin will be printing a story about how the Navy responds to a red alert, as a sort of public-spirited promotional feature designed to bolster the PR the Navy is building around the new fleet of Trident submarines. All you have to complain about is that the admiral gave Mr. Tolbin preferential treatment out of friendship. But it was within his power to do so."

"I don't see it that way, Ski. Those body bags tell me there's a zingo of a story. I think your pitch about a red alert drill is crap."

The waitress came with their drinks and Ski put a five-dollar bill on the waitress's tray. "Keep the change," he said, then took a long sip of the Scotch and soda. "Believe what you want, Fay. The body bags are filled with dummies, props used to train our medical personnel in casualty evacuation maneuvers. We use dummies instead of live personnel to prevent personnel from becoming actual casualties during the rehearsal."

"I'm still not convinced."

"Yes, you are. And I'll tell you how I know. If you were sure a disaster'd taken place, you wouldn't have bothered to call me. You'd have released the story immediately. Instead, you're here trying to pry something out of me that doesn't exist. Go ahead! Write a story! Put those pictures in your newspaper. But don't be surprised if you and your newspaper are the objects of ridicule around Washington for being alarmists. Tomorrow the *Washington Chronicle* is going to print a story that will explain what really took place. Mr. Tolbin will be printing facts. Your story will be based on fiction, a figment of your own silly imagination."

"I'm willing to take that risk, Ski," Fay said, but she was bluffing. Without details of a disaster, her photos would look foolish in the newspapers.

"Go ahead. But if you do, I'm going to let it be known that you tried to blackmail me. That's a criminal act, Fay."

"Blackmail is a harsh term. All I wanted to do was persuade you to be fair."

"I'm willing to be fair. I'll give you the same story about our red alert exercise that Mr. Tolbin is being given. How's that?"

"It's not exactly what I had in mind."

"Well, I can't give you what I don't have . . . so I guess I have nothing to trade. However, if you want a story to wrap your snapshots up in, I strongly suggest you write what I just explained about the body bags." He glanced at his wristwatch. "We're still at red alert. I have to get back to the base now. Will you be going back to Washington?" He hoped she would.

"That all depends upon what my managing editor wants me to do. I am a working woman. I take orders, too."

"All the more reason to think before you leap. You might wind up out of a job if you cry wolf and can't produce one." He saw her taking out a cigarette and lighter. He took the lighter out of her hand and lit the cigarette for her.

Fay released a stream of cigarette smoke that sent a blue cloud billowing up over her head. "Thank you," she said. She accepted her lighter back, still feeling impressed with the Navy Intelligence captain's manners. It was his explanation of the body bags that she was unimpressed with. She just couldn't put her finger on what it was that didn't gel.

"Well, I guess this is good-bye then," Ski said as he got up to leave. He shook her hand. "I hope you have a pleasant trip back to D.C. when you do go. Again, if you're interested in sharing the story with Mr. Tolbin, I'll see what I can . . ." He noticed Fay was staring at something behind him. When he turned to see what it was, his eyes met Janet's.

"There you are, Ski," Janet said, then nodded at Fay. "Hello, Fay." Fay returned her nod. Looking at Ski again, Janet went on, "I see you got my message after all, Ski."

"What message?"

"I called the base and told the CIC duty officer to tell you to meet me here when the red alert was over. What were you doing at the base hospital? Are you feeling ill or something?"

"It was just a routine visit with Doc Hilderbrand, Janet. I'm fine."

"Well, I'm glad you made it. Sorry we're having our tennis meeting on such short notice, but Jack Morrison and I are leaving for Boston tomorrow. He simply must be there early to arrange the Interstate Tennis Tournament matches."

"I'm not going to be able to attend the tennis meeting, Janet," Ski said. "We're still at red alert and I have to get back to the base."

"Then why on earth did you come here if . . ." She narrowed her eyes. "Ski, you didn't even get my message, did you?" She shifted her stare to Fay, then back to Ski. "Why are you here?" she asked suspiciously. "More chaperon duty?"

"I had to give Fay some information about the red alert for her story."

"Oh. And you're finished now?" Janet asked as she eyed their drinks on the table.

Ski looked down at Fay. "I hope so." He grew tense when Janet noticed Fay's snapshots. Fearing Janet might also question the body bags in the photos and rekindle Fay's suspicions about their meaning, he took Janet by the arm to lead her away. "I really have to go now, Janet. Sorry we had to cut your visit short, Fay." He tugged on Janet's arm. "I'll walk you to the meeting room, Janet."

As Fay thumbed through the prints again, she began to feel as though the expensive developing equipment she had purchased had been an unnecessary extravagance. She thought her managing editor might even refuse to reimburse her if she returned to Washington without a big scoop.

Fay was about to slip her prints back into her purse when suddenly she realized what it was that had disturbed her about the snapshots. Ski had said the body bags contained dummies and were being used as props to train medical personnel in handling corpses. She thought it strange that *none* of the props were dressed up as wounded. And there were no plasma or IV bottles being used to make a staged maneuver more realistic. She wondered why medical personnel needed to practice moving corpses around, when it would be more beneficial to train them to handle *wounded* personnel. Another thing bothered her terribly: why were body bags needed if only dummies were being used in the red alert rehearsal.

An electrifying feeling raced through Fay's body. Something told her she had just been lied to. Something told her Ski's big hurry to get back to the submarine base might be because more body bags were about to be flown in by helicopter. And something told her that if she returned to the river's edge where she'd taken the snapshots earlier that morning, she'd have her proof.

With the check paid by Ski, Fay left a generous tip and hurried off to her motel room. She decided jeans, a warm sweater, and her running shoes would be appropriate. Realizing it was getting late, she was frightened about the idea of crossing the graveyard and the railroad tracks in the dark, but she'd brave the challenge somehow. Anything for a possible Pulitzer prize story. Anything.

## Chapter Twenty-one

Dave had diligently and pleasurably prepared the *Trident*'s sonar tape for playback while Ski was away at the Holiday Inn. Then, to amuse himself while waiting for his CO to return, he delved into the intricate functions of the sound laboratory's sophisticated apparatus and made notations on a pad about some interesting segments he wanted to bring to Ski's attention. He was just listening to the last segments of the new submarine's crash-surfacing sounds when he noticed Ski step into the room. He switched off the sonar tape, then removed his headset and asked, "How did things go with Fay Parks?"

"She missed her calling in life," Ski commented. "She should have been a covert operative instead of a newspaper reporter. She had every damn detail of my return to the base with the bodies this morning captured on film. But I think I managed to convince her for the time being that her snapshots are meaningless. I'm hoping she'll be on a plane and heading back to D.C. in the morning." He sat down in the reviewing armchair next to Dave and removed a pint of Southern Comfort from a paper bag. He had purchased the whiskey to ease the tension the long day's activities had caused. "How are things here?" he asked as he unscrewed the bottle cap.

With his eyes glued to the bottle of Southern Comfort, Dave replied, "I reviewed the segments of the *Trident*'s arrival at its coordinates, then replayed the segments of the crash-surfacing noises. There didn't seem to be anything in the latter segments that Bentsen might have thought peculiar, so I synchronized the voyage recorder disc with the sonar tape and replayed them simultaneously. That function brought the sounds of the whale echolocations over my headset in unison with Bentsen's statement of something being peculiar. But everything was so loud and happening so fast, that I couldn't discern what Bentsen might have been referring to. The next thing I did was use our sound-separation system."

Ski took a swig of the Southern Comfort, then offered the bottle to Dave. "Have a belt of this. You deserve a drink. It sounds like you've been quite busy while I was gone."

Dave took a swig of the liquor and gasped when it burned his throat on the way down. "My God, Ski! How can you drink that stuff?"

"It hurts on the way down, but it feels good once it gets to your head," Ski said. "How does this sound-separation system work, Dave?"

"It isolates the sounds being monitored on sonar in various individual recording modes. It's called audio phasing, or mixing down onto channel separators. By playing each recorded source of sound on different channels, we can listen to them independent of the entire sound source."

"Maybe you'd better show me how it works," Ski said. He took another sip of the liquor, offered it to Dave, who declined, then screwed the cap back on and sat back to listen. "Should I slip on a headset?"

"No. I'll play the segments over the speaker system first, Ski," Dave replied. He flicked a number of switches on his remote-control module and sat back. The voyage recorder disc and sonar tape rewound to the desired setting, then clicked. "What you're going to hear first is the whale echolocations that were occurring outside the submarine at the precise time Bentsen made the statement 'Isn't that peculiar?' " He flicked the playback switch.

When the playback ended, Ski nodded. "I see what you mean, Dave. I can't figure out what Bentsen might have thought to be peculiar, other than how loud the whale echolocations seemed to be."

Dave flicked the rewind switch, then, as the disc and tape were being automatically brought back to the same starting segment, he said, "Now I'll replay each audio segment being monitored on sonar without the accompanying voyage recorder dialogue. There are three major sounds: a rather faint and continually fading noise, which I challenged for an identification. The computer declared it was surface screw noises that cross-referenced to a Spruance Class destroyer."

"That would have been the *Dart* in the *Trident*'s area," Ski said.

"Exactly. The second sound you'll hear will be the very distinctive whale echolocations. Backgrounding the whale noises will be an almost inaudible third sound, which thus far I have been unable to identify." He flicked the start switch and selected the first sound source mode.

Ski listened to the faint droning noise that the computer had identified as the surface destroyer's engine-driven propeller sounds. He nodded to Dave as the screw noises faded off. Dave flicked the switch for the second sound source, and immediately the Dolby speaker system in the room blared with whale echolocations that pierced their ears with the excitement-filled mammal noises. Soon the whale echolocations faded, then stopped.

Dave flicked the third sound-mode switch, then turned up the volume to its maximum setting. "You'll barely hear this, Ski . . . even at max volume. But see if you can identify it."

Ski leaned forward in his seat and listened to the faint humming noise. When it suddenly vanished, he shook his head. "I have no idea what it might be, Dave."

"Even the computer couldn't identify it. But I am pretty sure that sound arrived with the whale and came close to the *Trident*. It abruptly ends just before the whale echolocations fade off. I'm going to play that segment once more. Listen this time to how that humming sound has the same duration as the whale echolocations.'' He gestured to the headset hooked to the side of Ski's chair as he picked up the headset clipped to his seat. ''Let's listen through these this time. You'll get a clearer sound.''

Dave flicked the replay switch. There was a silence that preceded the whale echolocations, then, just as Dave had pointed out, the whale echolocations were joined by the faint humming sound. As both sounds grew more intense, Ski envisioned the whale drawing closer to the submarine. Then the humming sound ended abruptly, and the whale echolocations began to fade away.

Dave stopped the sonar tape.

''I get your drift, Dave. The humming sound seems to arrive with the whale, then linger outside the sub before ending.''

''Right, Ski. And I think the humming sound might be what Bentsen was questioning when he stated something was peculiar. Even though Bentsen was a sonar expert, he might not have been able to identify that humming sound either.''

''The *Trident* is equipped with sound-separation phasing apparatus, isn't it, Dave?''

''Just like the one we're using.''

''Well, if Bentsen wasn't sure about what he was hearing, why didn't he use his SSP system?''

''It could be he'd been about to when Mr. Hobart interrupted him with the annunciator problem. If he had, its isolation effects would have also been recorded on the sonar tape and I wouldn't have to be using SSP now.''

''Fine, Dave. We'll assume that Bentsen was unfamiliar with the humming sound, but his reaction still has me convinced the sound caused him concern.''

''Well, according to Commander Buel, the *Dart*'s sonar didn't detect anything in the area of the *Trident*'s holding coordinates for about a hundred miles. The only thing that was in close proximity to the sub was this noisy whale. Therefore, we have to conclude the whale was making the humming sound. But just to be sure we didn't have a seagoing tanker overhead of the *Trident* at that precise time, as Doc Hilderbrand's theory suggested, I went further into the recording with a little experiment of my own.''

''Which is?'' Ski asked with interest.

''Well, the humming sounded a little like the noise pumps make. So I replayed the segment covering the sounds sonar recorded during the *Trident*'s crash-surfacing.''

"And?" Ski prodded.

"Rather than explain what I heard, I'll let you listen to my little experiment yourself, Ski," Dave said, then advanced the sonar tape to that recorded segment. He gestured for Ski to put his headset on again, then, after doing likewise, he flicked the playback switch. Ski listened intently to the commotion the emergency crash-surfacing was causing. Then, utilizing the sound-separation phase feature, Dave isolated the ballast pump noises and rewound the sonar tape once more. "Those defined humming sounds were unquestionably made by the *Trident*'s ballast pumps. Did you hear them clearly?"

"Yes," Ski replied.

"Good. Now I'm going to replay the humming sound accompanying the whale echolocations. Only this time I'm going to use a little trick called mixing down. What I'll be doing in effect is lowering the louder mammal noises so that it will seem the humming sound is dominant, just as I did with the crash-surfacing and ballast-pump noises."

Ski listened to the sounds and nodded in recognition when he heard the humming sound come over his headset. He waited through the duration of the sound. "The humming noise does sound similar to the sound made by the ballast pumps."

"Exactly, Ski. End of experiment," Dave said proudly. "We can't be sure, even by using sound-separation phasing, if the humming noise is coming from the whale. For all we know it could be undersea current noises around the whale or the submarine, either of which might make a similar sound to running pumps. All we can be sure of is that the sound occurred at the same time the whale visited the submarine. Now, if we accept the possibility that Bentsen couldn't be sure of the origin of the humming sound either, we can understand why he thought it was quite peculiar."

"Go on," Ski said.

"We thought it sounded like pumps. Perhaps Bentsen did as well. He was listening to whale echolocations at the time. Now, he knows whales don't have pumps, but his submarine does. And he was well aware his sub was rigged for quiet running. Maybe he thought one of the *Trident*'s pumps was actuated in breach of quiet-running requirements. Maybe a head was being flushed at that moment and echoed out in the close proximity to the whale. You know how sound travels under the sea and how tricky sounds can be when mixed with sea currents. Add whale echolocations of the intensity we have on the sonar recording and anyone, even a sonar expert, as you say Bentsen was, might be fooled about their origin and meaning."

"Dave, I just can't bring myself to believe anyone aboard the *Trident* would disobey silent-running procedures at such a critical time. You said it yourself. Sound carries through the sea. With a surface patrol ship in her area, it seems very unlikely that anyone aboard the *Trident* would risk running a pump."

"Okay, Ski," Dave said. "Maybe it was sea currents that sound like a pump, then."

"I'm sure that as a seasoned sonar instructor and veteran submarine skipper Bentsen would have been able to tell the difference between sea currents and . . . that sound."

"Then maybe it was part of the whale echolocations, Ski. Maybe the whale was making different pitched sounds at the same time. Only an ichthyologist would know that. Do you think we should get one to listen to these tapes?"

"Yes. We need to know whether the humming sound is mechanical or natural."

A red light flashed above the window of the sound control booth, indicating there was an incoming phone call. Dave picked up the phone extension attached to his armchair. It was the CIC room duty officer. Dave listened, then acknowledged the caller and returned the phone to its cradle. "That was CIC. They just got word that the Bull is about to enter the Thames River with the *Trident*. He wants us to get over to the new sea hangar to meet him when he docks."

## Chapter Twenty-two

Nearly an hour had elapsed since Fay had climbed the sloped landscape, made her way past eerily shadowed tombstones and crypts, and crossed the railroad tracks to the sandy beach where she had taken her snapshots that morning. Crickets chirped all around her. The weeded swampy riverbank rustled uneasily in the warm breeze. Her flashlight picked up fiddler crabs crisscrossing along the sand in front of her and a horseshoe crab lying upside down on the riverbank some ten feet away. An occasional fish jumped out of the water, making a splashing sound that chilled her. Across the rippled surface of the Thames River, the lights of the submarine base glowed and flickered under a moonlit summer sky.

Fay used the telephoto lens that was attached to her camera, loaded with black-and-white special surveillance film, as a telescope as she kept a determined watch on the Naval shore installation. Thus far, except for an occasional pair of headlights moving along the roads on the submarine base, there had been nothing to see. As the minutes ticked away, the lack of activity was reducing the enthusiasm that had been afire when she'd left the Holiday Inn to a smoldering hope that seemed doomed to go out if something didn't happen soon.

A mosquito buzzed near her face annoyingly. It landed and bit her on the cheek, forcing her to lower her camera and slap the insect, then wipe her face clean of blood with her handkerchief. It wasn't the first sting she had gotten since she'd arrived. She heaved a sigh of exasperation, then lit a cigarette in the hope that the smoke might chase the annoying mosquitos away from her face. Instead the pesty insects seemed to buzz around her more. She threw the barely smoked cigarette into the river and moved away from the biting insects, smacking at the pests as she did.

Fay was about to give up and leave when a rumbling sound upriver along the opposite bank caught her attention. She aimed her camera lens in the direction of the sound and watched with interest as one of the huge doors on the new sea hangar began to rise. A brilliant white light spilled out across the surface of the river as the door climbed higher and tucked away into the rooftop, then ended its rumbling growl. She focused her lens on the figures moving around inside, then zoomed in on a uniformed officer and found herself staring at the familiar face of Ski. She panned to the officer standing next to him on the center pier and recognized Dave. Checking the other activity inside, she noticed sailors busily readying lines and preparing the submarine slip.

Excited all over again, Fay panned back to Ski's face, then a massive blackness filled her lens. Uneasily, she lowered the camera, then stood gaping at the monstrous object passing offshore of her. Her eyes blinked in disbelief as she took in the immenseness of the submarine with its winged sail seemingly bridging out across the river to her. She shook the daze from her head, then quickly panned the bridge deck and focused the camera on the meaty face of Admiral Pulvey. With professional instinct she began clicking snapshots of the admiral and of the tall white numbers seven-two-six that were backgrounded by the sharklike fin that was the submarine's conning tower. As the giant submarine turned to maneuver for entry into the new sea hangar, she panned the inside of the structure once more and focused on Ski's face. She snapped the shutter.

It seemed to Fay, as she lowered her camera and looked on, that the supersubmarine couldn't possibly fit inside. Yet, after some skillful maneuvering, it was swallowed up by the building and came to a stop alongside the long center pier. Fay raised her camera again and began clicking off shots of the U.S.S. *Trident* at rest in its berth, as the overhead door rumbled and began lowering behind the submarine. In a few moments the white light spanning the river drew back like a shade, returning the surface of the Thames to darkness.

"Jackpot!" Fay shouted as she jumped into the air. The U.S.S. *Trident*'s return home seemed to contradict what the Navy had claimed was the reason for its delay in getting into port. The supersubmarine had been sneaked back to port under cover of darkness. Now she knew she had been lied to. Now she was sure her sixth sense had been right—there *had* been some sort of disaster.

Something troubled Fay, though. She glanced around the rest of the submarine base and her confidence dwindled. There were no red lights flashing atop ambulances showing up to meet the submarine, no helicopters landing with additional body bags—no signs of urgency at all. In fact, there was very little activity to be seen anywhere on the other side of the Thames. That had her wondering what else the new submarine's unannounced return to home port might mean. She found herself entertaining the possibility that Ski hadn't lied to her at all when he'd said the activity she'd captured on film was just a training aspect of the red alert. It could mean that the U.S.S. *Trident* had really been delayed to participate in the Navy exercise and that the red alert maneuvers were now over.

Fay suddenly felt foolish standing at the river's edge, spying on the Navy base. If she was wrong, if there was no disaster after all, then all her snapshots were worthless, and her investment in the assortment of developing equipment had been a waste. She turned her back to the Thames and slowly began to walk away, accepting that perhaps she had made a mountain out of a molehill. Perhaps there was no Pulitzer prize story. Perhaps there was no story at all. Perhaps she'd better book herself on the first flight back to Washington before she did something to get herself fired.

## Chapter Twenty-three

*Tuesday*

After parking his new jet-black Corvette outside the sea hangar, Ski returned the salute of a Marine sentry and hurried into the new facility. As he approached the *Trident*, he marveled over how its dull-black rounded body filled Slip One. It was tied alongside the center pier, the overhead fluorescent ceiling lights gleaming down on its finlike conning tower to change its color to an eggplant purple. He noticed Troy Hanley standing on the aft deck atop the missile hatches, giving hand signals to a Navy crane operator who was working his boom out from the center pier to a position overhead of an open aft-deck hatch. Ski scurried up the aft gangway and joined Hanley. "Have you found out anything yet, Troy?"

"Plenty. My crew and I worked right through the night on the oxygen analyzer. We're about to raise it up from below decks now. Give me a minute and I'll tell you all about it."

Ski nodded, then stood a few feet behind Hanley and watched as the crane operator lowered the boom cable into the open hatch. The cable's cargo hook disappeared below decks for a few moments, then was raised back up. It brought up to the topside aft deck a cylindrical object that Ski thought looked like a very complex hot water heater, only much bigger. Two of Hanley's engineering hands steadied the object to keep it from swinging in midair at the end of the boom.

Hanley waved at the crane operator. "Hold it right there," he ordered, then regarded Ski. "There it is. It's supposed to be a model EOA dash seventy-one."

"Supposed to be?"

Hanley took a component identification nameplate out of the hip pocket of his khaki pants. "I removed this ident plate from the side of the unit. It's a nameplate for an EOA dash seventy-one, so whoever installed this oxygen analyzer aboard the sub was fooled into believing that's what he was putting aboard." He gestured for Ski to follow him over to the round-bodied life-support system component, then pointed to the area he had removed the nameplate from. "Take a close look at the model number embedded on the body."

Ski examined the area and found the nearly illegible model number. "It's an EOA dash fifteen."

"That's right, Ski. I was baffled when I tried to disassemble the damn unit last night. Nothing in the engineering specs for an EOA dash seventy-one that I was working from seemed to make any sense. We're not usually called upon to tear into these units, so I figured I must have been doing something wrong. Then, after mind-boggling hours of work that was getting me nowhere, I tried comparing the physical characteristics of this analyzer to other models illustrated in the repair and overhaul manuals."

"And you found you were trying to disassemble an EOA dash fifteen instead of an EOA dash seventy-one."

"You got it, Ski," Hanley said.

"Someone mistakenly labeled this component, and then someone else came along and installed it aboard as an EOA dash seventy-one?" Ski asked.

"It was no mistake at all. It was a deliberate deception," Hanley returned.

"By whom? And why?"

"Well, as soon as I realized I wasn't working on an EOA dash seventy-one, I removed the ident nameplate to see if I could determine how the mistake had been made. When I saw that the unit's original nameplate had been removed and this one put on the unit in its place, I knew it'd been no accident. I called Admiral Pulvey right away, and ever since he saw what I found he's been going over invoices in his office. What the Bull came up with was some mighty convincing evidence that the builder substituted an inferior oxygen analyzer for the one our Navy specs clearly specified they use aboard Trident submarines. And it seems the builder did so with the intent of ripping off the Navy for some real big bucks."

"Fraud!" Ski said sourly.

"So it seems, Ski," Hanley said. "They provided us with what we thought was an EOA dash seventy-one. Then their own engineering tech rep, who we incidentally learned was the one they assigned to go along on the *Trident*'s maiden voyage, unknowingly authorized the wrong analyzer for installation aboard the sub. I say unknowingly because I seriously doubt he would have intentionally installed an inferior unit aboard a sub he knew he was going to spend considerable time aboard. If he'd survived I'd be suspicious, but his corpse is over in the hospital morgue right now."

"Didn't this engineering tech rep have a problem hooking up the wrong unit to the *Trident*'s life-support system components?''

Hanley shook his head. "Surprisingly enough, the electromechanical hookup was no different. The difference was in its operational performance. It was compatible with the type scrubbers and model Detection and Warning system used with an EOA dash seventy-one. But the EOA dash fifteen is far less sophisticated and was therefore classified obsolete by BUSHIPS tech ops bulletins. The bulletins described the older model as being incapable of handling a number of comtaminants known to be harmful to humans, like this methyl mercury, which is both odorless and colorless. The EOA dash fifteen wouldn't have known it was encountering methyl mercury if the poison had introduced itself as it came aboard. The oxygen analyzer passed on the mercury unchallenged. In turn, the scrubbers passed it along because they're not engineered to do the oxygen analyzer's work. Finally, the Detection and Warning system wasn't triggered by the odorless, colorless mist, and SAM's sensors didn't react to it either. In a matter of minutes after being taken aboard through electrolysis, the lethal composition was circulating through the air-conditioning ducts and . . . well, you know the rest.''

Ski nodded solemnly. "I'm heading over to the admiral's office now to have a look at those invoices he's found. Is there anything else I should know?''

"Only what we learned by following up on the maintenance gripe sheets in the ship's logbook,'' Hanley replied matter-of-factly.

"Which is?''

"To start with we had to reassemble the ship's annunciator in order to return to port under the sub's own power. The engineering tech rep had mentioned there was something wrong with it, but it seemed fine to me.''

"Perhaps it was just some freak malfunction that taking it apart had fixed,'' Ski suggested. "Anything else?''

"We had time to kill while waiting to come back to port under cover of dark, so we looked into another gripe the builder's engineering tech rep made out in the Mid-Atlantic. The ship's log noted it was a breach of quiet running caused by the diving plane slaving servo.''

"Interesting.''

"The tech rep, Nelson Hobart, claimed the slaving servo was making excessive noise.''

"Might it have been a humming noise?''

"The kind of sound wasn't mentioned in the log."

"In your learned opinion, could this slaving servo make a hum-ming sound if it were malfunctioning?"

"Not to my knowledge, Ski. I'd be more inclined to think it would make a growling or shrilling sound. But there are a lot of engineering quirks built into this new sub that the builder knows of and our Navy tech engineering people have yet to become familiar with. If it's important enough to know, you could check with Marine Dynamics' engineering people. They should know. Only I doubt they'll be interested in talking to Navy people when they hear about the Bull's accusation of fraud."

"Call someone over at the defense plant and make an appointment for me to see the engineering honcho over there tomorrow morning, Troy. Someone will talk to me, I promise you."

"Roger that, Ski. And while you're there, ask Engineering if they ever installed something with an adhesive binding in the slaving servo access compartment. We found the floor of the compartment had an adhesive imprint that was caused by something, yet we couldn't find anything out of place or missing. I'm just curious about what that something might have been."

"I'll do that, Troy . . . and get word back to you on what I find out. Give me a call later and let me know what time my appointment is. I'll be at the sound lab after I see the admiral."

Admiral Pulvey studied the bitter look on Ski's face as his future son-in-law seated himself across the desk from him. "I gather you just came from the new sea hangar?" he asked. A nod confirmed his guess. "Then Troy Hanley explained everything to you about the deception." Another nod. Holding a smoldering cigar in one hand, he passed some documents across the desk to Ski. "These are the purchase invoices covering the sale of an EOA dash seventy-one to the Navy, Ski. Notice they've been declared paid in full. Notice also that the price paid to the builder for that particular model oxygen analyzer is a whopping four million dollars."

Ski studied the information on the documents, then returned them to the admiral and accepted another set of invoices. "What are these, Admiral?"

"They're invoices pertaining to past sales, Ski. Sales involving the purchase of a model EOA dash fifteen. You can see by the price tag that its cost is half that of the new model." He waited for Ski to digest the information on the second invoice.

"I can't believe that anyone at Marine Dynamics would chance such a deception, Admiral," Ski commented.

"Why not, Ski? As long as an unusual chemical like this methyl mercury didn't happen along to spoil their deception, who would ever have reason to tear into the device and discover that a substitution had taken place?"

"But sooner or later something might have gone wrong with the unit, necessitating a repair, Admiral," Ski insisted.

"Not according to Troy Hanley. He said an oxygen analyzer's life expectancy is so long that it could outlast the submarine itself. Its mechanical performance is known to be virtually trouble-free. What malfunctions might occur would most likely involve the scrubbers, the D and W system, or some external parts of the oxygen-manufacturing plant. Not the oxygen analyzer itself. In fact, the only reason we tore into that major component was because we were unable to locate a problem anywhere else in the life-support system."

"Admiral, I just can't believe the builder would be so pressed for profits."

"We've witnessed petty ripoffs right along, from the day the *Trident*'s keel was first laid. I must admit I'm rather shocked to learn of a big-scale cost-cutting venture such as this, but when we consider all the cost overrides Marine Dynamics was constantly plagued with, we can readily understand the firm's financial desperation. Spiraling costs were eating away like a cancer at the profit yields, which they expected to realize in spite of the very risky underbidding they did to get the entire *Trident* submarine contract away from their arch competitor."

"I recall some of that, Admiral," Ski agreed. "But I had no idea they were desperate enough to resort to fraud."

"Well, let me enlighten you, Ski," Pulvey said, exhaling blue cigar smoke that billowed up into a thick cloud above his head. "At the time the bidding was shaping up for the Trident submarine program we had only two firms capable of constructing such an immense vessel. Marine Dynamics' competition submitted a bid of two billion per submarine, and Marine Dynamics placed a bid in of one point eight billion per vessel. They were lowballing and they knew it, but they also knew they could submit cost-override claims in the hope of recovering the two hundred million dollars they underbid by. Influenced by the lower bid, the Defense Department awarded the entire Trident program contract to Marine Dynamics, which as you know was to build ten such Trident class submarines."

"Then the cost overrides came flowing in?"

"Exactly, Ski. They came in over a period of time and under threat of work stoppage on the prototype. The builder claimed that changes the Navy demanded in design and material used were not within contract specifications and therefore a burden that the Defense Department *must* subsidize, or they were going to renege on the contract. With completion of the new fleet of submarines already running behind schedule, the Defense Department allocated the additional two hundred million dollars to pay for the changes the Navy'd called for. In effect, that nullified the underbidding of point two billion dollars, which was the basis for awarding the contract to them in the first place."

"I don't understand, Admiral," Ski said. "If the builder recouped its underbid, and its financial plight was resolved by doing so, why would they need to substitute an inferior oxygen analyzer for the more expensive one?"

"Simply because their financial plight didn't end there. One, they experienced labor problems with built-in cost factors that further burdened their treasury. Two, they suffered from an attrition problem and had to pay more to replace supervision that either quit or was fired. And three, the most taxing cost factor of all, they were caught using materials that didn't meet Navy specs and were forced to replace those materials at their own cost. Those cost overrides they next claimed they should be reimbursed for were flatly turned down by the Defense Department. They were told they weren't getting a penny more, and if they reneged on the contract the remainder of the submarines would be built by their competitor. Add all these financial adversities up, as I have done in going over these invoices, and we can readily see that unless they did something drastic to recover from their encountered losses they would have been behind on the profit projection by some two million dollars. It was a figure they just had to recoup."

Ski slammed a closed fist down on the admiral's desk in anger. "And they did recoup it, didn't they? To protect their profit yield they resorted to reckless endangerment. Or perhaps it's criminal negligence they're guilty of."

"I'm not exactly sure what they can be charged with, Ski."

"As an intelligence officer I know something about the law, Admiral. And I think they can be charged with one hundred and sixty-one counts of murder."

"With all due respect to your knowledge, Ski, I prefer to leave the classification of charges to a military tribunal. I was on the phone with Admiral Preston before you got here. The CNO is sending a judge advocate general and other tribunal officials here to New London this evening. It'll be an informal inquest at which my evidence, that of Troy Hanley, and the autopsy findings of Doc Hilderbrand will be presented. I want you to attend, of course. And I also want to have Commander Buel on hand to answer any questions the board of inquest might pose. If you have any evidence to offer, by all means bring it with you. If the builder is guilty of fraud, as this evidence seems to suggest, I want to see to it that Marine Dynamics Corporation attorneys find no legal loopholes.''

"All I have is what was recorded on the *Trident*'s voyage disc and sonar tape, Admiral. Frankly, I did think for a time that I was on to something when I reviewed those recordings. But now that I've seen Troy's evidence and yours, I'm not so sure I have anything to offer.''

The desk phone rang and Pulvey answered it. He acknowledged the caller. "Yes, he is, Dave.'' He handed the phone across the desk. "It's your XO.''

Ski stared at the phone uneasily for a moment. He anticipated Dave was calling to let him know he had managed to get an ichthyologist. After the meeting he'd just had with the admiral, he felt unenthusiastic about proceeding with the marine specialist. Certain it would be embarrassing if the Bull overheard that he'd called an ichthyologist in to listen to whale echolocations, he accepted the phone and held it close to his head. "Yes, Dave.'' He listened as Dave told him the ichthyologist already had his test meters hooked up in the sound lab. Rather than appear foolish and tell Dave to send the specialist away, he decided to go through with the tape evaluation. "Fine. I'll be right there, Dave.'' He returned the phone to the admiral.

Pulvey took notice of the strange look on Ski's face. "Is anything wrong, Ski?''

"No, sir. It's just a routine detail that I have to handle back at the Intelligence Center. I may as well shove off and get it over with.''

"Perhaps you can fit in another small detail for me, Ski.''

"Which is, sir?''

"Stop off at CIC and see to it that Commander Buel is notified by ship-to-shore radio that he's to fly to the base by chopper and attend the inquest this evening. Tell him to be here by, say . . . eighteen hundred hours.''

"Aye, aye, Admiral. Will that be all, sir?"

"There is one other thing, Ski. Janet mentioned that she saw you at the Holiday Inn with Ms. Parks yesterday evening. What was that all about?"

Ski cleared his throat. "The incident is resolved now, sir. That's why I didn't mention it to you. Fay managed to take pictures of my return to base with the casualties yesterday. She had hoped she was on to a disaster story and was using the threat of early publication to pressure me for a share of what she thought was Toblin's exclusive."

"I just knew Ms. Goddamn Liberal Bitch would stick her nose in where it didn't belong," Pulvey growled, banging his fist on the desk. "What did you tell her, Ski?",

"That what she saw was all part of a training exercise held in conjunction with the red alert."

"Good thinking, Ski. Ray Tolbin has an article coming out in the papers today, confirming that story."

"I couldn't very well explain to Janet why I met with Fay without revealing the *Trident* catastrophe to her."

"Leave Janet to me, son. However, do avoid seeing Ms. Parks unless you let me know first."

"Aye, aye, Admiral. I plan to stay an ocean away from her," Ski said.

"Carry on, son. See you tonight at the inquest."

## Chapter Twenty-four

Fay Parks sipped the piping-hot container of coffee she'd brought back to her room from the Holiday Inn restaurant as she sat on the edge of the double bed waiting for her call to Washington to go through. She had purchased morning editions of the *Connecticut Herald* and the *New London Times* at the cashier's counter, then darted back to her room to make the urgent call to her managing editor. The news in the *Connecticut Herald* hadn't prompted the call to D.C.; the article Ray Tolbin had syndicated under his name in the *New London Times* had. She had her legs crossed and was swinging one impatiently as she took intermittent puffs on a cigarette. Finally someone answered at the other end.

"*Washington Globe,* copy desk. Can I help you?"

Fay recognized the voice at the other end as that of her colleague, Pam Wilson. "Pam, this is Fay."

"Hi, Fay! Where the hell are you?"

"I'm still here in Connecticut, and I've got to speak to Tom Hurt right away."

"Just hang on, honey. I'll page him for you," Pam Wilson promised.

Again Fay began rocking one leg as she held the *New London Times* in front of her, ready to cite passages from Ray Tolbin's article to her managing editor. She heard Tom Hurt's voice come on the line and said excitedly, "More hot developments took place here last night, Tom."

"What have you got, Fay?"

"I followed a hunch last night and returned to the spot across from the submarine base where I took my snapshots. Guess what I saw, Tom?"

"More body bags?" Tom Hurt asked with interest.

"No. But I did see the U.S.S. *Trident* being sneaked back into home port. It's in a building they call 'the new sea hangar' and it's behind closed doors."

"What do you make of it, Fay?"

"Well, at first I thought this red alert exercise that was said to be delaying the *Trident*'s return home had ended. So I was going to hop aboard a Washington-bound flight this afternoon. Then I picked up copies of the *Connecticut Herald* and the *New London Times*, and I was flabbergasted. The *Connecticut Herald* didn't carry the story, but lo and behold, an article written in the *New London Times* by none other than good ol' Ray Tolbin clearly states that the red alert is still on. And there's a quote by Admiral Pulvey, the submarine base's commanding officer."

"Isn't he the Navy brass that sent us the invitation to the open-house weekend?"

"Right," Fay returned. "Admiral Pulvey is quoted as saying the date of the *Trident*'s return to home port remains indefinite while the red alert exercise is still going on." There was a long silence on the other end. "Don't you get it, Tom? I've been lied to. There is definitely some sort of cover-up going on at the submarine base!"

"I get the picture, Fay," Tom Hurt finally said. "And it sounds like you might be on to a real smoke screen up there." He thought for a moment about the possible repercussions of allowing Fay to expose the lie Ray Tolbin had obviously been a party to, then said,

"Okay, babe. This is how it'll be. You stay on at the Holiday Inn and stick close to the phone. I'm going to put our top-notch trouble-shooter on the job at this end and see what we can pick up on Capitol Hill about why the Navy dropped a lie on you. If anything breaks, I'll get back to you and give you the green light to pressure the Navy for a share in the story. Now, get a pen and paper and jot this name down."

Fay took a pen and pad out of her purse. "Go ahead, Tom."

"Mickey Langly."

"Who is he?"

"He's the senior editor of the *Connecticut Herald*. It's apparent his newspaper is being bypassed on the developments at the Navy base, too. I'm an old friend of Mickey's, going back to our college days. If you get something hot, give it to Mickey and he'll give you the by-line credit on the scoop. Okay?"

"Okay, Tom," Fay said excitedly, feeling she was finally becoming a real pro investigative reporter.

"If we pick up the story at this end, the *Globe* will feature you as the by-line reporter. So either way, if a story breaks, you come out looking good. Okay, babe?"

"Sounds real good to me."

"Now, do as I said. Don't aggravate whatever is going on by going off on your own to smoke it out. Sit tight by the phone and wait for me to get back to you. Then we'll take it from there, Fay."

"Talk to you later, Tom," Fay said, then hung up the phone. She hadn't been hungry when she first got up, but now she suddenly felt famished. She picked up her room phone again and the motel operator got on the line right away. "This is Fay Parks in room ten. I'm going to step out to the motel restaurant for a bite of breakfast. If a call comes in for me, please page me there at once."

## Chapter Twenty-five

Dr. Raymond Foust, the ichthyologist, mumbled to himself as he listened attentively through a second playback of the whale echolocations over his personal earphones. He had brought the earphones and dual megahertz meters along with him from his office at the Mystic Seaport Aquarium and Marine Life Museum, where he was employed as a director in charge of the facilities. He had to splice the megahertz meters into a wiring trunk beneath the sound laboratory audio control booth console so that he could measure the noise registrations and identify the particular mammal that was making the echolocations. A short, plump man in his mid-sixties, he possessed a mild manner and a boyish voice. When he spoke about his profession, his warm blue eyes twinkled from behind horn-rimmed eyeglasses. He referred to the creatures he cared for as fellows, friends, and family members. He had mentioned he rarely left the confines of the museum or aquarium grounds, and made it well known that his only reason for responding to Dave's request was that he felt obliged to the Navy for the many times it had assisted his ichthyology, marine biology, and oceanography colleagues.

With his glittering eyes locked on the bouncing needles of his dual megahertz meters and his chubby hands poised purposefully on the volume knobs that gave the needles life, he nodded repetitively to every sound dancing through his acutely tuned ears as though he understood what every noise meant. When the sounds abated, he removed his earphones, then announced, "Without a doubt, that was a *Balaenoptera musculus.*" He grinned gayly and added, "More commonly known as a blue whale."

Dr. Foust opened his attaché case and thumbed through a stack of 8 x 10 black-and-white photos of mammals, then selected one and handed it to Ski. As he watched Dave looking over Ski's shoulder at the mammal, he recited, "Up to thirty meters in length and upwards of 136,000 kilos." He produced another photo. "As you can see by the physical characteristics, a *Balaenoptera musculus,* or blue whale, has a rather pointy nose in comparison to this chap." Pointing to the second photo, he explained, "This fellow is a *Physeter catodon,* or sperm whale. His nose is quite blunt shaped."

Quickly converting the metric measurements mentally, Dave said, "A hundred feet long and a hundred and fifty tons! Is this blue whale the biggest mammal in the sea, Dr. Foust?"

"Yes, Lieutenant Lee."

Ski glanced at the photo with disinterest, then hurried the meeting with the ichthyologist along, wanting to end it as quickly as possible now that he regarded it a waste of time. "What we had wanted you to do was tell us if you found anything peculiar about the whale echolocations on the tape recording, Dr. Foust."

"The barking, cracking, moaning, and screaming noises we heard are typically the forms of communications mammals use. The dear fellows can even make whistling sounds, although such noises were absent on your tape recording, Captain Kowalski. Mammal echolocations basically register in the twenty-hertz range as low-pitched sounds and are therefore audible to human hearing. However, the echolocations we just listened to do seem particularly excessive in volume and duration.'' He rubbed his chin as he thought more deeply, then nodded his head rapidly. "Yes, Captain. I'd definitely say they were a bit peculiar in that sense. Extreme volume and excessive duration. So much so that I didn't hear the accompanying humming sound until you isolated it on the mix-down panel.''

"Could this whale have been making the humming noise, Dr. Foust?'' Ski asked.

"Absolutely not, Captain. The sounds I've mentioned are the only ones we know our mammal friends are capable of making. The humming sound seems to begin with the arrival of the dear fellow in close proximity of your submarine, then stop just before the *Balaenoptera musculus* leaves the area. The poor darling does seem extraordinarily upset the way he's screaming and moaning so repetitiously.''

"He was surrounded by dead fish,'' Dave mentioned. He immediately got a disapproving look from Ski.

"That would explain the excitement in his voice,'' Dr. Foust said. "Mammals are known to get quite upset around sick, dying, or dead animals—even of species other than their own. Indicative of their warm-blooded nature perhaps, they behave very sympathetically toward other creatures in distress. Yes, that might explain why this fellow was making so much noise. Mammals have been seen pushing dead creatures to shore from miles out at sea.''

Ski ignored the ichthyologist's animal behavior speech and narrowed his eyes at the picture of the blue whale Dr. Foust had insisted was the mammal that had made the echolocations on the sonar tape. He noticed that the blue whale was a finless mammal, yet he recalled Commander Buel had mentioned the whale that had surfaced near the *Trident*'s holding coordinates had a fin. Finding that curious, he interrupted Dr. Foust's lecture and anxiously asked, "Do these blue whales ever have fins, Dr. Foust?''

"Never, Captain,'' Foust replied, then thumbed through his assortment of photos and selected two, handing one to Dave and one to Ski. "The photo you have, Captain, is of a *Balaenoptera physalus*, or finback whale. The one you have, Lieutenant Lee, is of an *Orcinus orca*, or killer whale. These are the only two finned whales we know of other than a *Delphinus delphis*, or dolphin, which is also called a porpoise."

Pointing to the picture of the finback whale, Ski asked, "Is it possible that a finback made those echolocations?"

"Not according to the registrations the echolocations made on my hertz meters, Captain. The finback whale's echolocations are in the twenty-hertz range. Your recording reached fifty hertz, which is the range of a blue whale."

"You're certain of that, Dr. Foust?"

"Absolutely."

Ski glanced over at Dave and their eyes met. "Didn't Commander Buel say he saw a finned whale, Dave?"

"Yes."

"Perhaps this Commander Buel was mistaken," Dr. Foust suggested.

"Well, I'll be seeing him later today and I'll ask him again," Ski said. "Would it be possible to borrow a couple of your photos for a short period of time, Dr. Foust?"

"Absolutely, Captain. Which ones would you like?"

"Just the photos of the blue whale, the killer whale, and the finback whale. I'll return them to you as soon as I'm finished with them."

"Take your time with them, Captain," Foust said as he gathered those photos up and handed them to Ski.

"Getting back to the tape recording," Ski said, "you said the humming sound accompanying the echolocations was not made by the whale."

"That's correct. Although the humming sound registered in the twenty-hertz range, which is what the finback's echolocations reach, it is not a whale sound."

"Could sea currents have produced that sound, Dr. Foust?" Dave asked.

"Not unless they somehow reverberated off the hull of your submarine. In that case they might have registered in the twenty-hertz range. But otherwise, no. Currents in the sea usually register much lower. I think your submarine caused the humming noise and the high-frequency sound I also registered on my hertz meter."

"What sound?" Ski asked.

"Sort of the sound your ship's radios might make when transmitting frequency waves."

"I didn't hear a high-frequency sound," Dave said.

"Neither did I," Ski added.

"You wouldn't have. I didn't hear it either," Dr. Foust said. "We didn't because it registered in the two-hundred-hertz range on my sound meters. That's well above the range of human hearing, and beyond the operational range of sonar as well. One would have to have a special radio receiver or sound-measuring instrument, such as my hertz meter, to detect such a high sound."

"You say it might be a radio frequency wave being transmitted?" Ski queried.

"Well, at first I thought it might be the echolocations of another whale some distance away, answering the echolocations the whale near your submarine was producing. Cetaceans produce two types of sounds. One is a low-pitched signal predominantly in the human audible range, used mostly for social communications. The other is a high-intensity signal that gets up into the two-hundred-megahertz range and is used to navigate, much like sonar or radar. However, it would have been a clicking sound if a mammal were making it. This high-frequency signal was steady." He observed the puzzled looks on the faces of the two Navy officers. "Might your submarine have been broadcasting a high-frequency signal?"

Not wanting to furnish the civilian with critical information that would reveal the *Trident* disaster, Ski replied, "We'll have to check on that sound further."

"And the humming sound," Dr. Foust said. "Might that have been produced by your submarine?"

"We'll have to check further on that sound as well," Ski replied. His intention was to do so tomorrow during his meeting with someone from Marine Dynamics engineering. Now, instead of just a humming sound to identify, he also had a high-pitched noise that sounded like a radio frequency signal. The ichthyologist's evaluation of the sonar tape had confused rather than cleared up the problem.

"It appears I haven't been of much help to you and Lieutenant Lee. Perhaps if you could tell me what it is you're concerned with in particular on your tape recording, I might be able to listen more profitably. Is this some sort of Naval Intelligence project you're working on?"

"Sort of," Ski replied.

"I think I get the idea now, Captain. Your work is of a classified nature, isn't it?"

"More or less."

"I understand. I didn't mean to pry into secret military business. I just wish I could help you more."

"That's quite all right, Dr. Foust," Ski said as he patted the aging ichthyologist lightly on the back. "Perhaps you have been more of a help than you realize."

## Chapter Twenty-six

Admiral Pulvey leaned forward in his executive swivel armchair and answered the buzzing intercom on his desk. "Yes?" He listened, then said, "Tell the switchboard operator to go through the motions of putting her call through to BOQ. Then have her bring the call in on my special line instead." Pulvey looked at Ray Tolbin, who was seated on the other side of the desk with a telephone extension in front of him. "Wait for my cue, Ray. Then answer her call. If I give you the high sign, make some excuse to leave the phone, then cup the mouthpiece."

"Leave it to me, Admiral," the *Washington Chronicle*'s senior investigative reporter said, then waited for the admiral's cue. When the signal light on Pulvey's special line began to flash, Tolbin picked up the extension in sync with Pulvey's lifting his receiver. "Fay! Is that really you?"

"Yes, Ray," Fay replied at the other end. "I've been trying to get through to you at the BOQ building for over an hour."

"I was having a bite to eat, kid. Where are you calling from?"

"The Holiday Inn in Groton."

Tolbin winked at the admiral. "Hell, I thought you'd gone back to D.C. Lieutenant Lee told me that you and the others went back to Washington yesterday morning."

"Didn't he also tell you that I had a little meeting with Captain Kowalski last night?"

"No." Tolbin got a cue from the admiral to move things along. "I was told you called about an urgent personal matter. What's wrong, kid?"

"Cut the crap, Ray. I read your article this morning. The one that mentions the *Trident* is still out at sea."

"What do you mean, kid?"

"I mean . . . I have some very interesting snapshots that I took of the new submarine last night. I was right across the Thames River from the new sea hangar when Admiral Pulvey brought the *Trident* back into port. Your article contradicts what my own eyes saw last night," Fay said angrily.

Tolbin quickly read the note Pulvey passed across the desk to him. "What you probably saw was another submarine that looked just like the *Trident*."

"Bullshit, Ray!" Fay snapped. "I'm looking at a picture I took of that submarine. Standing on the bridge deck is Admiral Pulvey. And in bold white stencil on the conning tower sidewall are the numbers seven-two-six."

Pulvey sighed in exasperation, then quickly scribbled another note.

"Ray! Are you still there?" Fay asked.

Reading the admiral's second note, Tolbin said, "Hell, if that was the *Trident* submarine you saw the admiral aboard, it's news to me that it's back in port, kid. What do you make of it?"

"I think there's been some sort of disaster, Ray. And I think the Navy is trying to cover it up. And . . . I think you're helping them, just so you can get an exclusive on it."

Tolbin laughed heartily. "Disaster! Surely you jest, Fay."

"Don't try to snow me, Ray. I smell a story, and I also smell a rat."

"Fay, I honestly don't know what you're talking about. If there'd been a disaster, I'd be aware of it, kid."

"Why did a Navy tribunal just board a plane in D.C. that's bound for New London?"

"What?" Tolbin said, surprised as he looked across the desk at Pulvey.

"That's right, Ray. My managing editor called me about an hour ago. He told me that one of the *Globe*'s ace troubleshooters got wind of a military jet taking off from Andrews Air Force Base. The jet is bound for Quonset Point, where it's to be met by a helicopter that's to airlift the tribunal to the submarine base."

Tolbin saw Pulvey waving fiercely and picked up on the cue at once. "Hold on a minute, Fay. Someone is at my room door. I think it's the drink I ordered from the BOQ bar. She knows everything, Admiral," Tolbin said, his hand cupped tightly over the mouthpiece.

Holding his hand tightly over his mouthpiece, Pulvey said, "We have to stall her, Ray. She could get something out tonight over radio or TV and if this tragedy becomes public, the press will attack the submarine program like vultures swooping down on a cow's carcass.

They'll undermine the belief in the sub's invincibility. They'll claim the *Trident* is too vulnerable to play a key role in the nation's defense program.''

"Admiral, she's shouting on the other end. I'd better get back on before she becomes suspicious.''

Pulvey stared up at the ceiling. "Tell her that you don't know a thing about a tribunal arriving here tonight. Tell her that . . . maybe some sailor or officer is getting a court-martial. You'll ask around and see if there's anything to it. Act cooperative. Tell her that if there is a story, you'll get to the bottom of it, and that you'll be happy to share it with her.'' He looked across the desk at Tolbin as the reporter got back on the line, pretending he'd had to wait for change from the BOQ waiter who'd just brought his drink to his room. Tolbin repeated the admiral's instructions. After doing so, there was a pause on the other end that told him he and the admiral had Fay wondering. That was good for their side, he thought. "Fay, are *you* still there?''

"Oh, I'm here, Ray,'' Fay returned sarcastically. She digested what her colleague had told her, then said, "I'm still convinced this tribunal has something to do with a disaster, Ray.''

"I truly wish you were right. I'd like nothing more than to go back to D.C. with a nice hot piece of investigative reporting like a disaster at sea or something. But as I said, nothing's going on here at the Navy base that I'm aware of.''

"Ray, if you're lying to me, your name is going to be mud around D.C. Tom Hurt is following through on my hunch, and if he finds out I've been tricked, he's going to kick the seat of your baggy pants in.''

"Trust me, kid. I'm giving it to you straight. But I will have a look-see around and see if something is brewing.'' He saw Pulvey making slicing gestures with a hand across his neck. "Listen, let me get off the line and I'll scope things out. I'll get right back to you if I learn anything. And thanks for tipping me off that something may be brewing right under my nose, kid.''

"All right, Ray. I'm going to believe you. But do it my way. Call me here at the Holiday Inn tonight, whether something's going on or not. I won't be able to sleep a wink until I know one way or the other.''

"I'll do that, kid. Maybe we'll have a drink together before you head back to D.C.'' He returned the extension phone to its cradle. "Well?''

"You did fine, Ray," Pulvey said as he hung up his phone. "You have my promise, the Navy won't forget the *Washington Chronicle* for cooperating with us on this goddamn catastrophe." He glanced at his wristwatch. "The members of the tribunal should be landing at the heliport momentarily. We'd better get over to the new sea hangar to greet them."

## Chapter Twenty-seven

Ski looked bored as he sat next to Dave at one of the tables arranged into a U-shaped configuration in the new sea hangar's Slip Two area, where the admiral's press conference had been held just days ago. Along four tables set to Ski's right sat the presiding judge advocate general and the other half-dozen members of the board of inquest. Directly across from Ski at a table slightly larger than the one he and Dave were sharing were Admiral Pulvey, Troy Hanley, Doc Hilderbrand, and Commander Buel. Buel had arrived at the base late, and the tribunal had been well under way when he'd entered the new sea hangar. Now Ski anxiously waited for the inquest to end, his mind on the questions he wanted to ask the skipper of the U.S.S. *Dart*.

Dangling from the crane on the center pier behind Ski was the inferior oxygen analyzer in question, which all of the members of the board of inquest had examined, along with the identification nameplate that disguised the unit. The tribunal members then got right down to scrutinizing the purchase invoice documents Admiral Pulvey presented as supporting evidence.

Ski accepted that it was just an informal inquest, to establish whether or not there were grounds for formal charges against Marine Dynamics. He also noticed an urgency about the proceedings caused by the fear that the remainder of the Trident submarine fleet was on trial along with Marine Dynamics. The Navy wanted desperately to separate the submarine from the cloud of guilt enveloping the builder.

The board of inquest took a brief recess, then reconvened with the presiding judge advocate general reciting the tribunal's findings and decisions. The Marine Dynamics corporate heads were to be notified by telegram that night that the company was being cited for fraud and one hundred sixty-one counts of murder. The company was to respond to the charges at a formal inquest in Washington the following week. A motion was presented by Pulvey and unanimously carried to seek a court injunction barring the builder from continuing work on the remainder of the Trident submarine fleet contract until the formal inquest was held. And the tribunal granted the admiral's request that a conjunctive court order be obtained to pave the way for a fleetwide investigation, to determine whether the builder's fraudulent deception might be widespread and involve life-support systems aboard other submarines. A final resolution suggested by Pulvey was to seek approval to revert the remainder of the Trident submarine fleet contract to the next eligible bidder and have construction commence at the earliest possible date.

Ski listened to the presiding judge advocate general approve Dr. Hilderbrand's request for release of the bodies of the *Trident*'s crew to their respective relatives for burial. They had been kept in the base hospital morgue pending the results of the informal inquest. A news release was also authorized, which was to be drafted by Ray Tolbin under the supervision of Admiral Pulvey, as program liaison for the Pentagon, and the judge advocate general, as legal representative of the Defense Department. Public disclosure meant that Ski would now have to inform Jack Bentsen's wife, Donna, of the heartbreaking news.

When the inquest was over Ski saw that Buel was getting up to leave. He hurriedly said, "Dave, I'm going to chat with Bad Ass Buel, then I plan to stop off at Donna Bentsen's house on my way home. You can secure for the day. I'll see you at muster in the morning." Ski dashed across the concrete shoulder of Slip Two and caught up with Buel just as the destroyer skipper was about to step into a waiting jeep. "Commander Buel!" he called out.

Buel stopped and faced Ski. "Yes, Captain?" he asked as he eyed Ski's captain's eagles.

"I'm Kowalski of base intelligence. I'd like to ask you a few questions."

"Haven't I seen your name on communiqués coming aboard my ship?" Buel asked.

"That's right, Commander. I'm also skipper of base CIC."

"Ah, yes. I was just about to head back to my chopper. Will it take long, Captain? I'm expected back aboard the *Dart* now that the inquest is over."

"I'll give you a lift to the heliport in my car," Ski said as he pointed to his Corvette. "We can talk on the way."

Buel turned to the jeep driver. "That'll be all. I'm getting a ride from Captain Kowalski."

Ski led Buel over to his car. When Buel was seated inside, Ski flicked on the courtesy lights and brought out the mammal photos he brought along. "I understand you saw a whale out in the *Trident*'s area on the night before the sub crash-surfaced."

"We saw a whale that night and on the two preceding nights, Captain. Gave the son of a bitch chase all three times, thinking maybe it was your sub playing hide-and-seek with us."

Ski handed Buel the photo of the finless blue whale and asked, "Did the whale you saw look like this, Commander?"

Buel studied the photo, then pointed to the mammal's back. "The whale I saw had a dorsal fin on its back that looked something like a submarine's conning tower," Buel replied firmly.

"You're quite sure?"

"Absolutely. I saw it, and my bow lookout saw it, too. We also saw it clear its blowhole."

Ski handed Buel the photo of the finback whale. "Then the whale you saw looked more like this one."

"Just like that, Captain. Maybe the fin was shaped a little different. It was dark out. I can't be sure. Our spotlights were splashing shadows on the sea ahead of us, distorting things. But I'm not mistaken about seeing a fin."

"Did all three whales have a fin?"

"We never saw the first two. We only saw the one the night the *Trident* got back because I got annoyed about being toyed with. I gave chase that time, determined to make sure it was a whale and not a sub. You see, I was turning my crew out to GQ every time the son of a bitch was picked up on sonar. My XO was getting a tight asshole over my doing that. So, just to appease my exec, and to satisfy my own curiosity, I was going to fire warning depth charges at the bastard. Before I could, up it came, bigger than life, its dorsal fin slicing through the sea ahead of our bow."

"Then you can't be sure if it was three different whales you encountered. It might have been this finned whale each time."

"I have no way of knowing, having only seen the son of a bitch on the surface once. Why all these questions about whales, anyway?"

Ski decided to level with Buel, and he explained what the ichthyologist had told him. When he'd finished he asked, "Wouldn't you say it was a little peculiar that you saw a finned whale out there and a whale specialist insists that a finless mammal made those echo-locations?''

"Yes, and so is the accompanying humming sound you mentioned. And that high-pitched radio frequency signal coming from a sub rigged for quiet running is rather queer-sounding too.'' He shifted his bulky frame in the bucket seat. "What do you make of it all, Captain Kowalski?''

"I'm not sure, Commander.''

"Do you think the Russians were involved?'' Buel asked.

"The Soviet Union would certainly gain if they caused the Trident submarine program to fall into disfavor and be scrapped for good.''

"But the evidence presented by your sub engineering officer and by COMSUBOPS himself was leaning pretty heavily toward industrial fraud.''

"Frankly, that's another thing that's bothering me. The evidence so obviously points to the builder. You'd think, if they could construct a submarine as sophisticated as the *Trident*, they'd have been more skillful in committing fraud. Yet, with little effort at all our tech engineering people discovered the deception.''

Buel shook his head. "I've only known one other intelligence guy, and just like you, he was the diehard suspicious type. It seems all you G-Two people are that way.'' Ski started to defend himself. "You needn't explain, Captain. Curiosity is a quirk of mine, too. Maybe I'd have made a fair G-Two guy, myself.'' Buel's smile was friendly. "Know what I always say?''

"What's that, Commander?''

"Never accept the obvious. Question everything that doesn't seem right. It's a rule I sternly enforce aboard my ship. And when I catch one of my officers or enlisted hands veering from that rule, I kick them square in the fanny to wake 'em up. No one aboard the U.S.S. *Dart* uses guesstimation as standard operating procedure. The SOP I enforce is ABC. Always Be Curious. Always Be Careful. Always Be Conscientious. And by doing so, one will always be confident rather than confused.''

"I didn't get to go aboard your ship the other day, but after meeting you, I'd be willing to bet the U.S.S. *Dart* is one sharp tin can,'' Ski said in praise of Buel.

Buel glanced at his wristwatch. "Say, it's been a pleasure talking with you, Captain. But I really should shove off for my ship. I'll be out on patrol along the Long Island coastline right through to next

Monday. Don't hesitate to call me ship-to-shore if there is anything further I can do to help.''

"Thanks, Commander," Ski said, then shut the courtesy lights off. He turned the ignition key and brought the rumbling sports engine to life, then streaked away from the front of the new sea hangar with a jerk that put an impressed look on Buel's smiling face.

## Chapter Twenty-eight

*Wednesday*
Fay adjusted her robe, then opened her door for the friendly and accommodating bellhop who'd been seeing to her room-service needs during her stay at the Holiday Inn. She eyed the inviting breakfast tray and the two newspapers neatly folded and placed to one side of the pot of coffee and muffins, then gestured to the table and chair set in front of the picture window that looked out over the city of Groton. "I'll have breakfast over there." She waited at the door while the bellhop placed the tray on the table, then tipped him a dollar on his way out. "Thank you, Richard."

"Thank you, Ms. Parks. Have a nice day," the bellhop said, then closed the door after him.

Fay seated herself at the table and poured herself a cup of coffee. Before taking a bite of one of the appetizing muffins yellowed with melted butter, she unfolded the first of the two newspapers. "Bastard!" she shrieked at seeing the headline on page one.

### TRAGEDY ABOARD TRIDENT SUBMARINE
#### ENTIRE CREW DEAD
An exclusive by Ray Tolbin, investigative reporter with the *Washington Chronicle* and syndicated news columnist to the *New London Times*.

---

New London, Sept. 4th. Last night at an informal military inquest held at the Naval Submarine Base, a judge advocate general, presiding over a six-member tribunal sent from Washington, heard Rear Admiral William Pulvey, the base commanding officer, and other investigating officers at the base present evidence that charged Marine Dynamics Corporation of

Groton, the builder of the first Trident class submarine, with fraud. In a brief prepared by Admiral Pulvey, the giant submarine builder allegedly substituted an inferior oxygen analyzer, a component vital to the submarine's life-support system while operating submerged, which subsequently led to the deaths of the 160 men and officers aboard. Another casualty in the undersea disaster was one of the builder's own engineering technical representatives, been assigned to assist the Navy on the sub's maiden voyage. . . .

Liars, Fay thought after absorbing the story. Tolbin had lied to her, Admiral Pulvey had lied to her, Ski had lied to her, and Dave had lied to her. Her instincts, her journalistic ingenuity, her intuition all had been right. And the twerp and the Navy brass had tricked her into doubting herself. She looked again at the closing statements of the article, which mentioned that the Marine Dynamics corporate heads had declined to respond to the Navy's allegations and remained unavailable for any comment to the media.

Fay quickly picked up her copy of the *Connecticut Herald*, the local newspaper whose managing editor was a close friend of Tom Hurt's, but there was nothing in that newspaper about the *Trident* tragedy. She hadn't really expected there would be, but looked anyway to be sure. It told her that good ol' Ray had hogged the story for the *Chronicle*, and shared it only with his close crony of the *New London Times*. She was bitter. It was a real blockbuster scoop, a Pulitzer-type story if there ever was one.

Fay pushed her muffins to the back of the breakfast tray and lit a cigarette. She was no longer hungry. She stared out the picture window at the rush hour traffic building up in the streets of Groton. Groton, she mused, the town where the submarine builder's defense plant was located. She thought about that, and about how a follow-up article covering the submarine builder's reaction might at least give her something to bring back to Washington with her. It would be a meager offering to her managing editor when she submitted her expenses for her investigative efforts, but it would be better than going back to D.C. empty-handed.

Fay knew that every newspaper and every radio and television station would be hounding Marine Dynamics corporate heads for a response to the Navy's charges. She wondered how she could hope to overcome that stiff competition and get an exclusive interview for the *Washington Globe*. She had failed miserably to worm anything out of the Navy. How could she hope to wrangle anything out of the accused?

She knew she had to win the submarine builder's confidence—get the Marine Dynamics corporate heads to believe she was a friend, not another enemy. She wasn't really their enemy anyway. After all, the submarine builder hadn't been proven guilty of the charges yet. Until he was, it was her duty as a journalist to represent both sides of the story fairly. But would they believe her if she told them that was her intent?

Accepting that they probably wouldn't, Fay racked her brain for another way to penetrate the protective barrier the submarine builder was now hiding behind. She realized she'd have to lie her way into the defense plant. She thought of a way that would serve to convince the bigwigs at the defense plant she could be trusted, then moved over to her bedside phone and lifted it from its cradle. In a moment the Holiday Inn switchboard answered. "Yes. Can you get me through to the Marine Dynamics Corporation's defense plant, please?"

The cabin motor launch rounded the west end of Martha's Vineyard, leaving the high seas and its mother ship well behind over the southern horizon. The launch pilot idled the engine back, then negotiated the flotation pier that was the Martha's Vineyard Fueling and Bait Station. Two line handlers jumped aboard the pier and secured the launch to bow and stern eye pads, then stood by as Felicia Marlow stepped off and hurried up the gangway.

Felicia went inside the wooden structure and purchased a copy of each of the Connecticut newspapers. She glanced at the front page of the *Connecticut Herald* first, then eyed the headlines featured in the *New London Times* next and smiled. She stepped outside and entered a phone booth, then quickly dialed the familiar number of the Fisherman's Wharf Marina and Restaurant in Montauk Point. After two rings, the throaty voice of Tony Capobianco came on at the other end. "Have you read the Connecticut newspapers?"

"I have a copy of the *New London Times* on my desk in front of me," Capobianco replied.

"Good. You can proceed with finalizing things with the Boyds," Felicia instructed.

"We'll do so tomorrow night."

"I thought you were anxious to receive the final installment on the contract."

"We are. But we ran into two complications, one of which has already been resolved."

"What happened?"

"The old man had an incriminating letter in safekeeping with a relative but we managed to take possession of it."

"You came highly recommended. This is a disappointment."

"Mr. Boyd was cagier than we'd anticipated."

"So I gather. What's the other complication?"

"He panicked because my associates leaned on him a little hard about the fucking letter and left his house, went into hiding."

"Great! Since when?"

"We found out about it last Friday when we called him for the coordinates."

"Why didn't you let me know then?"

"We wanted to find him ourselves. And straighten out the letter problem. I had to send my associates all the way to West Germany to take care of that little snag."

"Interesting. I wasn't told you operate internationally."

"Normally we don't. But don't worry, there's no extra charge for the trip."

"What do you propose to do about Boyd?"

"He gave us instructions to communicate with him through the personal advertisement section of the *New London Times*. That's why it's going to take an extra day to finalize things. We'll put the ad in tomorrow afternoon's edition. He'll see it and keep the meeting as already arranged."

"You are sure of that?"

"We still have his daughter here, and he knows we have her alive and healthy. He isn't going to go very far without her. He'll be reading the papers every day, waiting for our message. That takes all the doubt out of it for me."

Felicia thought about that for a moment, then said, "All right. I'm convinced. I'll inform my superior that the work will be done and the final installment can be paid tomorrow night."

"You do that. The work will be done. That I guarantee."

"Until tomorrow night," Felicia said, then hung up the phone and hurried down the gangway to the waiting *Brighton Explorer*'s motor launch.

## Chapter Twenty-nine

When Ski arrived at the spacious Marine Dynamics Corporation's submarine defense plant complex on this first visit, he was directed to check in at the administration building by the main gate security guard. In the lobby of the building he signed the visitors' registry for another security guard, manning numerous closed-circuit TV monitors. He was told to take the VIP elevator up to the top floor to see Arthur Harrowman, the plant vice-president. Ski found VIP country to be plushly decorated with living room-style furniture, wall-to-wall pile carpeting, and framed pictures of a half-century of submarine construction at the Groton, Connecticut, plant.

After introducing himself to a young and very pretty blond receptionist, Ski took a seat in the lounge area. He scanned the reception room, noticing the six doors, each with a silver nameplate. The door to the customer relations lounge was partly opened and revealed more comfortable furniture and a complimentary refreshment counter. Other rooms were the industrial relations conference room, labor relations conference room, board of directors conference hall, and the corporate president's and vice-president's private offices, which adjoined each other and were probably connected by an inside door.

Ski waited briefly, then the receptionist ushered him to the vice-president's office and opened the door for him. He was greeted by a tall, brawny man with black wavy hair and a swarthy complexion.

"Welcome to Marine Dynamics, Captain Kowalski. I'm Arthur Harrowman, plant vice-president."

Ski shook Harrowman's hand and smiled back at him. "My pleasure."

"Sorry our plant president, Elliot Claybar, couldn't receive you himself, but he's a rather sickly man. Over seventy-five, you know. I'm afraid this shocking unpleasantness was too much for him. He's at home under his physician's care."

"As a matter of fact, I really wanted to see someone in Engineering. Security sort of directed me here to you."

"I asked them to, Captain Kowalski. To honor your lost submarine crew I've ordered the plant closed today. There's no one in engineering to receive you. However, I was the engineering department head before I became vice-president. I thought I might be sufficiently qualified to meet you on behalf of that department.''

"I really don't want to impose on you," Ski said. He didn't want to discuss the nature of his visit with a corporate VP. He preferred speaking to someone beneath the executive level, someone with less concern about the ramifications of the fraud charges. "Perhaps I should come back tomorrow when the plant is open.''

"You're here now, Captain. Allow me to at least try to help you." Harrowman gestured to an armchair close to one side of his large maplewood desk. "Please sit down.''

Ski sat down, then gazed out the large picture window behind Harrowman's desk. It framed a panoramic view of the rear of the defense plant, where several submarine construction piers were outstretched like fingers to the Thames River. There were three submarines under construction simultaneously, which he knew would be additions to the new Los Angeles Class antisubmarine fleet when completed.

Harrowman seated himself. "Before we cover the nature of your visit, may I express our deepest sympathy for the loved ones of the deceased crewmen. We here at the plant are at a loss for words. We lost one of our finest engineering tech reps along with the crew of the U.S.S. *Trident*. We shall miss him terribly. Did you by chance know Nelson Hobart?''

"No, sir. In fact, I just recently came upon his name in the *Trident*'s logbook. In a way, it's because of something Nelson Hobart entered in the maintenance gripe sheets that brings me here today.''

"Oh! How so, Captain?''

"While the *Trident* was out in the Mid-Atlantic, Mr. Hobart made a surface repair on a noisy diving plane slaving servo. By way of routine follow-up, our Navy engineering tech officer, Lieutenant Troy Hanley, was double-checking all repairs made during the maiden voyage, and detected a peculiar humming noise, the source of which has us puzzled.''

"Well, if this humming noise is also a breach of quiet running, trust SAM to locate it for you.''

"This humming noise isn't exactly a breach of quiet running, sir. Therefore, SAM wouldn't be of any help in isolating it aboard ship. It was a steady humming noise with a set duration, but its volume was extremely low. With the slaving servo being the last electromechanical device to be worked on, Troy and I were wondering if it might have acted up again and produced such a noise."

"Can you describe this humming noise?"

"It's similar to the sound pumps make when they're running. A mellow sound, very low in volume."

"But loud enough for you to hear?"

"Barely."

Harrowman shook his head. "The slaving servo comprises mechanical linkage that is electrically driven. The diving planes it actuates are quite heavy. I think the servo would probably make a loud growling or shrilling noise. I think a faulty pump is the source of your humming noise."

"Finding the pump will take some doing," Ski said.

"It certainly will. Especially without SAM to assist you. There are countless pumps aboard a submarine. Was there anything else you wanted to discuss?"

"We also registered a high-pitched sound, similar to a high-frequency radio signal."

"How the hell did you manage to hear it?"

"We used a megahertz meter."

"That's a rather unusual instrument to be using for troubleshooting a noise problem. Did you know the sound you were searching for was inaudible to human hearing at the start?"

Ski could sense Harrowman's suspicious tone. He had wanted to make his question appear routine because he still wasn't sure what was making the sounds. And, if there was foul play involved, he didn't want the Marine Dynamics corporate heads to know where his investigation was leading.

"We just happened upon this high-pitched sound while conducting a sonar experiment," Ski said casually.

Harrowman relaxed only slightly. "Perhaps your ship's radios were transmitting at the time your experiment was being conducted. Maybe someone aboard forgot to shut them down."

"As part of being rigged for quiet running, the sub was observing radio silence."

"Interesting. Well, was anything else puzzling you?"

"Yes, while Troy was inspecting the slaving servo access compartment, he found an adhesive coating on the floor. It seemed to him that something might have been installed there and had freed itself, so he searched the compartment for something that might have come dislodged, but found nothing."

Harrowman leaned forward in his chair. "Installing a device with an adhesive backing aboard any part of a submarine is not a wise practice. Changes in depths under the sea, extreme variations of temperature, even vibrations might disturb its mounting and dislodge the device. We use rivets, anchor fasteners, set screws, locknuts, and bolts for our mounting materials. We'd weld a device aboard before we'd chance installing it with an adhesive binding. That's the sort of mounting technique a professional would use only for a temporary installation or if there was no other available means."

"I see," Ski said with interest.

"There's one other thing, Captain. The area Troy Hanley found this adhesive coating in is a watertight compartment. If anything had been installed in it and worked itself free, it couldn't have gone far. Also, anything installed in a component compartment has a specific function. If the device were to become dislodged, its function would cease. You'd have some indication of a failure if the device was a component of some system aboard."

"You have a point there," Ski admitted.

"I have another point, Captain."

"Which is?"

"Why is a captain of Naval Intelligence here, asking the questions an engineering officer should ask?"

"Under the strange circumstances surrounding the tragedy, we've all been asked to pitch in and . . ."

"I think you're probing a breach of national security and I think you're investigating the possibility that sabotage was behind the submarine disaster."

"I made no mention of sabotage."

"You didn't have to say it outright, Captain. Your line of questioning tipped me off."

"My questions were purely of a routine nature."

"Come now, Captain Kowalski. I would expect Admiral Pulvey or Lieutenant Hanley to discount the possibility of espionage or sabotage, but frankly not you. As an Intelligence officer, surely you entertained the idea that our plant might have somehow been infiltrated by enemy agents. Our security is tight but not impenetrable. Neither is yours at the submarine base. If we have been victimized by enemy agents, they are our common enemy. And that makes us allies. I'd like you to hear me out."

Ski nodded slowly. He now realized that he had been suspecting sabotage all along, but had gotten swallowed up in Admiral Pulvey's and Troy Hanley's evidence and refused to admit openly his doubts about the convenient and quiet fraud charges. "Just what is it you have to say?" he asked.

"I know no one above me was a party to this deception. I also know that no one subordinate to me or Elliot Claybar would have had anything to gain from fraud. The money saved would never line their pockets unless we at the top had a part in it. But obviously someone did switch the *Trident*'s designated oxygen analyzer for an inferior model. The Trident program might be stopped as a result of stringent pressure from opponents of the new submarine, who would use the tragedy to support their arguments. Therefore, wouldn't it be logical to assume the Soviet Union or any other of our nation's enemies would commit sabotage to accomplish that goal?"

"I've thought of that. But . . ."

"But you can't seem to tie these puzzling noises in with such a sabotage plan."

"Right. Just switching the analyzers wouldn't accomplish a damn thing for saboteurs. How could they be sure the submarine would come in contact with the methyl mercury?"

"That makes sense."

"But if they intended to kill the crew by making the switch, and knew where the submarine would be spending some time, all they'd have to do is put the lethal chemical in the submarine's path."

"Hence your strange noises," Harrowman put in. "And perhaps an explanation for that adhesive coating."

"Maybe."

"Then we have two questions: Did a breach of plant security occur and how did the methyl mercury happen to be in the path of the *Trident*?"

"I think the mercury was transported to the *Trident*'s holding area. By whom and when I don't know."

"Well, I'm sure you're the expert to find out, Captain. As for saboteurs penetrating our plant security, we already have our own Intelligence people going over personnel files. The problem is we have thousands of employees to investigate and very little time."

"Are you asking for my assistance?" Ski asked with a warm smile.

"Frankly, we can use all the help we can get."

"Suppose I do a little checking into some of your past employees. It seems to me that the people involved would certainly be looking to move on."

"Do you believe that I was not involved?"

"I'd rather not commit myself yet. I warn you in advance, though, if it turns out to be you . . . I'll not be merciful."

"I have no fear of that. Care to join me in our personnel records office?"

## Chapter Thirty

It was late afternoon when Fay approached the security desk in the lobby of the Marine Dynamics Administration building. She signed the visitors' registry and noticed the name of the last visitor. Interesting, she thought, wondering why Ski had visited Arthur Harrowman. She made a mental note of the times the Navy Intelligence captain came and left and took the elevator up to the VIP level. After she crossed the spacious room to the receptionist and identified herself, she was shown right into Harrowman's office.

"So you're a journalist friend of the governor's," Harrowman said with a congenial smile and an extended hand.

Shaking his hand, Fay replied, "More so of the governor's press secretary. Realizing that your trouble with the Navy might result in the shift of numerous jobs to another state, the governor expressed immediate concern."

"Have a seat, Ms. Parks," Harrowman said. "Can I offer you some coffee or tea?"

"No, thank you. I just had a late lunch. But I would like to smoke, if I may."

"By all means," Harrowman said. "What can I do for you?"

"I think it's more a matter of what I can do for you."

"Oh!" Harrowman said with raised eyebrows. "How so?"

"Before I get into that, may I ask you what Captain Kowalski was here to see you about?"

"You know him?"

"It was my misfortune to make his acquaintance."

"You sound bitter. What has he done to you?"

"He, his executive officer, Admiral Pulvey, and a very untrustworthy colleague of mine, all conspired and lied to me. And I hate liars with a passion."

"I see. I'll have to remember not to lie to you myself."

"That will be a welcome change," Fay said. She explained the past days' events to Harrowman and in summarizing said, "That's why I want to know if this Captain Kowalski and you are on friendly terms. If so, perhaps you and I won't be of any help to each other."

"I admire your frankness, Ms. Parks. I . . ." His intercom buzzed. "Excuse me a moment, please." It was his receptionist, summoning him out to her desk. "I'll only be a moment, Ms. Parks." He left Fay seated beside his desk and stepped out to the reception room, closing the office door behind him.

"Step in here a moment, Art," Elliot Claybar said from the open doorway of his office, his shriveled, pale face full of excitement.

Harrowman followed the president of Marine Dynamics into his office and closed the door. Seated at a conference table that formed a T headed by Claybar's immense desk was Christopher Yates, the company's attorney.

Yates switched off the tape recorder that was hooked up to a hidden microphone situated in a desk plant inches away from where Fay was seated in Harrowman's office. "We're going to shoot for a new angle with this female journalist, Art," he said, sounding excited.

"I'm listening," Harrowman said as he seated himself at the conference table.

"Ms. Parks wants to help us, and from a legal standpoint she can do so more than you realize," Yates said. "Her animosity toward the Navy Intelligence captain will smooth things nicely in that direction. I advise you to let her use the power of the press, Art. Pretend you're taking her into your confidence and tell her everything Captain Kowalski said about sabotage. Tone it up to be a notch more interesting to her, of course. But get her interested in releasing that sabotage angle to the public and we'll get the time needed to prepare our defense brief."

"Chris, I worked hard to get Captain Kowalski interested in helping us. As a Naval Intelligence officer, he might be extremely important in proving our innocence," Harrowman said. "He's the first one from the Navy who's offered to help us. Now you want me to betray his trust before he's even had a chance to initiate an investigation. Why, he'll sour on us the moment he learns I've turned our little meeting against him."

"Art, be realistic," Yates said. "It's going to take Kowalski more time to investigate this matter than we can afford. I have to prepare a defense brief in time for the formal hearing we're to attend next week in Washington. If I can't offer anything to counter the charges, we'll be standing in front of a grand jury in short order, hearing indictments read to us. Once that takes place, things are going to move very fast. Before I have a goddamn chance to prevent a verdict against you, you and Elliot might be sitting behind bars.''

''What is it you want me to do?'' Harrowman asked.

''Don't wait for Captain Kowalski to save the day,'' Claybar said. ''He might have been stringing you along.''

''He seemed sincere to me,'' Harrowman insisted. ''He even took along some dossier copies of former personnel to start his investigation.''

''Time, Art,'' Yates reminded Harrowman. ''We don't have it to spare. You've got to lie through your teeth to Ms. Parks. You've got to tell her Captain Kowalski suspects sabotage. Tell her the Navy Intelligence captain is on his way back to the submarine base right now. Tell her Ray Tolbin is going to outscoop her again if she doesn't act fast. Then tell her you're willing to give her the exclusive story because you're angry about the way the Navy mistreated her.''

''But even if I talk her into printing the sabotage story, Captain Kowalski is sure to deny he ever mentioned sabotage.''

''That won't matter, Art,'' Yates said. ''Once the story is out, we'll have the reasonable-doubt defense motion I need to fire back at the Navy. We'll move for time to investigate the claims of sabotage further. Remember, the Navy has evidence, but the prosecution brief I read made no mention of witnesses. That will put the burden of proof on the Navy. And by the time they get their trial date, we just may have the kind of proof we'll need to enter a motion to have the charges set aside.''

''It's our only hope, Art,'' Claybar pleaded.

''Very well,'' Harrowman agreed.


## Chapter Thirty-one

*Thursday*

''Captain Kowalski! Are you there?'' Buel said into the ship-to-ship radio mike. He was in the *Dart*'s radio shack, responding to a call Ski had patched through base CIC to Buel's ship.

''I'm here, Commander Buel,'' Ski replied.

''Where are you, Captain? You sound quite far away.''

''I'm aboard my sloop in a yacht club here in Connecticut,'' Ski

aid as he looked down at a sea chart he had been studying since
he'd come aboard *The Smile* last night.

"What can I do for you, Captain?"

"I slept aboard and just woke up, and while I was having a cup of
oe, something occurred to me."

Buel glanced out of the bridge windows at the early-morning sun
climbing the eastern horizon ahead of the *Dart*'s bow. "That's the
est time for thinking, Captain. Rising with the sun while sipping a
up of coffee. I gather it has something to do with whales again?"

"You're right on the money, Commander," Ski said. "Some-
hing dawned on me as I looked out at the bay and saw some dead
ish floating along with the outbound current. My question is, the
ery first time you passed over the *Trident*'s holding coordinates on
he night the sub got back into home waters, did you notice any dead
ish floating on the surface in the area of gas hole Alpha?"

"Stand by a minute, Captain," Buel said, then turned to Ensign
Schmidt. "Schmidt, did we have dead fish on the surface the night
efore we found the *Trident* crash-surfaced?"

"Negative, Skipper," Schmidt replied firmly.

"You're sure, Schmidt?"

"Positive, sir."

Buel returned to the ship-to-ship radio mike. "Captain, that's a
irm negative. According to my OOD on the bridge watch that night,
ve first encountered the dead fish approximately the same time we
icked up the *Trident* crash-surfaced. Is that any help to you?"

"A big help. One more quick question and I'll let you get back to
unning your ship."

"Take all the time you need, Captain."

"We know your third whale sighting took place in the vicinity of
as hole Beta."

"Roger that, Captain."

"Fine. Now please check and let me know where the first and
econd whale sightings occurred."

"Standby one, Captain," Buel said, then ordered Schmidt to
heck the whale sightings through ship's CIC. In a few moments
chmidt hung up the bridge phone and relayed the information to
im. Keying back on with Ski, Buel said, "The first and second
ightings took place in the vicinity of gas hole Alpha, Captain."

Ski made some notations on his sea chart. "Now, once again, are
ou quite sure there were no surface ships or submarines in the area
f gas hole Beta during that time?"

"That I can confirm myself, Captain. I run a very disciplined ship. If there had been, I'd have been made aware of it. Of course there was the Soviet submarine I reported to your CIC on Friday, but that one I know for a fact left our international waters that day and didn't return."

"One final question, Commander. Have you sighted a whale since?"

"Negative, Captain."

## Chapter Thirty-two

Dr. Phillip Grant switched his stateroom radio off. "Sabotage," he said in a low voice. He regarded Felicia and Captain Horthorne. The ship's master had brought to Grant's and Felicia's attention the radio news release about sabotage being suspected in the submarine disaster.

Later, they'd listened to a second broadcast of the shocking news.

"Perhaps Kowalski is merely assuming sabotage," Felicia suggested. "He's a Naval Intelligence officer, and as such is probably just routinely investigating that possibility."

Grant stared into Felicia's eyes. "I wonder—have we thought of everything?"

"There was no mention of any details supporting Captain Kowalski's suspicions," Captain Horthorne said. "And there was no mention that construction on the remainder of the Trident submarine fleet had resumed. That seems to suggest that sabotage hasn't been fully substantiated."

Grant nodded. "Perhaps so. My guess would be that our Mr. Boyd might have panicked. Perhaps he and this Captain Kowalski were confiding in each other."

"But would Mr. Boyd risk his daughter's life?" Felicia asked.

"Perhaps he told Kowalski about his daughter's captivity and was promised protection."

"If Mr. Boyd did reveal anything, it must have been very recently," Felicia said. "And if he did, that would explain . . ." She fell quiet.

"Explain what, Felicia?" Grant challenged.

"When I spoke to Mr. Capobianco last, he mentioned that Boyd had vacated his home and gone into hiding," Felicia said. "He's been instructed by Mr. Boyd to communicate through messages in the personal advertisement section of the newspapers."

"I'm extremely disappointed in your connections ashore, Felicia," Grant commented.

"We're not certain Mr. Boyd did talk, Phillip," Felicia said. "Perhaps the two events are unrelated. And, as Captain Horthorne points out, it appears that Kowalski's mention of sabotage to the media hasn't changed the charges Admiral Pulvey has brought against Marine Dynamics. So if Kowalski meets with an unfortunate accident, there will be nothing more said about enemy agents and sabotage."

Grant weighed the possibilities and said, "We'll not be weighing anchor for the Montauk Point anchorage tonight, after all, Captain Horthorne. We'll remain at anchor here until the Kowalski problem is resolved." He regarded Felicia next. "Felicia, you may proceed with your round-robin to Martha's Vineyard as planned. But instead of informing Mr. Capobianco that his final installment will be paid tonight, you advise him I'm not at all pleased with the turn of events. He must arrange a most convincing accident for Kowalski before we can proceed with Mr. Boyd and his daughter. He's to cancel his rendezvous tonight with Rudolph Boyd and concentrate on Kowalski."

## Chapter Thirty-three

Ski drove from the yacht club to his garden apartment building in Ledger, Connecticut, with the car radio off so that he could think quietly. He had the photocopied personnel dossiers Arthur Harrowman had provided him with yesterday on the seat next to him, but he knew looking into those half-dozen former employees would be a lengthy undertaking. On the rear window deck behind him was the notated sea chart, which he planned to set up in his den for further study.

He pulled into his assigned parking spot and hurried into the building, the dossiers and chart tightly tucked under one arm. When he arrived at his door he heard his phone ringing and quickly let himself in, bringing the rolled-up newspaper in with him. He dropped everything on the living room couch and lifted the receiver.

"Ski, it's me," Admiral Pulvey said excitedly at the other end.

"Where the hell have you been? I've been trying to reach you since early this morning."

"I spent the night on my sloop to think things out, and I've stumbled onto some very interesting—"

"I know all about what you've been doing behind my back, Ski," Pulvey interrupted. "I was quite concerned about your absence from the base most of yesterday and wormed it all out of Dave! You've been listening to the *Trident*'s voyage recorder disc and sonar tapes, listening to Bentsen's cries for help till it got you so emotionally upset that you've taken to drinking excessively. You bring a whale specialist to the base to listen to classified military recordings and keep a secret rendezvous with Ms. Parks, knowing she could mean trouble for the Navy. You've gone too far!"

Ski was at a loss. "All I've been doing is some routine checking—"

"You've been panicking everyone. It's in all the goddamn newspapers. Where do you two get off claiming sabotage was the cause of the tragedy aboard the *Trident*?"

Ski was dumbfounded. He ripped the rubber band off the morning newspaper and unfolded it. There it was, headlined in the *Connecticut Herald:* NAVY SUSPECTS SABOTAGE ABOARD TRIDENT SUBMARINE. An Exclusive by Fay Parks of the *Washington Globe* "Admiral, I had nothing to do with this. The last time I saw Fay was at the Holiday Inn."

"Then how come the goddamn article reads: 'Arthur Harrowman, vice-president of Marine Dynamics Corporation, who yesterday was accused of cheating the Navy of two million dollars substituting an inferior life-support system aboard the new submarine, reported that he was visited by Captain Allen A. Kowalski of Naval Intelligence, who shared Harrowman's suspicion that saboteurs infiltrated the defense plant here in Groton.' I won't go on, Ski. All I'll say is, this was one hell of a blunder. You've succeeded in giving Marine Dynamics corporate heads just the kind of legal loophole they've been looking for. And your sabotage claim has caused alarm in Washington. Enemy agents? Have you gone mad, Ski? On whose authority are you claiming sabotage?"

Ski was flabbergasted. He had somehow been betrayed. He guessed Harrowman and Fay had secretly gotten together after his visit and obviously twisted his words to serve their own purpose. "Admiral, it would be on my authority if *I* had claimed sabotage. But I didn't! That was Harrowman's idea, not mine. I merely asked some routine questions and he suggested enemy agents might have infiltrated his plant.''

"Bullshit, Ski! According to this article you were checking Marine Dynamics' personnel records, searching for an enemy agent who *you* think committed the sabotage. I'd hardly call that a social call, Ski. I'd call it an overt investigation, and an unauthorized one at that!''

"Admiral, I've been a victim of manipulation. Everything I said was exaggerated and twisted into lies.''

"You had no business going there without my approval. Ray Tolbin is drafting a retraction for you right now. It'll be out in tomorrow's newspapers. You'll be quoted as denying you ever mentioned sabotage or enemy agents during your visit. Also, you're to stay away from Fay Parks. You're not to ask any more questions at Marine Dynamics. You're to forget this nonsense about sabotage entirely. Marine Dynamics is at fault here! They're lying through their teeth to save their own asses, and you've been playing right into their hands.''

"Admiral, what the hell purpose do I serve as an Intelligence officer if the Navy is going to tie my hands? It's my duty to investigate any potential threats to our national security. And if I feel there are grounds to, I intend to do just that.''

"Ski!'' Pulvey shouted. "You buck me on this and you're not going to be an Intelligence officer much longer!''

"If that's how it is, maybe I should consider resigning my commission.''

"I have a less drastic idea, Ski. I'll put Dave in charge and cut leave papers for you.''

"Admiral, are you relieving me of my command?''

"You'll still be CO of the Intelligence Center when you come back, but I'm ordering you now to take a thirty-day leave.''

Ski realized that being on leave would give him an opportunity to continue his probing full time. "I'll go on leave, as ordered, Admiral. But I'm making you no promises that I won't continue to probe this matter.''

"Son, if I learn that you have caused further problems for the Navy's case against Marine Dynamics, you may find yourself facing a court-martial.'' Ski angrily hung up the phone.

## Chapter Thirty-four

It isn't fair, Fay thought as she drove out of the Holiday Inn parking lot. In the trunk of the car was her luggage and the expensive developing equipment she had bought, which she now thought was an unjustifiable extravagance. In her attaché case were the six personnel dossiers Arthur Harrowman had furnished her with. She had spent all day tracking down the former employees, only to learn that three of them were deceased, one was hospitalized for breast cancer, one confined to a wheelchair as a result of a stroke. The last name on her list was an employee who requested early retirement from the firm to leave the country for good. She had managed, with the help of a friend in the Washington Bureau of Passports, to learn that Rudolph Boyd, a former captain of the Marine Dynamics Security Police Force, was relocating to West Germany with his daughter, but hadn't left the country yet.

By late afternoon, she had tracked Boyd to his former residence in Norwich and had been told by the occupants that they had bought Boyd's house through a realtor. The realtor had had no forwarding address for the Boyds, and she had returned to the Holiday Inn. Waiting for her at the check-in counter had been a Western Union telegram, which read:

> FAY:
> KOWALSKI DENIES SABOTAGE. NAVY DEMANDS YOUR STORY BE RETRACTED. THE *GLOBE* INTENDS TO COMPLY. STOP INVESTIGATING THE NAVY AT ONCE. RETURN TO D.C. ON CONNECTICUT AIR LINES MIDNIGHT FLIGHT NUMBER 7 OUT OF HARTFORD. FAILURE TO COMPLY WILL RESULT IN DISMISSAL.
>
> TOM HURT

The telegram was shattering to Fay. Arthur Harrowman had duped her. He had assured her Ski wouldn't deny that he was investigating sabotage. Now her article was to be retracted. She had made a fool of herself and the *Washington Globe*. She could just see Ray Tolbir having a good laugh on her.

Twenty minutes after she left the motel parking lot, she found herself crisscrossing highways she had never seen before. After two miles of dark surroundings, a road sign told her she was heading for the submarine base. Her sense of direction told her the Thames River Bridge would be the opposite way from the Navy base, but she was paranoid about turning around. Her job depended upon her getting back to Washington on the Midnight Express. She drove on for another mile, then caught sight of a flashing neon sign that announced: Dino's Den and Motel. Deciding she'd better recheck her directions, she pulled into the crowded parking lot.

Dino's was a western-style pub with a three-piece country rock group playing ear-piercing music right near the entrance. She made her way over to the bar. "Excuse me," she said loudly to the brawny bartender, "I'm trying to"—the band suddenly ended their song to go on a break, and Fay's voice shrilled in the sudden silence—"get to Rentschler Airport in Hartford and I seem to have gotten lost."

With his uniform tie loosened at the collar, his captain's gold-embroidered cap placed on the bar stool next to him, and his eyes drooping from the half-dozen Scotch and sodas he had consumed since he'd arrived at Dino's from Bentsen's wake, Ski recognized the female voice coming from four bar stools away. Anger gripped him as he saw Fay poised against the bar, listening intently to the bartender. Overhearing Fay mention the Thames River Bridge, an irresistible urge overcame him. "When you get to the middle of the bridge, do me a favor and make a sharp right, then stomp on the accelerator." His outburst immediately drew Fay's attention and the bartender's.

"You know him, lady?" The burly bartender grunted.

"It's okay," Fay said to the bartender. "Thank you for the directions."

"Careful what you say to her, pal," Ski slurred to the bartender. "She's Ms. Journalist, and that makes her a doubly dangerous female. You just might find yourself in the newspapers tomorrow as a caricature in one of her storybook tales." He took a sip of his drink. "Women . . ."

Fay reassured the bartender that she could handle the situation, then walked over to Ski. Speaking slowly and in a low voice suggesting composure and confidence, she said, "It's men who are living in a storybook fantasy, not women. Admiral Pulvey is Dumbo! David Lee is Daffy Duck! Ray Tolbin is . . ."

"Bozo!" Ski put in for her, remembering the nickname Admiral Pulvey had given the hotshot reporter.

"Bozo!" Fay repeated with an approving nod. "Arthur Harrowman is Pinocchio, the long-nose liar!" She noticed Ski chuckling and thought he was laughing at her. In retaliation she grunted loudly, "And you . . . you're Dopey the dunce cap dwarf!"

"And you're Alice in Wonderland!" Ski retorted through more laughter.

"No, Ski. Janet Pulvey is Alice in Wonderland," Fay hissed. "I'm just a working woman, trying to earn a living. I don't have a rich father to pay my way through life. If trying to do your job is funny, then go ahead and have a big laugh at my expense." She turned to walk away.

Ski grabbed her by the arm to stop her. His smile had left his face. "No, Fay," he said in a serious tone. "I actually don't think it's funny at all. As a matter of fact, I think it's sort of a sad reality in learning you've been lied to. Understand me. Arthur Harrowman lied to me as well." With the wave of his hand he dismissed Fay's attempt to say something. "But Arthur Harrowman was a stranger, and that makes his manipulating of me a little easier to take. What really hurts is when you learn that people who are supposed to love you and be on your side are just using you for their own selfish needs. I'm wide awake now, though. After all these years I've finally realized that Janet Pulvey has been manipulating me, and Admiral Pulvey has been bullying me. And up until now the joke has been on me. Well, they made a drastic error in judgment. They mistook kindness for weakness. Now they're in for a crude awakening."

"You're beginning to sound like Doctor Jekyll, Ski," Fay commented as she took the seat next to him at the bar.

"Maybe that's because it's become time to produce Mister Hyde," Ski said, then gestured for the bartender to come over. He looked over at Fay. "Care to join me in a potion?"

"Thanks, but no," Fay replied. "I have to catch the Midnight Express flight back to D.C., or else."

"Or else?" Ski questioned.

Fay removed the telegram from her purse and handed it to Ski. "Or else I'll be looking for a new job."

Ski quickly read the telegram, then in returning it to her he said, "It seems we're two peas in a pod. I've been told to back off or else, too." He glanced at his wristwatch. "Listen, you have time for one drink before you catch your flight." She shook her head decliningly. "Please, Fay. I'd feel better if we left off on friendly terms."

"I'd like that, too," Fay said. "But it's late and I'm going to have a time of it finding that damn airport in the dark."

"Please," Ski insisted. "I'll be leaving after one more drink myself. I promise I'll get you on the right road to Rentschler Airport right after that."

"A whiskey sour, then," Fay agreed, deciding she preferred to leave off on good terms with Ski. He had been nice to her in the beginning, until the submarine incident happened along and got everyone up tight. She took out a cigarette and allowed him to light it for her. She thanked him and under her breath complimented his gentlemanly manners. A very handsome gentleman at that, she concluded as she raised her glass. "To being friends," she toasted.

"To staying friends," Ski added over the rim of his glass. He was glad she agreed to sharing a farewell toast. But for some reason he was wishing they weren't saying good-bye.

Parked inconspicuously toward the back and off to the side of Dino's parking lot was a gleaming Lincoln Continental Mark IV. Butts, the driver, sat chain smoking behind the wheel. Mr. A sat restlessly in the front seat next to him, chatting with Mr. B, whose huge body took up nearly the entire back seat. Tony Capobianco had called the Navy base early that morning and introduced himself as a restaurant owner attempting to return some personal property Captain Kowalski left behind in his establishment. The unsuspecting Navy yeoman he spoke to provided Capobianco with Kowalski's address in Ledger, Connecticut.

An hour later, Mr. A had landed his Cessna 150 at Tweed-New Haven Airport, where Butts met him and Mr. B then drove them to Kowalski's home. They had followed Kowalski to a funeral parlor, where he remained until early evening. Kowalski had next led them to Dino's. Mr. A ordered that they wait until Kowalski's visit to the pub was over, so it would be dark by the time he took to the road again.

It was well after 10:00 P.M. when Mr. A spotted Kowalski. He happily announced, "Here comes our hotshot Navy captain now. Judging from his wobbly legs, he's tipped a few martinis too many."

"He's got a goddamn dame with him," Butts said.

"Tough for her ass if she's planning to go home with him," Mr. B said.

They watched Ski kiss the woman lightly on the cheek, then help her get in behind the wheel of her Cutlass. They were relieved when Ski climbed into his Corvette and led the way out of the parking lot.

"She's not going home with him after all," Mr. A said.

"She's one lucky broad," Mr. B commented.

"Wait till he gets a little distance between him and the bar, then overtake him, Butts," Mr. A ordered.

"Don't forget to tell Capi he's footing the bill for whatever dents I put in my machine," Butts reminded.

"Capi's paying you enough to buy two more of these lead sleds," Mr. B grunted. "Just make sure you don't get squeamish about putting some dents in the fucking thing."

Soon after Fay left the parking lot, four high-beam headlights came crashing into her rearview mirror. The bright headlights were more than a mere annoyance to her, since they made it extremely difficult to negotiate the dark and deserted road ahead. She searched for the catch that was usually on rearview mirrors to change them to tinted glass, but the Cutlass didn't seem to have that option. The bright lights continued following behind, spilling their glare into the sideview mirror as well. "Damn it! Are you blind?" she said angrily to the spread of light in the mirrors. She did her best to focus on Ski's taillights.

"The fucking broad is following him," Butts said unhappily. "She's going to see us give it to him."

"Just keep your high beams welded on the back of her car," Mr. A said. "They'll make her so goddamn bug-eyed, she won't know what the hell is happening when we pass her."

"Why don't we make our move now," Mr. B put in. "There ain't a fucking soul on the highway but them and us."

Mr. A got a glance from Butts. "Might as well. Floor it, Butts."

Fay squinted when the bright headlights suddenly began to gain on her. After the speeding car passed her with a thunderous roar, its taillights and the taillights of Ski's car vanished around a curve in the road ahead. She followed on, her eyes adjusting to the darkness.

Ski flicked the tint element on his rearview mirror in response to the bright headlights that suddenly turned the highway behind him into near daylight. The car seemed to be closing on him fast. The road straightened ahead and it became apparent the car had moved into the oncoming lane to pass. Not wanting to get too far ahead of

Fay, he eased the accelerator up a little. The action quickly brought the car abreast of him. Looking over at it, he saw three men inside. Noticing the man in the passenger's seat was brandishing a gun, he pressed the accelerator to the floor and the Corvette leaped ahead of the Mark IV.

"Stay with him, Butts!" Mr. A shouted, his weapon held at the ready out the open window.

Butts stomped on the gas pedal and the Mark IV's carburetor growled as its four barrels opened wide. The car lunged after the fleeing Corvette as it slowed down for a curve and quickly was abreast of it again. Then, with a light nudge that he gradually intensified, Butts began to sideswipe the sports car, cracking its fiber glass body.

With stiffened arms Ski tried to fight off his intoxication and keep the small sports car on the road, but the ramming from the heavy car was overpowering. One final sideswipe sent the Corvette out of control. It skidded off the shoulder, then sailed down the steep ravine that paralleled the highway. Fighting the wheel as he bounced down the brush- and rock-covered slope, Ski stared wild-eyed at a thick tree trunk standing in his way at the bottom of the ravine. Unable to get the car to turn, he hit the tree head on. The impact mangled the front of the car, and chunks of fiber glass flew into the air as Ski's head was thrust into the windshield, which shattered and made an outline of his head. Stunned, he fell back in the bucket seat, blood trickling down his face. Steam from the mangled radiator gushed up into the air in a thick column.

Panic-stricken, Fay, who'd seen the assault, raced to the skid marks leading across the highway shoulder and down the ravine. She screeched to a stop, looked quickly at the taillights of the Mark IV as it vanished around a curve, then got out and hurried down the ravine toward Ski's wrecked Corvette. She pulled on the driver's door frantically, then finally got it open and cringed on seeing Ski's face covered with blood. "My God! Ski! Are you all right?"

Ski moaned, then shook his head. "I think so. My head feels like someone hit it with a sledgehammer and my arms feel like I was wrestling with a grizzly, but I'm alive."

"It's a miracle you still are, Ski. Your car is a mess."

"Never mind the car. Help me get out."

Fay strained to support Ski's brawny frame as she assisted him out of the bucket seat. She steadied him for a moment, then moved him a few feet away to a tree and rested him against it. "Do you have a handkerchief?" she asked as she examined his wounds more closely.

Ski removed a handkerchief from his hip pocket. Handing it to Fay, he asked, "Am I going to need stitches?"

Fay gently dabbed at the cuts to clear the blood away, causing Ski to grimace. "I don't think so, Ski. You've one cut over your right eyebrow and another knick on your jawbone. But I think some antiseptic will take care of them." She managed to clean the blood off his face, then looked into his eyes. "Ski, it looked to me like that car was deliberately ramming into you to push you off the road."

"It was, Fay. The reasons might have a lot to do with your sabotage article, I'm sure."

"My God! You mean I caused this to happen?"

"Don't blame yourself. Let's just get the hell out of here before those bastards come back to see what kind of a job they did on me."

"We'd better get to a phone and report this to the police, Ski."

"No police, Fay," Ski said. "They'll see I was driving a sports car, detect that I've been drinking, and throw me in the slammer for drunken driving."

"Well, what are we going to do?"

Ski glanced at his wristwatch. It was nearing eleven o'clock. "What I'm about to suggest is going to cause you to miss your midnight flight back to Washington, but would you mind giving me a ride back to my apartment?"

"I'm certainly not going to leave you stranded out here."

"What about your managing editor's ultimatum?"

"He'll just have to understand," Fay said firmly.

"What if you were able to return to D.C. with that big exclusive you've been hoping for? Would that square things for you with your managing editor?"

"It sure would," Fay said. "Why?"

"Because I'm pretty damn sure that in time I can substantiate that sabotage article you wrote. Just take me back to my apartment and I'll explain everything. I'll take care of getting my car out of here tomorrow."

# Chapter Thirty-five

Ski unlocked his apartment door, pushed it open, and stepped aside to let Fay enter first. She took one step inside and froze in her tracks. Ski did the same. Returning their stunned expressions from her seat on the living room couch was Janet Pulvey, who rose from her seat and stared coldly at Fay.

Embarrassed over what her presence suggested, Fay said, "I'm here to discuss a professional matter with Ski."

"Let me see," she said. "The last time you discussed things of a professional nature with Ski, the topic was sabotage of a submarine. What's it this time . . . the sabotage of an engagement?"

"Janet, I can explain everything," Ski said, sharing Fay's embarrassment over his fiancée's accusation.

Janet noticed the slight cuts on Ski's face which in her anger she hadn't seen before. Thinking they were scratches, she said, "Don't bother, Ski. By the looks of your face it seems I wasn't enough of a tigress for you in bed. I'd stick around and take lessons from Fay on fiery lovemaking, but I'm afraid I'd be a poor student." She moved toward the open door.

"Janet, you're acting like a jealous schoolgirl," Ski growled. "Now, do you want to hear my explanation or not?"

"No, Ski," Janet snapped back. "I thought I owed you one last chance to work out a reconciliation, but it seems the joke is on me. While I was taking the initiative, you were out on the town with her, having a ball." She took out her keys and removed the one for Ski's apartment from the ring. Tossing it at Fay, she said, "Here. It looks like you'll be needing this now." There were tears in her eyes. "Fuck you, Ski!" she said and stormed out of the apartment.

"Janet! Wait!" Ski called out as he hurried after her. He grabbed her by the arm at the top of the stairs leading down to the street. "Please. Come back inside and let's talk this out."

Janet slipped off her engagement ring and tried to throw it in his face, but it fell to the floor. "What's to talk out, Ski? Everything is very clear."

Ski sighed. "I'm tired already but your constant jumping to conclusions would exhaust me anyway."

"Now it's all my fault," Janet screeched.

Ski could feel a headache developing. "Janet, you and your father are driving me nuts. I've had it. Go back to your father and tell him to arrange for someone else to marry you."

"I'd never be happy with you."

"Fine! Then we have a meeting of the minds. Now get out of my life and stay out!" Ski searched the top of the landing for the ring as Janet hurried down the stairs. When he found it, he was going to throw it down the stairs at her, but she had already exited the building. "Fuck you, too!" he called down the stairs, then slipped the ring in his pocket.

"What's going on out here?" a male tenant called out to Ski from behind his partially opened apartment door.

"I just became a free man again."

When Ski stepped back inside his apartment, he found Fay in tears. "Hey! Why are you crying? I'm the one who just got screamed at."

"I feel so responsible for what's happened to you," Fay sobbed. "I got you in trouble with the Navy. I almost got you killed. I—"

"You got me unengaged," Ski said with a smile.

He crossed the room to her and took some Kleenex out of a nearby box. Dabbing lightly at her tears, he said, "Janet and I were on our way to a breakup before you ever came to New London. And you didn't get me in trouble with the Navy, I did. By bucking Admiral Pulvey. As for your sabotage article—think of the brighter side. Now I *know* I'm dealing with saboteurs."

Fay looked into his eyes. "Here I am bawling away like a baby and your cuts need attending to."

"See how uncaring you are?" Ski teased. Pointing to the master bedroom, he added, "You'll find the bathroom in there. I should have some iodine and gauze in the medicine chest. You take care of that while I make us a drink. Then I'll tell you some things I found out that just may give you the granddaddy of scoops. But, you have to promise not to print a word of it until I give you the okay."

"After what my sabotage article caused you, I'm not about to print anything without checking with you first."

"Scout's honor?" Ski asked.

Fay kissed him on the cheek. "Will that do? I was never a Scout."

"It'll do for now."

Fay got up and headed for the bathroom. When she stepped into the master bedroom, she glanced around at the furnishings. She was impressed by the bachelor chest and vanity that matched the king-size bed. The bedroom furniture looked expensive to her, as did the attractive flower-patterned bedspread. She noticed the ceiling over the bed was covered with mirrored tiles and smiled. She found the bathroom to be twice the size of the one in her Washington apartment. After getting some iodine and gauze out of the medicine chest, she returned to the living room.

Fay noticed a room adjoining the living room that was furnished with a desk, worktable, and bookcases. To one side of the living room were a light blue couch and matching armchairs arranged around a glass-topped cocktail table. There were two smaller glass-topped tables that accommodated two beautiful crystal lamps. Hanging on the wall above the couch in a night setting, with its suspension cables aglow with miniature lights, was a painting of the Thames River Bridge. Occupying the opposite side of the living room and close to the adjoining kitchen was a richly polished hutch and serving bar fronted by a modern dining room table and six chairs with armrests. She peeked into the kitchen next and found it to be equipped with, seemingly, every conceivable modern convenience. "You have quite a nice place here, Ski," she said as she joined him at a long counter.

"It's all I can afford on captain's pay," Ski replied modestly.

"It's a lot more than I can afford," Fay said as she accepted the drink Ski offered her. "Whose idea was it to put mirrored tiles over the bed? Janet's?"

"Mine."

"Why, you pervert," Fay teased.

"What's perverted about watching yourself making love to someone?"

"I don't know. I never tried it."

"You should sometime. Maybe you'll become perverted, too," Ski said, then gestured for them to go back into the living room. He waited for Fay to seat herself on the couch, then sat down close to her. "Here's to our partnership in trust," he said. They both took a sip. "Boy, I needed that."

"So did I," Fay said. She glanced at the apartment door. "You should put the safety chain across the door. Those creeps might come back here and kill you when they don't find you in your car."

Ski pointed to the desk in the den. "If they do, they'll find me armed. I have a Python .357 magnum in that desk drawer." He noticed the worried look on her face. "If it'll make you feel safer,

I'll set the chain." He got up and set the safety chain across the door. "What I have to tell you may take some time to explain. Are you at all squeamish about spending the night in a bachelor pad?"

"What if Janet decides to come back and make another scene?"

Ski took the engagement ring out of his pocket and showed it to Fay.

"It's that final?"

"It is as far as I'm concerned," Ski said firmly. "What about staying the night?"

"Well, to tell you the truth, I'm not any too enthusiastic about going through that door when killers may be lurking outside."

"Then it's settled. I'll take the couch and you can sleep in the bedroom."

Fay took a turn at offering a toast. "You now have an overnight roomie. And a partner in the detective business."

"You're a detective now?"

"I've had occasion to do detective work investigating missing persons for the *Washington Globe* as a cub reporter. In fact, I was running down some leads on a former Marine Dynamics Security Police captain when my managing editor ordered me back to D.C."

"You can fill me in on that when I finish telling you what I've been doing."

For an hour, with her shoes off and her legs curled up comfortably under her, Fay listened as Ski revealed what he had learned thus far. "Then you believe the saboteurs are trying to blame Marine Dynamics for what happened to the submarine?" She got a nod. "Why, Ski?"

"It seems by doing so they will either stop or delay construction of future Trident class submarines. Now, I'm not saying I totally go along with that. Harrowman could still be behind the sabotage and the motive could still be profits. But if it was enemy agents who switched the oxygen analyzers, then tampering with the sub's life-support system was only half of their murderous act. A defective oxygen analyzer wouldn't necessarily endanger the crew unless it came in contact with a lethal chemical it couldn't handle. Surely, if the saboteurs wanted to be certain the crew would be killed, they wouldn't leave it to chance that methyl mercury would be in the submarine's path."

"That makes sense, Ski."

"If we rule out the possibility that the methyl mercury and the inferior oxygen analyzer are unrelated events, we can't suspect

Marine Dynamics of fraud. They certainly wouldn't substitute an inferior oxygen analyzer, then deliver a deadly chemical to the submarine so their deception would be uncovered."

"That makes sense, too."

"Here's something else that makes sense. If the methyl mercury was deliberately delivered to the *Trident*'s holding coordinates, then we aren't just looking for saboteurs who infiltrated the defense plant. We're also looking for a spy or spies who managed to violate our security at the submarine base. There's only one way they could have known precisely where the submarine would spend enough time for the methyl mercury to kill the crew. That's by visiting our CIC room at the Intelligence Center."

"If a violation of security did take place, then maybe I should continue searching for Rudolph Boyd. He's a former captain of the Marine Dynamics Security Police. Maybe he didn't have anything to do with the sabotage, but he just might have some ideas on how plant security could have been breached."

"Where did you leave off with him?"

Fay explained her findings to date. "What I was about to do when I got that telegram from my managing editor was go to the Connecticut Motor Vehicle Bureau and see if they had a lead on his whereabouts."

"Good idea. I'd like to use your car to take care of my chores. Could you go to the MVB by cab?"

"Sure."

Ski went into the den and took some cash out of his desk drawer. Returning to Fay, he said, "Here's a hundred dollars. Use what you need for expenses."

"Boy, I wish you were my managing editor. He rarely gives me expense money in advance."

"If you're going to work with me on this, I'll be footing the bill. And I'll be giving the orders, too. You be sure that you follow them to the letter. Do you roger that?"

"Does that mean yes?"

"It does."

"Roger that," Fay said.

"Your first order is if you get a lead on Boyd's whereabouts, come right back here and wait for me before you go any further." He took her face in his hands and held it gently. "I don't want anything unpleasant happening to you." Sensing she wouldn't object, he kissed her on the lips. "There. Now we've sealed our association with a kiss."

Fay felt tingly all over from the kiss—the same way she felt when they'd kissed good-bye outside Dino's Den. Only this time it was a more promising kiss. She thought about the mirrored ceiling tiles in the bedroom and returned his kiss without masking her true feelings for him.

Her kiss aroused Ski, and he drew her closer, wrapping his arms around her, his lips refusing to leave hers. He then lowered her onto the couch and covered her with his body.

After long kisses and fiery grinds, Ski lifted Fay's willing body up from the couch and carried her into the bedroom.

## Chapter Thirty-six

*Friday*

It was just after 2:00 P.M. when Fay paid the taxi driver outside Ski's apartment building. Seeing her rented Cutlass parked in Ski's assigned space, she wasted no time in getting upstairs. She let herself in and heard Ski call to her from the bedroom.

"Hi, Ski!" she sang out happily.

Standing in only his Jockey shorts, Ski said, "I gather by your cheery mood that you managed to get a lead on Boyd's whereabouts."

"Not Boyd. Krantz," Fay replied. "That's Boyd's real surname. Boyd was his stepfather's name. It's listed in the family history section of his dossier," she explained. "He has an uncle named Hans Gunther who lives in West Germany. His resignation papers state that he and his daughter, Helen, plan to live with his uncle, but no address is mentioned." She paused and looked at Ski for a reaction.

"Don't stop now," Ski said as he put on a pair of Levi's jeans.

"I also learned at the Motor Vehicle Bureau in Norwich that a driver's license under the name of Rudolph Francis Boyd had recently been surrendered, and that a 1980 Toyota Celica registered under the name of Rudolph Francis Boyd had been transferred to a Francis Rudolph Krantz about the same time. Krantz was recently issued a valid Connecticut driver's license. To sum it up, Boyd stated he's relocating to West Germany with his daughter, but it appears he's planning to stick around here in Connecticut as Krantz. Why stay? And why all the switching around of identification?''

"Perhaps he has some unfinished business he has to conduct incognito. Did you manage to get an update from the MVB on where 'Krantz' lives?''

"Number Ten Driftwood Drive in White Sands Beach. Now, I always thought most people moved *out* of their summer residences at the season's end, not in."

Ski gestured for her to follow him into the den where he leaned over the sea chart stretched out on the worktable. The chart of the Long Island coastline also depicted the outline of the Connecticut shores, and after running his index finger along the Block Island Sound area, he spotted White Sands Beach. "There's our next destination, Fay," he said, pointing it out to her.

Fay looked at the area Ski had pointed to and she noticed all the notations he had made on the chart. "Ski, what do all these dots and lines represent?"

"The black notations pertain to the *Trident*'s course to its overnight holding coordinates. The blue notations are the search patterns of the patrol destroyer. The red ones are the activity the whale was detected making, and the large red dot next to the black one shows where the whale and submarine spent some peculiar time together before the *Trident* was found crash-surfaced in a sea of dead fish.''

Fay looked up from the chart. "You've really done lots of homework on—" She stopped when she saw Ski remove a huge gun and two boxes of ammunition from his desk drawer. "Do you think that's necessary?"

"The saboteurs are responsible for the deaths of a hundred sixty-one people, including Bentsen, whose funeral I attended today. They already tried to kill me once just last night and may try to do so again when they find out their first attempt failed.''

"You think Boyd's involved?"

"I don't know, but we'll find out soon.''

# Part Four

## Chapter Thirty-seven

*Late Friday afternoon*

A billboard just ahead caught Fay's eye. "White Sands Beach . . . a quaint, quiet summer resort edging the shores of Block Island Sound. Turn left one mile ahead on Beach Boulevard."

Ski moved into the left-hand lane and signaled, then made the turn headed by a sign that said "TO BEACH." He found Beach Boulevard to be a narrow paved road that cut straight through tall sand dunes and wild brush to a cluster of wood-framed bungalows set on quarter-acre plots that were surrounded by still more dunes and brush. Every bungalow in sight was tightly shuttered in preparation for the coming winter.

"Let's find Driftwood Drive and take a look at Number Ten," Fay said.

Ski could see that the resort development was small and that only four streets crossed Beach Boulevard. He passed Seashell, Seahorse, and Starfish Drives. Driftwood extended only to the left of Beach Boulevard and ran parallel to the sandy white beach of Block Island Sound. Ski made the turn and for a hundred yards there were no other bungalows in sight on Driftwood Drive. Then Driftwood came to a fork at a steep sand dune, and he took the road finally finding ten bungalows.

Number Ten was as shuttered and lifeless as the rest of the development.

Filled with disappointment, they started back and then, halfway down Driftwood Drive, they saw a red van come speeding toward them. The van continued past them, the driver not even glancing at them.

"I wonder where he's going in such a damn hurry," Ski said, then brought the Cutlass to a stop at the curbside and eyed the van through the rearview mirror. He watched it make a U-turn, then stop outside Boyd's house.

Fay craned to look out the rear window of the car, and watched with Ski as a bearded man got out of the van, hurried up the front walk of Boyd's house, heaved a rolled-up newspaper onto the porch, retraced his steps, and drove off. As the van sped past them again, Fay said, "Why would anyone be delivering a newspaper to a shuttered up-house?"

"That's what I'm about to find out, Fay," Ski said as he got the Cutlass going and headed after the van. He caught up to it and began blowing his horn to get the driver's attention. The driver finally responded and pulled over to the side of the road. Ski hopped out of the car and hurried over to the driver.

Fay watched Ski engage the driver in conversation. After a few moments she saw Ski take out his wallet and hand the van driver some money. He returned to the car carrying a newspaper as the van pulled away. When he got in, she asked anxiously, "What did he say, Ski?"

"I asked him how long he's been delivering the newspaper to Ten Driftwood Drive and he said since Labor Day. He was around making some final collections in the area and Krantz gave him twenty bucks to deliver the paper to his bungalow for the next two weeks, without fail. When he came to deliver the paper yesterday, which happens to be the day your sabotage article hit the front pages, he found the house all shuttered up. When I asked him if yesterday's paper was still outside the door, he said no, someone had picked it up."

"Maybe Boyd was so frightened by my article, he decided to hide out in his shuttered house."

"That's possible."

Fay took the rubber band off the newspaper. Opening it to the front page, she scanned the columns of print, then found what she was looking for and showed it to Ski. "Look, Ski. Here's a retraction of the sabotage article I wrote."

"If Boyd is hiding out because he's involved and your sabotage article scared him, then the retraction might be just the thing to relax him enough to leave."

"Making his next move what?"

"He couldn't have handled switching the oxygen analyzer without help. He had to have accomplices to do that, and to get the methyl mercury delivered to the *Trident*'s coordinates. Maybe he's holed up here, waiting for his accomplices to come here or contact him somehow."

"He's pretty concerned about getting the newspaper every day."

"He's probably using the paper to follow the events pertaining to the *Trident*."

"Perhaps. But he might have another reason, too," Fay said, then began thumbing through the pages. "Every newspaper has a personal ad section. People sometimes use it to send messages. It just might be that his accomplices keep in touch with him that way."

"I doubt we'll be able to pick out a message meant only for his eyes even if there is one in with all those damn advertisements."

Reciting the ads aloud, Fay said, "Sometimes these ads get to be real bizarre. 'Ray, I must have you again soon, most passionately, Patty.' 'Lost earring, reward offered.' 'Found ring, owner must be able to identify to claim.' 'Baby sitting, sleep over okay.' " Skipping over several ads pertaining to lost pets and personal items, Fay found one at the bottom of the second column of advertisements that caught her eye. "Here's an interesting one, Ski. 'Daddy, we got the wrong information yesterday. That's why we didn't come. Everything is okay now. Be sure to come tonight or it'll be too late. Love, Helen.' Ski, that could be for Boyd. His daughter's name is Helen. That statement about getting the wrong information yesterday just might pertain to my sabotage article. And they could be referring to the retraction when they say everything is okay now."

"How could they know about the retraction when it's in the same day's newspaper as their message is in?"

"News of the retraction was also on radio, on TV, and in this morning's newspapers. This is an afternoon edition. They could have heard of the retraction this morning and still had plenty of time to put in a personal ad."

As Ski made a U-turn, she asked, "Where are we going now, Ski?"

"I want to take another look at Number Ten Driftwood Drive."

Fay watched out of the corner of her eye as Ski made a U-turn in front of the house. "Ski! The paper that was just delivered is gone."

"I see that." Ski, carefully looking away from Boyd's house, glimpsed a road leading down to the beach, paralleling Driftwood Drive from a few yards behind the development. From what he could see the beach access road would allow them to watch Boyd's cottage without being observed. As he headed for the access road he said, "Assuming that message was for Boyd, it instructed him to keep a meeting with his daughter tonight. Maybe his daughter is an accomplice or maybe the name Helen is just a code name for his accomplices. If we stick around and stake out his house, he just might lead us to whoever else is in this with him. When we have them all together, we can call the police to round them up.''

"Okay, Ski."

Ski parked the car on the access road in front of a steep dune to their right that blocked the bungalow from view. "Let's climb to the top of that dune. We should have a bird's-eye view of Boyd's house from there." As he got out of the car and joined Fay at the bottom of the dune, he added, "I wish I had my Vet here. I keep a pair of binoculars in the glove compartment."

"I have a telephoto lens on my camera."

"That'll do."

An hour of darkness blanketed White Sands Beach. It brought with it a bone-chilling mist from Block Island Sound, dampening Fay and Ski's clothes and everything around them as they lay side by side at the top of the dune. For the umpteenth time, Ski panned the porch and side of the bungalow with the telephoto lens but saw nothing but eerie shadows. "Come on, damn it," he said wearily. "Make your move." He lowered the camera and glanced at his wristwatch. It was nearing ten o'clock. He settled down for more waiting. Fay sighed, and then a loud rumble echoed out over the quiet development from the direction of bungalow Number Nine.

The rumbling noise sounded to Ski like a garage door being raised. A car's engine sprang to life as they listened and suddenly headlights illuminated the house across the street from Boyd's.

The car backed into the driveway. They heard the garage door close and saw the car drive off into the street and then in the direction of Beach Boulevard. Ski said, "Let's get after him. We don't want to lose him after sweating him out all this time." He grabbed Fay by the hand and helped her down the dune to the car.

He got the Cutlass going, and keeping the headlights off, negotiated his way back to Driftwood Drive. On reaching the intersection of Beach Boulevard, he caught sight of a pair of taillights leaving the development. With his headlights still off, he followed the car, staying a good thousand feet behind.

"Ski, are you sure that's Boyd?"

"I'm sure the car was a late model Toyota. He was cagier than we ever imagined. He was hiding out in the house across the street from his so he could keep an eye on his own house unobserved."

## Chapter Thirty-eight

Murderers, Boyd thought, as he reflected on the visit he'd made to the Gull Island meeting place last night. Now he was on his way there again. When he'd last spoken to Helen's captors on Friday night to give them the *Trident*'s overnight holding coordinates, he had also told them that he was going into hiding. After shouting fiery words of warning over the phone, Mr. A had conceded to his counter demands and agreed to keep in touch through the personal advertisement section of the *Connecticut Herald*. Boyd knew how anxious they were to get his copy of the incriminating letter, and as long as he had it in his possession, Helen would remain safe.

Their meeting place was an abandoned fishery, a gutted two-story structure situated across a narrow wooden bridge that spanned a creek at the end of Gull Island's dark and winding access road. It was surrounded by thickly weeded marshland.

Last night Boyd had found nothing of value inside the fishery. Its electrical fixtures and conduits had been vandalized and its plumbing and any building materials of any worth had been removed. The four walls were kicked in. The second floor had given way to decay and collapsed down to the first, littering it with piles of rubble that rodents had covered with droppings.

Boyd knew that when he met with the terrorists, they would relieve him of his service revolver as soon as he entered the structure, so he had decided to hide his .38 Smith & Wesson under a pile of rubble inside the gutted structure.

He turned off the main highway and drove down the Gull Island access road for the second night in a row. The headlights of his Toyota pulled the narrow wooden bridge out of the darkness ahead and he slowed down to cross it.

Ski pulled off the highway and came to a stop on the shoulder when the Toyota made a left turn onto a road that a sign announced was the Gull Island access road. He gave the Toyota a few moments head start, then entered the access road with his headlights off. Even taking the winding road at a slow speed, he nearly went off the pavement because of the darkness. Then the road straightened and he had the Toyota's taillights in sight to guide him. He slowed almost to a stop when the Toyota's brake lights flashed on brightly, then the car's high beams switched on and illuminated a bridge ahead. After the Toyota crossed the bridge and pulled up before a structure that peered out of the darkness on the other side, Ski inched his way toward the bridge, guided the Cutlass off the road, and shut the engine off.

Ski saw the high beams of the Toyota switch off and on, then a blanket of darkness swallowed up everything on the other side of the bridge. "That must have been a signal to his accomplices, Fay. I'm going to sneak across that bridge on foot just to see what we're up against. If I'm not back in ten minutes, go for the police. Tell 'em that a Navy Intelligence officer needs assistance."

"Where am I going to find a phone around here?"

Ski thought for a moment, then said, "We passed a gas station about a mile east of this access road. Head right as soon as you get back on the main highway and try there."

Fay watched Ski lower the driver's window, then raise himself up from behind the steering wheel to climb out. "Is there something wrong with the door?"

"Yes," Ski grunted softly as he made his way out the car window. When he was outside, he leaned back in and whispered, "Opening the door turns the courtesy lights on, so don't you open the doors while I'm gone." He gave her a reassuring kiss on the lips. "Don't worry. I'll be all right." He then hurried off toward the bridge.

Ski crossed the bridge and, from behind a crop of bushes, watched the man that emerged from the Toyota come to a stop outside the front door of the structure. There were no other cars in sight, but he knew someone was in the building when he saw the man fold his hands over his head as though he were being taken prisoner. A voice from inside ordered Boyd to enter, and Ski hurried over to the side of the building, where a window was missing, then carefully peered in. A flashlight was switched on and aimed at Boyd's eyes.

"Keep that light on 'im while I frisk him, Mr. B," Mr. A ordered as he stood behind Boyd just inside the front doorway. He ran his hands up and down Boyd's legs and torso from behind, then spun Boyd around and inspected his pockets and clothes. "He's clean."

After being spun around again to face Mr. B's flashlight, Boyd was unable to see anything inside the building. "Where's Helen?"

"I'm right here, Daddy," Helen called out from several feet in front of Boyd. Her voice brought Mr. B's flashlight beam crashing into her eyes, revealing tears flowing down her cheeks.

Boyd rushed over to Helen and took her in his arms. He sobbed uncontrollably as he hugged her. "Helen! Helen! Are you all right?"

"Hey! Get your ass back over here, old man," Mr. B ordered. "Who told you it was okay to hold a family reunion?"

With his flashlight also trained on Boyd and his daughter, Mr. A said, "Where're your manners, Mr. B? Let them say hello. They haven't seen each other for months."

With his lips close to Helen's left ear, Boyd whispered, "Don't react to what I'm saying. If you see me moving toward the pile of debris in the center of the room, be prepared to drop to the floor."

"Oh, Daddy . . . please don't do anything," Helen whispered back. "They'll kill us."

"Just . . . do as I say. I know what I'm doing."

"Okay, Rudy! Enough with the hugs and kisses," Mr. A demanded. "Let's have your letter."

Boyd took a few steps toward the pile of rubble that was between him and Helen's captors. He reached into his suit jacket pocket and removed a business envelope that Mr. A had failed to notice when he'd frisked him. Handing it to Mr. A, he said, "There's the letter. That concludes my business with you." He watched Mr. A open the envelope and remove the letter to read it.

With his flashlight trained on the lines of print, Mr. A said, "It certainly is what you said it was, Rudy. Listen to this, Mr. B 'Two men forced me to allow them into the defense plant to deliver something to the engineering department and take something in exchange. I'm sure they met a third man at the engineering department, probably a Marine Dynamics employee.' "

"Please, you have the letter. Can we go now?" Boyd was standing directly in front of the pile of rubble.

"Sorry, Rudy," Mr. A said drily. He nodded to Mr. B, who quickly removed a silencer from his jacket pocket and screwed it to the barrel of his revolver. "Give it to 'em quick and painless."

"I'd think about letting us go," Boyd said coolly. "I made a copy of that letter and put it in safe hands, with instructions to turn it over to the police if anything happened to me or my daughter."

Mr. A removed a photocopy of Boyd's letter from his inside jacket pocket and showed it to Boyd.

Astonished, Boyd asked, "How did you get that?"

"The night we surprised you in your house you dropped a telephone bill on the floor,'' Mr. A said. ''The toll call statement listed a lot of calls to West Germany, so we checked the phone number out and managed to get your Uncle Gunther's address in West Berlin. Then, over the past weekend, we paid Uncle Gunther a little visit.''

''Yeah, old man,'' Mr. B put in. ''And your Uncle Gunther gave us the copy of your letter, just before he fell out of his apartment building window.''

''You cold-blooded bastards!'' Boyd growled, then dove for the pile of rubble. Frantic, he tossed every bit of the debris off the pile until he reached the bare floor. The weapon was gone. He looked up tearfully at the familiar .38 dangling from Mr. A's index finger.

''Everybody freeze!'' Ski shouted through the open window, his magnum playing back and forth between Mr. A and Mr. B. He had heard enough to realize that Rudolph and Helen Boyd were being victimized.

Mr. A switched off his flashlight, dropped to the floor, shot two wildly aimed rounds in the direction of the voice, and rolled across the floor to reposition himself.

Mr. B directed his light at the intruder and opened fire.

Ski hugged the wall of the building to avoid the gunman's volley, then aimed at the huge frame standing behind the flashlight beam and squeezed off two rounds. The figure and the flashlight went crashing to the floor. The flashes from his magnum immediately drew fire from the other gunman and he was forced to duck below the open window. Ski had seen where the flashes of the returned fire came from and estimated it was close to where the Boyds were belly down on the floor. Fearful that he might hit the Boyds, he held his fire, then listened intently for sounds inside the darkened structure.

''Crap!'' Fay shrieked from behind the Cutlass. She had just finished relieving herself and was pulling up her panties when the firecrackerlike noises sounded. She pulled up her jeans next and dashed over to the driver's door. Uncaring about the courtesy lights, she pulled open the door and frantically, slid behind the wheel. After getting the car started, she hesitated, fearing that Ski might have been wounded or killed. When two more shots rang out, she put the car in gear and got it moving.

Good girl, Fay, Ski thought when the car's headlights splashed onto the side of the building as it screeched through a U-turn to head for the main highway. His last two shots had gone unanswered and he peered inside again. The flashlight beam was spilling across the floor from in front of the huge man he had brought down earlier.

The beam was partially illuminating a man and woman hugging each other tightly, who he knew were the Boyds. The flashlight beam made them easy targets, and Ski prepared to shoot it out, but Mr. A already had a bead drawn on Rudolph Boyd's head. He shot Boyd, then Helen, and rolled across the floor.

Mr. A fired his last two rounds at Mr. B's head. He wanted no survivors. Using Boyd's service revolver next, he quickly sent two rounds in the direction of the open window, then rolled side over side toward the direction of the rear door.

Seeing Mr. A shoot Mr. B made Ski realize that the remaining gunman was about to clear out. Hugging the side of the building, Ski reloaded as he inched his way toward the front, where Boyd's Toyota was parked. When he reached the corner of the structure, he paused and peered around to the front door, then quickly made a dash behind the Toyota to use it as a shield as he drew a bead on the partially opened front door. He waited, and instead of seeing the remaining gunman fill the doorway, he heard a loud roar coming from the rear of the building. He ran for the rear of the fishery and saw a large cabin cruiser pulling away from a pier. He charged after the yacht and at the pier's end he fired uselessly until the Python clicked empty. When the cruiser disappeared around a bend in the bay, Ski hurried back to the fishery.

Inside the building, Ski took over Mr. B's flashlight and played its beam down on the lifeless mass sprawled behind it. He could readily see that his magnum shots had done the real damage by ripping a huge hole in the man's chest and splattering his insides all over the wall. He trained the flashlight beam on the Boyds next. Helen Boyd's head was split open, brain matter oozing out all over the floor, and Ski saw blood trickling down from the old man's left temple. Then he heard Boyd moan and quickly took out his handkerchief. "Stay still. Just . . . stay still." He used the handkerchief as a compress and sighed with relief on hearing a police siren approaching the fishery.

## Chapter Thirty-nine

*12:01* A.M. *Saturday*

Unconscious and with the bullet from Mr. A's gun that filled him lodged precariously in his left temple, Rudolph Boyd was rushed by ambulance under police guard to Parkside Memorial, a small private hospital nearest to the Gull Island shooting incident. His condition was stated as most critical and removal of the ominous slug was a life or death situation. The O.R. needed a release and, pretending to be Boyd's next of kin, Ski signed the authorization for surgery in the hope his only living witness to the submarine sabotage would defy the narrow chance of pulling through that Parkside's head surgeon gave Boyd.

With Boyd under the knife, Ski put a call through to the submarine base and confidentially encouraged his XO to falsify venue documents that would gain him custody of Boyd upon his recovery. He also asked Dave to bring two armed Marines with him to Parkside to guard his witness to sabotage, expecting he would transport Boyd to New London to sign a deposition under the stunned eyes of Admiral Pulvey, who had hastily jumped to conclusions and acted upon circumstantial evidence. He was sure Vice-President of Marine Dynamics, Arthur Harrowman, would be quite grateful that a witness emerged, but his motivation for pressing on with his investigation was purely to avenge the dead crew of the U.S.S. *Trident*.

If there was anyone else he'd seek vengeance for, Ski was sure it was Helen Boyd, who, he learned from his intrusion at Gull Island, was a victim of the sabotage act along with the *Trident*'s 160 man crew. Helen and one of her assailants that Ski fatally filled had been taken by police van to the Connecticut State Police Mortuary in neighboring New Haven. There the police established that Helen's life-long ambition to become a doctor and devote her life to helping other people had been robbed from her by her heartless captors. He already avenged one of the culprits who the Boyds only knew as Mr. B. Since police had identified Mr. B through fingerprint and dental files as Frank Ford, and ex-Vietnam Army Corporal who had been dishonorably discharged from the service for immoral conduct and illegal dealings with the Southeast Asian "black market." Neither the police nor FBI had an MO on Ford and they were unable to establish if he had affiliations with organized crime. He was classified as a wolf torpedo, a killer for hire who worked as an independent contract filler, rather than for a mob.

An hour after Boyd had been taken up to the O.R. came the grim news that the former Captain of Marine Dynamics Security Police had succumbed to a cardiac arrest in the attempt to remove the slug. The news left Ski daunted. It seemed now that the assailant who fled Gull Island would remain at lodge, unscathed. So would whatever accomplices he had that were also guilty of sabotage. His XO arrived shortly after the bad news about Boyd, bringing him more discouraging information.

Dave told Ski that Janet Pulvey complained to her father about finding Fay Parks being *entertained* at Ski's apartment, overnight, Janet suspected, and that their engagement was now off. Bull Pulvey regarded the *sneaky* entanglement with the female reporter as a direct disobedience to his orders and ordered that Ski be arrested on sight and confined to base. He had everyone who knew of Ski's regular hangouts searching for him, with Dave placed in charge of the manhunt. In also defying the Bull's direct order to arrest Ski on sight, Dave brought only one Marine MP with him, Lance Corporal Donald Finch, who he knew would plead loyalty and secrecy to him and Ski. After feeling he was heading for deep gumbo in falsifying custody papers, Dave was relieved to learn they would no longer be needed. As it now stood, he would only be court-martialed for disobeying a direct order from the admiral, not for forgery as well, for he had signed the venue documents "Fleet Admiral William P. Pulvey."

With Fay, Dave, and Finch gaping on sad-eyed, Ski confronted State Police Sergeant Austin with his dilemma. Along with the others and State Troopers Baxter and Mathews, who responded to Fay's call for police help, they met with the hospital director to discuss a plan Ski had high hopes of initiating. He explained to all how meticulously the assailant at lodge called Mr. A had fired a series of coup de grace volleys into the Boyds, then his own partner, to insure he left no witnesses behind before fleeing. His point was that the escaped assailant couldn't know if Boyd actually died back on Gull Island, or in the Parkside O.R. Therefore, for all the killer knew, Boyd might still be alive. His plan was to somehow leak that information out in the newspapers, certain Boyd's killer would want to know how his shooting spree faired in the news. If it was carefully worded, the news release would claim he did leave a witness behind alive, which was certain to encourage him to make a reappearance to finish his work.

State Police Sergeant Austin and his two man team agreed to the plainclothes stakeout to lure the killer back for another try at Boyd; and with reluctance, the hospital director volunteered to vacate the fifth floor of Parkside Memorial for use in the police trap. Ski then pursuaded Dave and Marine Lance Corporal Donald Finch to stick around and join in on the plainclothes police dragnet, the civvies he agreed to furnish at his expense. The rest Ski left up to Fay's journalistic prowess in composing just the right kind of newspaper release to entice Mr. A to Parkside Memorial: Using the name of Boyd might be picked up on by either Admiral Pulvey or Arthur Harrowman, both of whom Ski didn't desire to have respond to Fay's article. Even Fay's name as investigative reporter would be withheld, and her managing editor's friend at the *Connecticut Herald* would get the credit for the scoop. To get around the name of Boyd they decided to use Boyd's alias and say that a Francis Krantz was in a coma at Parkside Memorial. Ski couldn't be sure if Boyd's assailants knew of him as Krantz as well, but they would certainly know who it was that had been shot at Gull Island on that particular night. Finally, to insure Boyd's killer would remain unsuspecting of a police trap, the article would claim that Krantz and his female companion who remained unidentified were obvious victims of a robbery in lieu of obtaining a statement from the coma-stricken male victim of the Gull Island incident. Using a fictitious name as well, Ski would be mentioned in the article as a private security police patrolman who happened upon the robbery in progress and fatally filled one of the assailants who also remains unidentified.

## Chapter Forty

*Late Saturday night*

Darkness had drawn down outside the hospital like a black shade, and the front of Parkside Memorial was a wall of yellow light spilling out of windows. Over the PA system the five-minute reminder that visiting hours would be over at 9:00 P.M. sharp was being announced as Ski stared out the window of Room 509 at a black Lincoln Continental Mark IV, which had stopped along the driveway a few feet short of the front entrance. A man got out, carrying a white box.

Mr. A moved through the glass double entrance doors, and slowed to pan the lobby for uniformed or plainclothes cops. Satisfied, he moved to the visitors' reception desk and presented the young woman seated behind it with a delivery invoice he'd obtained for the box of flowers he'd purchased on the way. "I'm supposed to deliver these flowers to a Francis Rudolph Krantz. Which room is he in, please?"

Fay glanced at the invoice, then brought both hands up to her hair as though tidying it, a gesture that was a signal to Dave in the visitors' lounge. "Krantz," she repeated, then began thumbing through the box of visitors' passes on the desk in front of her.

With the visitor's back to him Dave got up from his seat and carefully picked up his jacket, which concealed his walkie-talkie. He inconspicuously stepped over to a nearby phone booth, switched on the walkie-talkie, and keyed the mike button. "This is Dave. He's here. He's wearing black slacks and a waist-length brown leather jacket. Over."

Ski picked up the walkie-talkie and, with a three-man state police backup team watching, he replied, "And he's carrying a white box, similar to the kind florists use. He arrived in a black Lincoln Continental Mark IV. It's parked along the entrance ramp, and it looks quite a bit like the one that ran me off the road on Thursday night. Has he gone up yet? Over."

"Not yet."

Fay had stalled the visitor as long as she dared to and she pulled the pass for Room 510 out of the card file. "Sorry for the delay. Mr. Krantz is in Room 510."

"He's on the way up by elevator right now," Dave said when Boyd's visitor stepped onto a waiting elevator.

"Everyone stand by at your positions," Ski ordered. Then, leaving troopers Baxter and Mathews in Room 509 behind the closed door, he crossed the hall to Room 510 where Sergeant Austin lay waiting. After checking everything, he hurried down to the nurses' station and slipped on a white doctor's jacket. With his eyes on a mirror above the nurses' desk he studied the corridor as he got on the open line with Room 509. "The elevator is at the fourth-floor level now. He should be up here momentarily," he relayed.

Minutes passed then Ski shifted his stare from the elevator doors to a white-jacketed image that came into view in the mirror at the far end of the corridor. He saw the stairway door close behind the man. "I think I know what has been keeping our visitor," he whispered. "He stopped off to borrow a doctor's jacket."

Mr. A saw someone wearing a white jacket seated at the nurses' station with his back turned. He walked quickly to the door and quietly eased it open. The room was dimly lit, but he could see a bulky figure lying motionless in the bed, unattended. He let himself in and closed the door behind him, then crossed to the bed. He eased the oxygen tube out of the man's nose, then gently lifted the head to slide the pillow out. He placed the bed pillow over the expressionless face, then, just as he was about to apply pressure, he noticed the nurses' call button light on the wall behind the bed suddenly flash on silently and saw a hand bringing a gun into view from under the bed sheets. He drew his .38, and brought the butt of the gun crashing down on the man's forehead. There was a groan, then silence.

Mr. A realized he'd walked into a trap. The sound of footsteps racing toward the room made him drop to the floor and scurry under the bed. He aimed his weapon at the door as it was thrust open, then fired.

Trooper Baxter felt an explosion in his right shoulder, released his revolver, and sank to the floor on his knees.

Trooper Mathews had been standing right behind Baxter, and he was hit by the next two shots. His chest was torn open and he went sailing backwards out of the room, then came crashing to the floor on his back.

Mr. A rolled out from under the bed and dashed over to Baxter. Forcing him to his feet, he pointed his weapon at Baxter's temple, then shouted out into the hall, "Get back. I have my gun pointed at this cop's head."

Ski shouted back, "Give it up, friend. All exits are covered."

Mr. A strained to keep Baxter's body in front of him as he inched his way toward the elevator doors that were between him and the gun pointed at him from the nurses' station. "I'd better get out of here, friend! You've got three wounded cops down here. The longer it takes you to realize I'm not suited for prison life, the more blood they leak. Think about it!"

"Let me get some medical help up here first, then we'll talk about your demands," Ski stalled.

"No concessions, friend! I either leave right now and you arrange to have the front door cleared for me, or I'll waste this cop," Mr. A demanded. He knew he was running out of time. His hostage seemed bound for unconsciousness, and if he couldn't hold him up, he'd be face to face with the stubborn one at the nurses' station.

Fay had been relieved at the visitors' information desk by the regular volunteer worker. Restlessly, she waited for Ski's phone call to let her know the assailant was captured and it was all right to come up. She had her camera and was anxious to get on-the-spot snapshots of the arrest. Expecting that the arrest had already been made by now and that Ski might have forgotten to call her, she felt coaxed by a waiting elevator and rushed on just as the doors were sliding closed. She pressed the fifth-floor button decisively and envisioned having intriguing photos to accompany her story about the stakeout and arrest. A Pulitzer prize-winning article for sure, she thought. When the doors opened on the fifth floor, she spotted Ski standing behind a wall at the nurses' station and stepped right off.

"Ski, what . . ." She shrieked when she felt a hairy arm grip her by the neck from behind. Feeling cold metal pressed against the side of her head, she sobbed, "Ski! Help!"

Ski hadn't had a chance to even warn her. Everything had happened too fast. When she'd stepped off the elevator, the assailant had shoved Baxter toward him, then lunged for Fay. Baxter staggered a few feet in his direction before falling facedown. He lay there motionless between him and Fay and Boyd's killer.

"Fay, why did you come up?" Ski bellowed sourly.

"Oh. You two know each other," Mr. A said. "How nice. Fay, tell Ski that if anyone tries to stop me I'm going to splatter your fucking brains all over these hospital walls."

"Oh, Ski. Please do what he says. He'll kill me."

Mr. A felt the elevator doors start to close and put his body against one to keep them open. "What's it going to be, Ski—me or Fay?"

Ski picked up the walkie-talkie. "Everyone listen. This is Ski. The assailant is holding Fay as a hostage. He's coming down on the elevator. Stand off. That's an order. Do nothing to jeopardize Fay."

Mr. A pulled Fay backward into the elevator, which then left the fifth floor.

Ski keyed his mike again. "We have wounded up here. I'm on my way down. Get medics to the fifth floor on the double," he ordered, then raced down the hall toward Room 510. He found Sergeant Austin staggering toward the door, blood trickling down the front of his face from the deep gash in his forehead. "How bad are you hurt?" he asked.

"I'll live," Austin said.

"Take care of Baxter and Mathews till the medics get here. I'm going after that bastard," Ski said, then raced toward the stairs.

When the elevator doors opened at the lobby level, Mr. A found himself face to face with two armed men wearing street clothes. "Put those guns down on the floor or I'll waste this broad!" he growled.

Responding to Fay's pleas to comply, Dave nodded to Lance Corporal Finch. "We'd better do what the man wants, Finch."

When their guns were at their feet, Mr. A ordered, "Now kick them rods onto the elevator." As soon as they did, he pressed the elevator button for the fifth floor and let the door close behind the two weapons. "Get back," he demanded next. "Get back and don't try to stop me from leaving or Fay is going to get an earful of lead." He thrust her forward and marched her toward the front door, turning frequently along the way to face the two men he had disarmed.

Outside the front entrance, Butts saw Mr. A emerge with a female hostage held at gunpoint. He pressed the accelerator to the floor and pulled up to Mr. A. After thrusting the passenger door open, he barked, "I knew something would go wrong trying to hit someone in a fucking hospital!"

"Shut up and get us out of here," Mr. A demanded as he threw Fay into the front seat and climbed in after her. He pulled the large heavy door to the Mark IV. closed, then returned the barrel of his .38 to the side of her head. "You just better pray nobody tries to stop us, Fay. It'll be in your best interest if we make a clean getaway."

Ski made it to the lobby level and ran into Dave and Finch who were taking turns pressing the elevator call button repeatedly. "I'm going after that bastard in Fay's rented Cutlass. I'll keep my emergency flashers blinking so you can pick up my trail. Get the military sedan and join in on the chase. You can use your two-way radio to keep Sergeant Austin posted on the direction the pursuit takes us over the police radio band."

"Roger that, Ski," Dave said as the elevator arrived back at the lobby level. He joined Finch in retrieving their weapons, then they made a dash for the side entrance where the military sedan was parked.

Ski charged out the front entrance of the hospital just as the distinct taillights of the Mark IV were disappearing at the end of the hospital's circular driveway. He raced over to the Cutlass and jumped in, and in moments he was fishtailing down the exit ramp in hot pursuit of the Continental.

As they were heading down the ambulance ramp siding the hospital, Dave caught sight of Sergeant Austin. With Finch at the wheel, he lowered the passenger window and shouted to the state trooper, "I'll be in radio contact with you. Follow after us and hurry."

"I'm on my way!" Austin promised, then holding a bloodstained handkerchief over his wound, he raced over to an ambulance garage where he had his police sedan hidden.

The three cars raced through Parkside, disrupting traffic severely. Austin, some distance back in a fourth car, stayed in radio contact with Dave, requested additional units, and tried to anticipate the direction of the Mark IV so his men could clear the streets ahead of the speeding car. Ski and Dave, with Austin trailing, followed the Mark IV out of town. When Dave reported that they were on U.S. 1 heading south, Austin ordered a roadblock.

"Shit," Butts growled when he saw the flashing red lights atop the two police cars sitting back to back across the road up ahead.

"Go through it," Mr. A demanded, and braced himself.

"You can't," Fay said. "We'll all be killed!"

"Hang on!" Butts warned as he tightened his grip on the wheel. Savagely, the Mark IV plowed into the joined rear quarters of the two police cruisers, causing their rear wheels to leave the ground as they were banged out of the way of the Continental. The long nose of the Mark IV crumpled only slightly, but the collision had driven the radiator back into the fan. Seeing a cloud of steam billowing up ahead of the windshield, Butts grunted, "The radiator bought it. The engine's going to seize up before we make the airport."

"Keep going," Mr. A said. They were close to the private general aviation airfield, Harbor Airport, where Mr. A's Cessna 150 was parked. "When you get to the airport access road, kill your lights."

Ski sped through the broken barricade, with the taillights of the Mark IV still in view. He narrowed his eyes when the taillights suddenly vanished some distance ahead, and slowed so Dave wouldn't lose him when he made the turn.

After switching off his lights, Butts skidded through a right turn to get onto the airport access road, then negotiated the unlighted access road from memory, using the lights from airplane hangars in the distance to help him judge the road.

Butts eyed the flashing lights in the rearview mirror. "We're still being tailed, damn it," he growled. As he neared the Quonset hut that was Lynns Air Taxi Service office, where he had picked up Mr. A earlier, he saw two headlights suddenly pull out from an airplane hangar parking lot and head right for him. Butts shouted, "He doesn't see us!" At the last moment he switched on his headlights, but it was too late.

The aircraft mechanic, who had been working overtime in the hangar, was stunned when the bright headlights suddenly came crashing into his tired eyes. He hit his brakes and whipped the wheel to the right to avoid the oncoming car, then gripped the steering wheel when he careened off the Mark IV and sailed across the access road toward an airplane hangar across the street from his. The abrupt stop when he collided with the front wall of the hangar sent him lunging forward into the windshield, knocking him unconscious.

Butts skidded off the road, heading for the side of Lynns Air Taxi Service office, then came to a sudden stop on impact with the Quonset hut, sending pieces of shredded metal flying into the air. His jaw smacked against the steering wheel, knocking him unconscious at once.

Fay had sunk down in the front seat, doing her best to take cover on the floor of the car. Her head whiplashed backward and struck the lower part of the dashboard, stunning her.

Mr. A hit the windshield with the right side of his head, then fell back against the backrest of the front seat. He shook the dizziness from his head, and evaluated his situation quickly. The pursuing flashing lights were rapidly drawing closer. He took out his .38, aimed it at the back of Butts's head, and pulled the trigger.

The explosion shocked Fay into full awareness, and she saw that Mr. A's gun was an inch from her forehead. "Please! No!" she screamed. "I don't want to die!"

"Sorry, kid," said Mr. A, then squeezed the trigger.

Fay screamed hysterically as she heard the gun click a few times. Mr. A stopped squeezing the trigger after several tries. He realized he had failed to count the number of rounds he had fired. He raised the gun high over Fay's head, then heard a car screeching to a stop a few feet away. "You're one lucky bitch," he said, tossed the gun away, and ran for the air taxi service office.

Ski saw the assailant racing away from the car and fired a shot at him, but the figure kept running and disappeared behind the Quonset hut. Horrified by Fay's screams, he rushed over to the car and lifted her onto the front seat. "Are you all right?"

"Oh, Ski!" Fay sobbed hysterically. "He was going to kill me. He had his gun pointed at my head, but it just kept clicking."

"It's all over now," Ski reassured. He saw the military sedan speeding toward them. "Dave is coming. He'll look after you. I'm going to go after our friend."

"Oh, please don't," Fay pleaded. "He'll kill you!"

Just then Ski heard an airplane engine spring to life, and he saw the Cessna taxiing out from the parking apron. He fired a shot at the plane, then rushed back to the Cutlass.

Mr. A saw the headlights of the car charging toward him. He got the plane in position on the runway, lowering his flaps as he did. The wind sock showed he was headed into the wind. He revved up the engine, then released the brake pedals and rolled down the runway, quickly building up speed.

Ski turned onto the runway after the fleeing plane and pressed the accelerator to the floor. He pointed the nose of the Cutlass at the tail of the Cessna as it wobbled down the runway just ahead of him. "You're not getting away from me this time, you bastard!" Ski grunted, striving to narrow the gap.

Anxious to get airborne, Mr. A pulled back on the yoke to hurry the takeoff. "Rotate, damn it!" he growled as the airspeed indicator neared the lift-off range.

Ski was inches away from the tail when the nose wheel and main landing gear began to leave the ground. Uncaring of his or the pilot's safety, he struck the tail with the grill of the Cutlass. After taking a hard bounce back down onto the runway, the Cessna began to rise skyward again. Ski rammed the tail section harder and it came back into his windshield, shattering it and sending spears of glass into his face. He felt blood and took one hand off the steering wheel for an instant to touch his face. The car went out of control and swerved from left to right, then skidded sideways off the runway and rolled over on its roof. The rollover sent Ski's head crashing against the roof liner, stunning him momentarily.

The Cessna managed to get airborne and climbed skyward for nearly a hundred feet above the runway, but couldn't maintain its altitude. The car's ramming had seriously damaged the tail section and hampered the angle of attack on lift-off. The plane went into a stall and fell out of the sky, tail first. Then, before it returned to the runway, the weight of the engine pitched the nose down hard. Its nose wheel smacked the ground and sheared off, sending the Cessna's tail catapulting skyward as it stood almost straight up on its nose. For brief moments the propeller hurled up a windstorm of rocks and dirt as it tried to screw itself into the hard ground. Then its blades curled up into a spiral and the engine hissed to a stop. The impact had mangled the engine cowling and driven it toward the cockpit, forcing the fire wall and instrument panel behind it to buckle inside the cockpit, mangling Mr. A's feet as he hung from his seat belts, facedown.

Fearful that the engine might burst into flames, he screamed frantically, "Help! Someone! Get me out of here!"

Ski had shaken the daze from his head and was climbing out of the overturned car when he heard the shouts for help. He hurried over to the Cessna, climbed up on the left landing gear strut to peer into the cockpit, and then forced the pilot's door open. "I was hoping to see you jailed," he said. "Now you are."

"Don't just stand there!" Mr. A screamed. "Get me out. This thing might blow up any moment."

"All the more reason to start answering my questions, and fast."

"I have nothing to say. Now get me out of here, damn it!"

"Ever been in a burning cockpit before?" Ski asked. His question went unanswered. "No? Then let me tell you what happens to someone trapped inside like you are. First the engine catches fire and the flames start climbing up toward the cockpit. Then they wrap around the cockpit like a burning hot blanket. The flames eat everything up as they get inside to lick at your flesh. Your clothes smolder and become an oven with you closed inside them. You'll think you're going to die quickly as the radiant heat melts the flesh off your bones, but you keep on living to suffer through the agonizing pain of the hungry flames. Not until your blood begins to boil in your veins and your brain begins to fry inside your skull does death come to take the pain away. By then you're a raving maniac, and if anyone was to save you before you died, you'd live in such agony that you'd hate their guts for doing so."

"You're crazy! Stop it! Get me out! You can't leave me here to die like that!"

"Why not?" Ski asked. "A hundred and sixty of my shipmates were left to die aboard the *Trident* submarine."

"You're not a cop?"

"I'm Captain Kowalski of Naval Intelligence. Remember that

name?'' No answer. "You should. You left me to die at the bottom of a ravine the other night when you and your hood friends forced me off the road. You also left Rudolph and Helen Boyd to die. You killed your own partner. You just killed the driver of that Mark IV. And if you hadn't run out of ammunition, you'd have left Fay for dead, too.''

"Okay, damn it. You win. I'll tell you what you want to know. But get me out of this fuckin' cockpit first!''

"Talk first.''

"I'm just a gun. I was hired to fill a contract on Boyd. I don't know much more than the Boyds' part in the operation.''

"Then start by telling me who you work for.''

"Don Capi.''

"Who?''

"Tony Capobianco. He owns the Fisherman's Wharf. It's a restaurant and marina on the west bank of Lake Montauk in Montauk Point. He took on the contract. Some New York City family don recommended him.''

"Who took the contract out on the Boyds?''

"No names were mentioned. They came highly recommended and their dough was real good.''

"You're lying,'' Ski said angrily.

"It's the truth, damn it!'' Mr. A shot back. "In our line of work we often avoid using names. Names cause trouble later on. We agree to a price and the deal is sealed. Our part in it was to snatch Helen Boyd so we could force her father to get us on the defense plant. All we did was deliver that oxygen analyzer to the plant, then cart one away. One of their people took it from there.''

"Who?''

"An engineering guy by the name of Nelson Hobart.''

"Hobart?'' Ski asked, shocked.

"Yeah. He helped us snatch Helen Boyd. Then we kept her in the basement of Don Capi's place till—''

"Until her father was of no more use to you,'' Ski finished for him. "Before you left the abandoned fishery on Gull Island you made sure everyone connected with you was dead. Was that your idea or Don Capi's?''

"Don Capi called it that way and he's depending on me to get back to his place in time for the final payoff. He wants to hear from me personally that I took care of Rudy Boyd for good this time.''

"Tell me more about this payoff. When is it to take place?''

"I'm not telling you anything else," Mr. A said. "You get me out of here first."

Ski sniffed the air outside the cockpit. "I think you'll tell me more, and right now." He smiled. "Take a sniff for yourself. What do you smell?"

"Hey, the carburetor must be leaking gas all over that hot manifold. This thing is going to blow up any minute. Come on, get me out!"

"Tell me about the payoff. And you'd better hurry."

"It's set for closing time tonight at Fisherman's Wharf."

"What time is closing? Answer fast. I smell smoke."

"Two A.M. Sunday morning."

"*They* are going to have a surprise waiting for them." Ski released the seat belt that held Mr. A facedown in the pilot's seat. "Can you move your legs at all?"

Mr. A tried to and screamed. "They're pinned between the rudder pedals and the fire wall."

Just then Dave pulled up in the military sedan with Fay and Finch. "Stay on the two-way radio and give Sergeant Austin directions to where we are, Finch," he said, then ran over to Ski at the upturned Cessna.

"Our friend is stuck inside the cockpit, Dave," Ski said. "Climb up on the strut and help me haul him out." He waved Fay back. "Stay put where you are, Fay. This plane might blow up at any moment." With the flames curling up toward the cockpit from under the buckled engine cowling, Ski said to Dave as he joined him atop the landing gear strut, "His legs are pinned under the instrument panel. We're going to have to pull together on him to yank him free. On the count of two, let's pull together."

Mr. A screamed in agony. "You're tearing my legs off! You're going to cripple me!"

Finally the assailant's legs squeezed through the mangled metal and Ski wrapped his arm around Mr. A's torso. "You take his legs, Dave," he said, then together they raised him out of the cockpit and lowered him to the ground. Without delay they grabbed hold of him again and bodily carried him over to the military sedan to take cover.

Austin found the upturned Cessna just as it erupted into a fireball. With his roof light flashing and his siren shrilling, he raced over to where the military sedan was parked, then put a call in for additional police units and the fire department.

"Get down, quick," Ski said to Austin as he rushed over to him and the others. Just as he did, large pieces of metal and fabric were hurled high into the air from the burning plane when the gas tank exploded. One of the cockpit seats plummeted down, engulfed in flames, and landed just a few feet away from them. Pointing to the burning seat, Ski said to Mr. A, "you would have been strapped in that thing if you hadn't told me what I wanted to know, friend."

"What did you learn, Ski?" Austin asked.

"He's an underworld hit man, working for a small mob operating out of a seafood restaurant and marina over in Montauk Point. I want to get right over there and round up his boss. There's a payoff expected to take place tonight involving others."

"I have no jurisdiction over in Montauk, Ski," Austin reminded.

"No problem. I have," Ski said. "You just take care of this hood and leave the rest to me." He glanced at his wristwatch. "If we hurry, we can just make the last ferry crossing from Mystic Seaport to Orient Point. From there it's just a short drive to Montauk." He regarded Dave and Finch. "I'm assuming you two will face a little more risk and come along to help me." He got agreeing nods.

"I'm coming, too," Fay insisted.

"Okay, Fay," Ski agreed. "But this time do exactly what you're told and stay put when I say so. I don't want you having any more close encounters with death."

"I will. I promise, Ski," Fay said.

## Chapter Forty-one

*1:00 A.M. Sunday*
The military sedan had its red roof light and siren off as it sped along the winding hills of Old Montauk Highway atop Montauk Point's steep and sandy cliffs. A roadside billboard announced that Fisherman's Wharf was one mile away, and Ski slowed in anticipation of the turn. After making the left, they were on a narrow two-lane country road. From between dunes, tall weeds, and wild-growing pine trees and shrubs they caught glimpses of a large body of water to their right that was Lake Montauk. Another large billboard, announcing Fisherman's Wharf as the best place to eat in Montauk Point, directed them to take the next right.

Ski turned and headed along a gravel road that ended in a spacious parking lot. There were numerous boat slips to their left that comprised the marina area. To their right, with only three cars parked outside, was a teakwood one-story structure, with two bright spotlights atop the roof, set on a pier that fed out into the lake. Ski brought the car to a stop along the restaurant side of the parking lot, some distance away from the other three parked cars. The headlights of the sedan illuminated a ship's gangway that gave access to the restaurant through a ship's hatch. "Very nautical," he commented.

"It looks as though Don Capobianco's side business is very profitable," Fay said. "This place must have cost a million dollars to build."

"At least," Ski said. "Now, as per my briefing, Fay and I will go in first, pretending to be a married couple out for a few cocktails. Dave, give us about fifteen minutes, then you and Finch come, sit down and keep us in sight. Do nothing till you get my signal, then back my move without delay."

"Right Ski," Dave said.

Inside the lobby Ski marveled over the numerous decorative nautical devices and an encased board that neatly displayed every conceivable seaman's knot. They followed along a ship-styled passageway lined with framed pictures of old-time vessels that led to the bar and cocktail lounge, which fronted a highly polished hardwood dining room floor. The glossy, hand-rubbed bar running the full length of the building and facing the cocktail and restaurant tables was made of oak planking. The Montauk Lake side of the bar and restaurant afforded a panoramic view through two spacious picture windows and glass sliding doors. Outside the sliding doors was a large terrace with more tables and chairs and another gangway, which led down to the long pier that stretched out over Lake Montauk for some sixty feet.

What caught Ski's eye most as he and Fay seated themselves midway along the oversized bar was a thirty-eight-foot Egg Harbor cabin cruiser, with a flying bridge that looked familiar to him. "I'd safely be betting a year's pay if I wagered that that yacht tied up out there recently visited Gull Island."

"You think it's the one that assailant used to make his getaway in?"

"Yes." Ski looked around. There were only two other customers visible—an elderly couple seated at the terrace end of the bar, chatting with the young bartender. The bartender smiled at Ski and

Fay, then excused himself politely to the old couple. Embroidered over the left pocket of his gold bartender's jacket was the name "Joey."

"Good evening, folks. What's your pleasure?" Joey Wells said in a congenial tone.

"I'll have a whiskey sour, straight up," Fay replied.

"Make mine a Dewar's on the rocks," Ski said next. As Wells moved along the bar to prepare their drinks, Ski noticed a sailfish mounted on a piece of oak planking that matched the rest of the nautical decor. Hanging by brass chains from hooks under the sailfish was a bronze plaque that documented the catch:

Sailfish

8'3"                                              129 lbs.

Caught by

Tony Capobianco

2/4/1972                              Miami Beach, Florida

## Chapter Forty-two

The *Brighton Explorer* had left its anchorage off Martha's Vineyard over an hour before, sailed to a point some ten miles out at sea south of Montauk Point, and dropped anchor again. Captain Horthorne ordered the ship's twenty-four-foot cabin motor launch lowered on starboard and advised Dr. Grant when the launch was ready.

In his plush stateroom Dr. Grant neatly placed the last stack of crisp new hundred-dollar bills into the attaché case, filling it to the brim. After closing the case, he placed it by the door for Felicia to pick up on her way out. It totaled the second half of a million-dollar fee to be paid to Tony Capobianco for services rendered. "Mr. Capobianco's attention should be glued to the contents of your attaché case when he opens it, Felicia."

"I'm sure it will be," Felicia said as she screwed a silencer to the end of her revolver. After slipping the weapon into her purse, she said, "With the prevailing currents slackened, I'll arrive at Lake Montauk in under an hour."

"It's just one thirty now," Grant said as he glanced at his wristwatch. "You've time for a bit of brandy before you get under way. It'll help ease the sea's nightly chill." He poured a generous splash of brandy into two snifters and handed one to Felicia. "To finalizing with Don Capobianco," he said.

"Finally," she said. She took a sip of the brandy. "How long we've waited for this time to come, Phillip."

"To more rewarding times ahead," Grant said. "And to our long-awaited return to home port." He sipped his brandy and savored it. "Join me in the aft hold when you get back. I'll be there overseeing the scuttling preparations on *Scorpion*."

Dave and Finch walked into Fisherman's Wharf and headed down the narrow passageway. They took a seat at the entrance end of the bar after checking to see where Ski and Fay were seated and watched an old couple leave.

Ski saw the bartender heading his way. "I'll have another, Joey." As Wells refilled his glass with Scotch, he said, "I see Tony still has his prize catch."

Wells looked up at the sailfish Ski was pointing to. "Yeah. You know Tony?"

"We did some deep-sea fishing together a while back."

"Here in Montauk?"

"No. I know Tony from Miami Beach." Ski gestured toward Fay. "The wife and I are up for the summer. We're staying over in the Hamptons. I knew Tony owned this place and thought I'd drop in on him before we headed back down south. Is he around?"

"He's in the back office, catching up on some bookkeeping," Wells said. "If you stick around till closing, you can say hello to him then. Tony usually comes out to the bar for a nightcap."

"Thanks. I'll do that." He waited for the bartender to pick up his money, then, seeing no one else in the bar or restaurant area, he slipped out his magnum as Wells turned to ring the sale up.

"That's Tony's yacht outside at the pier," Wells said. "He goes deep-sea fishing every chance he gets." He turned to face his customers and saw the huge gun pointed at him. "Hey!" he said. He looked at the other end of the bar and saw his other two customers brandishing weapons. "What is this, a holdup? There's only about forty bucks in the register. That ain't worth getting shot for, so go right ahead and help yourself."

"It's not a stickup. Just stay cool and do what you're told," Ski said.

"You got it. I got a wife and three small kids that depend on my staying alive."

"Who else is still around besides you and Tony?" Ski asked.

"Louie Franchese is in the back office with Tony."

"What's Louie's function around here?"

"He's Tony's torpedo," Wells answered.

"A bodyguard?" Ski asked.

"You got it."

"Who is out in the kitchen?"

"No one. The restaurant closes at ten o'clock. All the help left an hour ago."

"I smell cooking."

"You smell the deep fryers. They're the last things the cook shuts down. They take a while to cool off."

"Fay, lock the front door. Finch, secure the terrace doors. Dave, keep an eye on Joey. I'm going to have a look in the kitchen," Ski said.

He pushed open the swinging kitchen door and scanned the area, then noticed the deep fryer. He walked over to it and examined it, noticing that the temperature indicator was still reading rather high. He held his hand above the tank of grease and could feel heat rising from it. Everything else in the kitchen looked secured for the night. Satisfied no one else was around, he returned to the bar. "Any other way in here besides the front and terrace doors, Joey?"

Pointing to stairs leading down from the hallway outside the kitchen and private office, Wells said, "There's an outside entrance to the basement, but the door is kept locked and bolted from the inside."

"What's down there?"

"A wine cellar, bar supplies, and a small room with a bathroom."

"Anyone occupying the room now?"

"Not anymore. That is, I think someone *was* living down there."

"Go on," Ski said.

"For months I saw trays of food being taken down there when I came on duty at six. But I was told to keep out of the basement and check with Tony if I needed bar supplies. Then yesterday I was allowed to go down and get my own supplies again. I took a peek and the back room and bathroom down there looked recently lived in to me."

"That could be where they were keeping Helen Boyd captive," Ski said to Fay and Dave.

"You people cops?" Wells asked.

"Naval Intelligence," Ski said.

"That's a relief. I thought maybe you were from some rival city family with a beef against Tony."

"Joey, I need your help. You cooperate and I'll see to it that no harm comes to you," Ski promised.

"What do you want me to do?" Wells asked. "I depend on this job to support my family."

"You can always get another job, Joey," Ski said. "One where you're not working for a bunch of gangsters. Now, how can we tell Tony and Louie apart?"

"Tony is the little guy with the jet-black hair. Louie is the big bruiser with thinning reddish hair."

"Is the office door kept locked?"

"Yes. In case of a holdup. But I think I can get Tony to open the door without becoming suspicious. As I said before, there's only about forty bucks in the register. Tony came out to collect most of the cash when the restaurant closed. I could knock on the door and tell 'em a customer can't pay his bar tab unless he gets change for a big bill."

"He'll buy that?"

"He don't let anyone welch on a bar tab. And he don't give credit. He'll make change for me."

"All right." Ski said. "Tell Tony a customer has a hundred-dollar bill and you need change. When you hear the door unlock, step aside and leave the rest to us." To Finch he said, "We're closed for the night if anyone wants in." To Fay he said, "Stay put at the bar no matter what happens. Dave, you take Louie when we go in. I'll deal with Don Capobianco myself." He nodded to Wells. "Lead the way, Joey."

Wells led Ski and Dave across the hardwood dining room floor, then apprehensively knocked on the office door. "Tony! It's me, Joey."

Capobianco had been engrossed in the figures in his ledger as he sat behind his desk. He threw his pencil down on the desk and said to Franchese, seated in a chair next to the desk, "We're never going to get done tonight. What the hell do you want now, Joey?"

"A customer has a ten-buck bar tab and all he has is a hundred-dollar bill. I need change."

"You would," Capobianco grunted. He shoved the ledger and adding machine over to Franchese. "Add that column of figures up again while I make change for Joey." He walked over to the open door of the safe and took out twenties and tens. Crossing the room to the office door, he glanced at his wristwatch. It was one forty-five They'd be closing in half an hour, and soon after that his after-hours visitor would show up. He wouldn't get his bookkeeping done in time.

Wells heard the door unlocking and stepped to one side.

Ski, with Dave right behind him, charged into the room as the door was opening. The door slammed into Capobianco's face, sending him reeling back into the room. Off balance, his nose bleeding, he fell on his back in front of his desk.

"Stay right there, cockroach!" Ski ordered, holding his magnum pointed at the little man. Franchese bolted out of his chair and drew his gun. Dave fired, catching the brawny man right between the eyes.

"That's the way you're going to wind up, cockroach, if you don't tell me what I want to know," Ski said to Capobianco. He saw Wells and Fay peeking in the door. "Take her back to the bar, Joey," Ski said.

"If you're in this with them, Joey," Capobianco growled, "you and your wife and kids are gonna be sorry."

"Shut up!" Ski said. "Go on, Joey." Wells and Fay left the doorway.

"Who the fuck are you!" Capobianco asked.

"I'm Captain Kowalski, Naval Intelligence," Ski replied. "Surely you recall my name? You sent your hoods over to New London to help me have an accident."

"I don't know what you're talking about," Capobianco insisted.

Ski ripped off one of the tie cords on the drapes covering the window behind Capobianco's desk, returned to Capobianco, turned him over, forced his hands behind his back, and tied them tightly. "You and I are going to have a little private chat out in the kitchen, cockroach." He jerked Capobianco to his feet and shoved him toward the door, then marched him out to the kitchen.

"You're jerking yourself off, pal," Capobianco insisted. "I have nothing to tell you."

Ski led him over to the deep fryer, and turned on the gas jet under the still steaming tank of grease. "How long do you figure it'll take your skin to melt off your face, cockroach?"

"Go fuck yourself," Capobianco grunted. "I don't scare easily."

"In that case, you'll die a hero," Ski said. He saw the grease in the tank turning into a frenzy of bubbling foam. Fine droplets of the hot brown liquid splashed up on the back cover like projectiles. "It looks like it's time to start cooking,'' he said, then lifted the little man off the floor and held him facedown over the boiling grease. ''Remember now?''

''Fuck you!'' Capobianco felt the intense heat of the bubbling grease as his face was pushed lower. It was like a blistering sun, drawing beads of sweat to his forehead at once. He felt splatters of the grease sting his cheeks as they shot up at him from the tank. ''Goddamn it! Stop with the fucking games and put me down, asshole.''

''I'm going to put you down, cockroach. Deeper into that tank of grease. Now this is your last chance. You're getting too heavy to hold up. Do you have something to tell me?''

Feeling himself sinking lower into the tank, Capobianco screamed out, ''You're crazy enough to do it! Okay! Put me down.''

Ski placed him back on his feet. ''If I don't like what I hear, I'll put you right back in there,'' he warned, then lowered the flame under the grease. ''You were hired to fill a contract on the Boyds, so your hood told me. Isn't that right?''

''Yeah. It's right. But you can't hold me over a deep fryer in court, asshole. So what good is it gonna do you to hear me admit it?''

''Who said anything about court?'' Ski asked. ''I'm my own court. Judge, jury, and executioner. I'm going to execute whoever killed that submarine crew. No sharp attorney is going to have a crack at getting the murderers off with a prison sentence.''

''Hey, I didn't put the hit on that submarine crew, pal,'' Capobianco said. ''My end of it was the Boyds and that's all. I ordered you hit only 'cause you got in the way.''

''Well, you're involved in sabotage, nonetheless, by taking on work from enemy agents. And you were aware at the time that they were going to put a hit on a submarine. That makes you just as guilty as they are. And as your judge and jury, I say you're guilty.'' He aimed his magnum at one of Capobianco's eyes. ''As executioner I've decided shooting out both your eyes would be a just sentence.'' He cocked the hammer.

''Wait, for God's sake!'' He turned and shouted toward the kitchen door. ''Somebody help me! Call the police, for God's sake! This guy is a maniac. He's gonna kill me!''

''Tell you what,'' Ski said matter-of-factly. ''Would you rather see those who hired you face the executioner?'' He got a nod. ''Well, if you're willing to help me round them up, maybe I'll just turn you over to the cops.''

"They don't mean anything to me. They're coming here tonight to pay me the balance on the Boyd contract. Do whatever you want to them, but let me live. I'll take my chances in the joint." Capobianco glanced at the clock on the wall. "She'll be here in fifteen minutes."

"She?"

"They use a broad to pass on instructions and deliver the dough. She comes here by boat. Ties up at my pier."

"Fine. I'll be with you in your office when she shows up."

"The guy that wasted the Boyds," Capobianco said, smiling.

"What about him? Does she know what he looks like?" Ski asked.

"No. But when she does meet him tonight, she wants to see him dead. That was part of the agreement. Those directly involved with the hit were to be eliminated after they wasted the Boyds."

"No problem. We'll show her Louie's body." Ski lowered his gun as he marched Capobianco out of the kitchen, then called everyone into the office. "Tony has agreed to keep his payoff rendezvous with one of the saboteurs. She's a woman, and she's coming here by boat. I want to let the payoff take place, then follow her in Tony's yacht when she leaves." Ski looked at Franchese's body. "Dave, you and Finch move this corpse to the walk-in freezer. And see if you can find a throw rug to cover the bloodstain."

"There's a throw rug by the front door," Wells volunteered.

"Why is your yacht the only vessel in the marina," Ski asked Capobianco.

"I only keep the bar and restaurant open all year," Capobianco said unpleasantly. "The marina closes at summer's end, and today was the last day for marina customers to move their boats out of the slips."

"Do your visitors know it's your yacht?" Ski asked.

"I never mentioned it to them."

Dave and Finch returned, and Ski said, "Finch, hide the military sedan in the weeds. Dave, I want you and Fay to move Tony's yacht out into the middle of Lake Montauk. Joey, do you have a flashlight?"

"There's one alongside the cash register," Wells said.

"Fine. I'll get it later," Ski said. "Dave, I'll give you two short flashes with the flashlight when I want you to come back with the yacht." To Capobianco he said, "Now for the keys to your yacht."

Moments after the yacht's twin engines sprang to life, Finch came back in. "There's still a Cadillac and a Mustang parked out in the lot."

"The Caddy is Tony's," Wells said. "I own the Mustang."

"The Caddy can stay," Ski said. "If they inspect the parking lot, they'll expect to see Tony's car still here. But I'd like to get Joey's car out of sight." He winked at Wells. "Let me see your driver's license, Joey." When Wells presented it, Ski copied down the bartender's address and got his home phone number. Then, returning the driver's license, Ski said, "How would you like to be able to go home to your wife and kids right now?"

"I'd like nothing better, sir," Wells said with a grateful smile.

"Keep yourself available for future questioning. Don't mention what happened here tonight to anyone. Finch, let Joey out, then lock the door after him." Ski glanced at his wristwatch. It was 2:15 A.M.

As Dave maneuvered the yacht out to the middle of Lake Montauk, Fay decided to look around. The cabin began with a roomy salon that was furnished with a divan and two lounge chairs that faced a television and stereo cabinet. The salon afforded a wide view on both sides from sliding glass windows. Forward of the salon was a full galley, with a sink, stove, and small refrigerator that was across the narrow walking aisle from a breakfast nook. On starboard, forward of the nook, was a helm station identical to the one on the flying bridge. Fay descended a small staircase, at the bottom of which was a standing head, complete with toilet, washbasin, and a closed-in shower. Two cabins lay adjacent to each other in the bow section. Each cabin had two bunk beds and built-in dresser drawers and closets. At the most forward part of the cabin the narrow aisle met another small ladder that accessed the bow through a lift-up hatch. Another hatch that faced aft covered the forecastle, a hold used to stow the anchor's nylon line. Fay was jarred when a noise overhead took her by surprise. Then, as the rumbling sound reverberated and seemed to shake the yacht, she hurried back to the aft deck.

"Did we run aground?" she called up to the flying bridge.

"No."

"Then what was that noise?" Fay asked.

"The automatic winch lowering anchor," Dave told her. "This yacht has every conceivable accessory. Up-and-down helm controls, auto pilot, radar, sonar, depth finder, dual throttles, an engine synchronizing indicator, a full panel of gauges, and a ship-to-shore radio. And this steering wheel is even padded with leather."

"There's a radio at the controls in the cabin, too," Fay said, "and—"

"Quiet," Dave ordered in a low voice. He listened intently in the direction of Gardners Bay, which was the mouth of Lake Montauk. "I hear a motor."

In also hearing the droning of a boat engine, Ski took Capobianco by the arm and said, "Remember, we'll have our weapons trained in your direction throughout the visit. Do anything to give us away and we'll gun you both down. That's a promise, cockroach!"

## Chapter Forty-three

The *Brighton Explorer*'s motor launch rounded Montauk Point light-house and turned left into Gardiners Bay, then entered the broad-mouthed inlet that was Lake Montauk. The launch pilot steered the vessel toward Fisherman's Wharf. Within a few minutes he had the launch secured at the marina's long pier.

Felicia Marlow got up from her seat in the cabin and picked up the attaché case. She stepped out on the aft deck, then onto the pier. "Keep the motor running. I'll only be a few minutes," she said to the launch pilot, and hurried up the gangway to the rear terrace doors. She knocked repeatedly, then heard the door unlock. It swung open. She hurriedly asked, "Has everyone left?"

"Yes. There's no one here but me," Capobianco answered.

"Rudolph Boyd?"

"He's been dealt with. This time for good," Capobianco assured her.

"And the man you assigned to do that task?"

"He's in the walk-in freezer out in the kitchen."

"Take me to him."

"You have the money?" Capobianco asked. He got a nod, then closed the door and led the way to the kitchen, knowing his moves were being observed from behind the bar. He opened the heavy hinged freezer door and gestured to the corpse lying face up on the floor inside.

Felicia stepped into the walk-in freezer and placed her hand on the jugular vein to feel for a pulse. Satisfied there was none, she stepped back out. "Your office?" Capobianco nodded and led her to the private office across the hall from the kitchen. Felicia placed the attaché case on the desk as Capobianco seated himself behind it, then slid it over to him with the side that opened facing him. "Please count your payment quickly. I wish to leave as soon as possible."

Capobianco raised the lid of the attaché case and stared down at the piles of hundred-dollar bills neatly stacked inside. He ran his index finger over the stacks of money, counting the piles as he did, then, hearing a familiar click, he looked up and saw a gun with a silencer just inches away from his face. "What . . ."

Felicia fired two shots. The first shot entered Capobianco's gaping mouth and came out the back of his neck. The other obliterated his right eye, and blood rained down onto the money inside the case. She quickly closed the attaché case, picked it up, and retraced her steps to the terrace entrance.

Ski watched Capobianco's visitor let herself out, still carrying the attaché case she had arrived with. He gave her a moment to get down the gangway, then dashed over to the private office, with Finch behind him. He looked at the bloody mess that was Capobianco's face. "What goes around comes around," he commented.

They both heard the sound of a boat speeding away.

"Get on the phone to the Long Island State Park Police, Finch. Tell them that you're with me unofficially and explain the situation here. Tell them to stand by here with a boat if at all possible. I'll get in touch with you and let you know where we're being led to." He jotted down Capobianco's phone number. "When the police get here, mention that incident over in Connecticut and have them call Sergeant Austin for verification."

Ski waited until the launch was well along its way, then cupped the lens of the flashlight to restrict the spread of its beam and gave Dave two quick flashes. When the yacht pulled up to the pier, Ski joined Fay and Dave on the flying bridge. As he seated himself next to Dave, Ski said, "Don Capobianco's visitor killed him." Ski broke the silence that followed. "Keep a safe distance behind them. I want them to think they got away clean."

Reaching the end of Lake Montauk, Dave moved the yacht out into Gardiners Bay, then caught sight of the launch's navigation lights as it began rounding Montauk Point lighthouse. When the launch's lights disappeared around the point, he chanced moving out a little faster. When they saw the launch again it was headed straight out to sea.

"I know of only one land mass," Dave said, "that's in the direction they're going, Ski. And I seriously doubt they're Bermuda bound in a small craft."

Ski watched the faint cluster of lights the launch seemed to be heading toward. "There might be another island that was recently put to the south of Montauk—a floating island as mobile as this yacht and that launch but considerably larger."

"A ship?" Dave asked.

"It makes sense, Dave. If my theory about a submersible tanker delivering the methyl mercury to the *Trident* is right, then it's also logical they'd need a tender ship for their operation."

"What's a tender ship, Ski?" Fay asked.

"A large vessel specially designed to handle—and in some cases even house—a submersible craft. The Navy employs such ships to service its submarines at sea—refuel them, replenish their supplies, repair them, at times, while still underway. Such a ship would not only be capable of servicing their submersible, if they have one—it could also serve nicely as their base of operation. They could stay out at sea for months at a time, making required trips ashore by ship's launch. Just as they did tonight and on past occasions. I'll bet their submersible was uniquely designed to imitate a finback whale."

"What do you think their next move might be?" Dave asked.

"I'm not sure. They might remain in the area and sabotage the next Trident class submarine or randomly kill crews of any submarine operating out of our base in New London. But I'm more inclined to think they'll be heading back to their homeland once they retrieve their launch. Their work here seems finished."

"You think their homeland is the Soviet Union, Ski?" Fay asked.

"Yes."

As they continued heading south a massive ship emerged on the horizon and it suggested without doubt that it was the launch's destination. Its size prompted Dave to say, "I wonder if the Coast Guard or police have anything on hand back in Montauk that'll stand up to a ship that size. They may have automatic weapons and hidden deck cannons aboard her."

"I think we can get hold of some very persuasive firepower," Ski said. "When I attended the military inquest in New London, Commander Buel reminded me that the U.S.S *Dart* was on an extended patrol for another week. He even gave me the *Dart*'s coded-call sign in case I wanted to get in touch with him on the QT. He should be running a patrol pattern somewhere west of us right now.''

''What are you waiting for, Ski?'' Dave asked. ''Get on the radio and give Bad Ass Buel a ship-to-ship jingle. Hell, he's always been fired up and ranting about how he'd kick Russian asses if he ever caught them inside our waters. Just last week—''

''How well I remember,'' Ski interrupted. ''For all we know, that same Russian sub might be waiting right outside our limits with orders to escort that tender ship back to home port.''

''Ski, that ship's radioman is probably monitoring all transmissions in the immediate area. You're going to have to be careful when you're talking to Bad Ass Buel,'' Dave reminded.

## Chapter Forty-four

Some thirty miles west of Montauk Point, heading westerly on its patrol course some ten miles out off the coast of Long Island, the U.S.S. *Dart*'s commanding officer was still awake and suffering from another attack of indigestion. Seated in his captain's chair on the bridge, Buel was growling at Ensign Schmidt, the bridge OOD, about the indigestible supper.

''Skipper!'' the *Dart*'s radioman interrupted as he stepped out of the radio shack. ''There's someone by the name of Ski transmitting on our coded-call signs. I think he wants to speak to you, sir.''

''What makes you think that, son?''

''He said he wanted to speak to Bad Ass and no one else, sir.''

Buel looked at Schmidt curiously. ''The only Ski I know is Kowalski over in New London,'' he said. Then he remembered he had given the Navy Intelligence captain the *Dart*'s special coded-call sign. He crossed the bridge to the radio shack with Schmidt right on his heels. ''This is Bad Ass. Over.''

''Bad Ass, this is Ski. I'm out in the vicinity where that big fish got away from you. The one you told me you used your ABC rules on. Do you copy that so far, over?''

''The area we all rendezvoused at on Labor Day?''

''Roger that,'' Ski said. ''I'm about five miles south of the big light. Copy that?''

Buel looked at Schmidt. ''He's talking about the vicinity of

Montauk Point where the *Trident* submarine crash-surfaced. He must be about five miles south of Montauk Point lighthouse.'' He keyed his mike. "Ski, do you have radar aboard? Over."

"Affirmative," Ski replied.

"Can you squawk for me?" he asked, hoping to locate Ski's vessel electronically on radar.

"Negative, Bad Ass," Ski replied. "I'm heading south on a vector straight up from the big light. I think I'm going to find the big fish. I think it's about five miles south of where I am now. I don't want any other fisherman picking up on me and interfering with the catch. Do you copy, over?"

"Standby, Ski," Buel replied, then looked at Schmidt. "Call down to CIC and ask Ensign Lichenberg what he has on radar about ten miles south of Montauk light. Also ask him if he's holding a vessel about five miles off Montauk, too." He keyed the mike again. "I believe I'm getting the picture, Ski. I'm checking my fish finder now. Give us a minute or two, over."

"I'm holding," Ski said.

Schmidt reported back. "CIC has the *Brighton Explorer* heaved to ten miles south of Montauk light, Skipper. That's the research ship that moved from its anchorage off Martha's Vineyard at about oh one hundred. And radar is tracking two small blips now seven miles south of Montauk light. They're heading south toward the big blip at about ten knots, less than a quarter of a mile apart."

"Roger on the big fish, Ski. Roger on you. And you have at least one other fisherman in your area. What is it you're asking of me? Over."

"I'd like to have you help me land the big fish. I expect it'll give me quite a fight when I hook it. And landing it is imperative. Do you copy that, over?"

"I think so, Ski," Buel replied.

"I may have trouble bringing the catch in. You'll be a big help in getting it back to land, over."

"Roger that," Buel said.

"How soon do you think you might be able to join up with me, over?" Ski asked.

"Give me a rendezvous ETA to ten miles south of Montauk light at flank speed, Schmidt," Buel said, then keyed his mike. "Checking that now. Standby, Ski." Schmidt obtained the information and gave it to Buel. "Thirty minutes, Ski."

"It'll have to do, Bad Ass."

"What further instructions do you have for me, over?" Buel asked.

"When you arrive, I hope to already have a hook in the big fish," Ski said. "Just join in on the fight. I don't want to let this one get away, over."

"Roger that, Ski. I'll get there ASAP. Bad Ass, out."

"Ski, over and out," Ski said as he looked ahead and eyed the huge ship growing larger on the southern horizon.

"Sound GQ, Schmidt," Buel ordered. "Watch. All ahead flank," he added. "Come about hard to starboard." "New course is zero-nine-zero." He got on the bridge phone and called down to CIC. "Mr. Lichenberg! Keep those surface contacts tracked. Advise me at once if there's any change." He saw his XO charge across the bridge toward him. "Good morning, Mr. Carwell."

"Another whale chase, Brewster?"

"You might say that." He keyed the PA mike. "Hear this. This is the captain speaking. This GQ is not a drill. I repeat. This GQ is not a drill. Go to your battle stations at once and standby for a possible enemy engagement. We are in pursuit of a surface vessel of a questionable status. I have been requested by Naval Intelligence to assist. We are to overhaul and board the vessel, and perhaps escort it to a Navy jurisdictional port. I want deck guns fore and aft loaded with live shells. Load port and starboard rocket launches with non-nuclear rockets. Keep all nuke weapons disarmed unless otherwise instructed. That is all."

"What the hell is going on, Brewster?" Carwell asked.

"Captain Kowalski of Naval Intelligence over in New London just recruited the *Dart*. Advise Newport by coded communiqué that we are turning about on a coastal defense-assist mission. We will advise further details when they become known to us. Copy New London on that, attention COMSUBOPS, Admiral Pulvey."

"If you're intending to engage the vessel in a combat action, shouldn't I ask permission to do so from COMDESOPS or COM-SUBOPS?" Carwell asked.

"If the need to do so arises, we'll consider it then, XO."

On the bridge of the *Brighton Explorer*, Captain Horthorne asked the radar operator, "Is the launch still being followed?"

"Aye, aye, sir."

"How far away are they now?"

"Less than a mile due north."

Horthorne looked at the radioman. "What are you monitoring on ship-to-shore?"

"Just the usual garbled chatter between fishermen, sir. Shall I radio the launch and advise Mrs. Grant she's being followed?"

"No. Maintain radio silence." Horthorne turned the bridge over to the first mate and headed down to the main deck.

Moments later, as the pilot maneuvered the launch alongside the starboard boarding ladder, Felicia looked out at the pitch-black sea. "I have no idea why I was followed," she replied to Horthorne. "But I intend to find out."

"Shall I advise Dr. Grant that there's an intruder?" Horthorne asked.

"No need to disturb his scuttling preparations on the *Scorpion* just yet. Let me investigate first," Felicia said. To the launch pilot, she said, "Take us back to the yacht."

"They're coming back, Ski," Dave said.

Ski kicked off his shoes and socks, then stripped down to the waist and gave his clothes to Dave to hide. "Dave, you know the plan. Follow me as soon as you can. Fay, remember, you and your boyfriend were out for a joy ride in your father's yacht. You had an electrical failure and all your lights went out. You went out too far off Montauk Point and followed their launch, thinking they would lead you back to land."

"Got it."

"Handling the yacht is easier than it looks. Dave is supposed to be seasick, so he can't help you. You have a wide-open sea to steer around in, so just handle the helm like you'd steer a car. Keep heading for their ship, pretending you were going over to it to ask for directions back to Montauk Point."

Ski quickly explained how to operate the controls, then wrapped his and Dave's guns in a plastic bag he'd found in the galley. He saw that the launch was drawing close, descended the bridge ladder, and went over the side.

A few seconds later the flying bridge was pulled out of the surrounding darkness by the blinding spotlight of the approaching launch. "Ahoy aboard the yacht!" Felicia called out over the bullhorn as they came alongside. "What are you doing out here? Why were you following us?"

"Hello!" Fay said, sounding relieved. "I'm so glad you came back. We were going to try and flag your ship down for help. My boyfriend and I were out for a boat ride and we had an electrical blackout. We followed you, thinking you'd lead us back to Montauk Point.''

"Montauk Point is in the other direction!" Felicia barked. "How stupid can you two be? Do you see that faint light flashing intermittently off your stern?" she added as she pointed to the north. "That's the direction your bow should be pointed in.''

"Thank you so much," Fay said.

"Why don't you let your boyfriend take the helm?" Felicia asked. "Or is he just as poor a seaman as you?''

"He's a little seasick," Fay answered.

"All you have to do is keep heading toward those flashes," Felicia said. "That's Montauk lighthouse. Can you at least do that?''

"I think so. Sorry to have caused you any trouble. We'll be on our way now. Thank you.''

Still suspicious of the yacht's presence, Felicia said, "Just a minute." She gestured to the two line handlers. "Board her and have a look around in the cabin. Make sure no one else is hiding aboard." She called over the bullhorn, "My crewmen are coming aboard to see if they can fix your power failure.''

Fay and Dave watched as two men brandishing handguns and flashlights boarded the yacht. Keeping up the pretense of innocence, Dave said, "What's going on here? What are the guns for?''

One of the men smiled grimly. "Stay cool, man. This won't take long. Be quiet and be safe.''

When the two men disappeared inside the cabin, Fay and Dave heard doors open and close and objects being shuffled about, then the two men emerged on the aft deck again below them. "Nothing, ma'am. Shall we check the flying bridge?''

"Don't bother," Felicia replied. "We've no more time to waste on them." The two line handlers crossed back to the launch. She nodded to the launch pilot and he began heading back toward the mother ship.

Dave waited for a couple of minutes, stripped, and went over the side to meet Ski. When he was clear of the yacht, Fay brought the yacht about slowly to head north, away from the ship.

## Chapter Forty-five

"And you can't get any more than two-thirds out of it?" Schmidt asked the *Dart*'s engineering officer. "Shit! Standby." He crossed the bridge to his CO. "Engine room reports they can only get two-thirds power out of our port turbine, Skipper."

Buel sprang from his captain's chair and rushed over to the bridge phone. "This is the captain speaking! You snipes have to pick a time like this to shaft me with engine trouble!"

"Skipper, there's nothing we can do to fix it while under way," the engineering officer said. "We threw a bearing on the main drive shaft. If we keep asking port engines to answer flank, we'll burn the whole goddamn turbine up."

"What do you recommend?"

"Reduce port and starboard engines to two-thirds. It's less strain for our starboard power plant if we keep port engine on line."

"Okay," Buel said. "But you keep your snipes turning two down there." He hung up the bridge phone. "Mr. Carwell, lay down to the engine room on the double. Kick ass if need be, but make sure everything is being done to restore flank speed. Schmidt, alert the air boss to get the Seasprite readied for scrambling on a moment's notice. But tell 'em not to launch the chopper unless I give the word personally." Buel slipped on his headset. "CIC from bridge!" he barked into the mike.

"CIC," Ensign Lichenberg answered wearily.

"Standby to brief the air group on a vector to that big surface blip of yours. Advise me at once of any hostile activity you detect."

"Just a young couple who ventured out too far and lost their running lights," Felicia informed Captain Horthorne as she came aboard the mother ship. "They couldn't find their way back to Montauk and were following us in the hopes we'd lead them there."

"But we were sure they began following you from Montauk," Horthorne insisted.

"Maybe your radar operator miscalculated how far out they were from land when he began monitoring them," Felicia said, certain the two foolish lovers she had seen aboard the yacht couldn't be any threat to them.

"I'll question the radarman about a miscalculation," Horthorne said. "I don't relish miscalculations aboard my ship."

"As you wish," Felicia said. "If it will make you feel more at ease, leave the launch over the side until the last possible moment before we get under way. If they fail to continue heading toward Montauk and come about toward the ship again, I'll ride back out to the yacht and make them wish they never left Montauk Point."

"Very well," Horthorne said, and led the launch pilot and the line handlers up to the bridge. He went over to the radarman. "Are you sure that yacht began following the launch in the vicinity of Montauk lighthouse? Might it have been further out from land when you first detected them astern of the launch?"

"I first picked the yacht up rounding Montauk light, sir," the radioman said firmly. "It might have been following the launch all the way from Fisherman's Wharf, but I can't be sure of that."

"Check your automatic weapons and standby here on the bridge," Horthorne said to the men.

When Dave finished his careful swim, Ski allowed him to rest for a couple of minutes. They climbed out of the water and sat on the boarding platform that the launch was tied up to. Ski removed the two weapons from his plastic bag and passed one to Dave. The guns had been kept bone dry through the quarter-mile swim. They didn't see anyone manning the top of the boarding ladder, so they eased their way up the metal steps. At the top step they crouched down and checked the main deck fore and aft, but that seemed unattended as well. They heard a faint noise, like that made by machinery, rising up from a metal canopied staircase on starboard abaft. Ski pointed to the tall superstructure's starboard bulkhead that was hatted by the bridge promenade deck overhang. In a whisper he said, "We'll make our way aft, hugging the side of the superstructure, then go below decks and see what's at the bottom of those stairs."

Out of the corner of his eye as he stared out at the sea, Captain Horthorne saw a figure emerge from the top of the boarding ladder, then dart across the main deck and disappear under the promenade deck he was standing on. He was about to rush after it, when a second figure quickly followed. He raced into the wheelhouse and faced the launch pilot and two line handlers, standing by with their machine guns. "It would appear the yacht was hiding two people who are now aboard my ship. Quietly come with me."

Arriving at a point aft where the superstructure bulkhead and promenade overhang that roofed them abruptly ended, Ski scrutinized the stern deck area. Voices were spilling out of the rear of the superstructure from an open hatch. The hatch door obscured their presence from anyone inside the aft compartment, and there was no one on the aft deck. Ski gestured to Dave to wait, then made his way over to the canopied staircase and hugged the side wall. After a moment, he signaled to Dave to join him. Together they descended the long staircase that seemed to be taking them to the lowest portion of the ship's hull. At the bottom was a closed hatch, behind which the sound of machinery had grown louder. Ski whispered, "It sounds more like a machine shop in there than an engine room."

"This is a wide-beamed ship, Ski," Dave whispered back. "The damn engine room could be centering the aft hold with a bunch of engineering shops surrounding it port and starboard. We might be walking right in on a bunch of crewmen working the night shift in there."

"Let's just hope none of 'em are looking this way when I open the hatch," Ski said softly, then quietly undogged the door latch. He eased the hatch door open a crack and peered inside. "Jackpot."

"Jesus, Mary, and Joseph," Dave said softly, catching a glimpse. "It looks to me like your submersible tanker theory was right on the money, Ski."

They noticed the submersible's striking resemblance to a finback whale. Then they saw a woman, Capobianco's visitor, standing in front of the craft, chatting with someone who seemed to be supervising the activity around the submersible. A group of silver-helmeted men were working from scaffolding resting against the submersible's hull. "I'd say they're preparing to scuttle the craft, Dave."

Ski observed the launching cradle the submersible was resting on, and the beveled-out basin under it, which resembled a large swimming pool emptied of water. He nodded approvingly at the tall stern doors that sealed the submersible craft inside the ship. "A seagoing dry dock," he commented. "Right down to an overhead crane." There were three heavy-duty fueling hoses draped above the submersible, and three closed hatches in line along the submersible's back. "I'd say the humming sound we heard on the *Trident*'s sonar tape were probably made by submerged boost or ballast pumps inside her pressure hull. And those fueling hoses above the submersible probably filled her inner hull with methyl mercury."

"I recommend we get to the engine room and do something to upset their plans to get under way, Ski," Dave said anxiously.

"And I recommend you both put down your weapons and face the wall with your hands folded over your heads," Horthorne called down to Ski and Dave from the top step of the stairwell. Flanking him were the launch's line handlers, their machine guns aimed down the stairwell.

Ski placed his magnum down on the bottom step and gestured to Dave to do the same.

"It was dumb of you not to dry your feet when you sneaked aboard," Horthorne said. "Your wet footprints led us right to you. Now do face the wall with your hands over your heads as I asked so one of my men can come down and collect your guns."

Ski noted Horthorne's distinctively British accent, his navy blue maritime captain's uniform and white uniform cap with the gold embroidered peak before he and Dave turned to face the wall. After the launch pilot picked up the two guns, Horthorne descended.

Dr. Phillip Grant's eyes widened in shock when he saw Horthorne and the launch crew marching two shirtless and shoeless men toward him at gunpoint. "What is this all about, Captain Horthorne?"

"I caught these two chaps sneaking aboard, Dr. Grant," Horthorne replied. "I've reason to believe they arrived here aboard that yacht."

"I wasn't aware there was a yacht in our vicinity," Dr. Grant said. "Why wasn't I informed?"

"Captain Horthorne told me the yacht was seen following me out from Montauk Point," Felicia said. "It had no running lights, and when I went back to challenge it, I found this one"—she pointed to Dave— "and a woman, pretending to be lost. The other one must have been in the water already."

"You should have brought this to my attention at once, Felicia," Grant said. "What are your names?" he asked, turning back to the men.

"I'm Captain Kowalski of Naval Intelligence, and this is Lieutenant Lee, my executive officer."

"I was under the impression you'd met with an unfortunate accident back in New London," Grant said. "This time I'll make sure." He turned to Horthorne and the launch crew. "See to that yacht. It's not to return to Montauk."

"I'll see to it myself, Phillip," Felicia said. "I don't like being made a fool of." She gestured to one of the line handlers. "You remain here with our two Navy visitors."

"As soon as the yacht has been dealt with, get us under way,

Captain Horthorne," Grant ordered. He smiled at Ski and Dave. "As you may have gathered, my submersible craft is being prepared for burial at sea. You both being Navy men, I think it would be fitting for you to join the *Scorpion* in her grave at the bottom. We plan to put her to rest over the continental·shelf, where the depths will be great enough to implode her pressure hull."

"What are you gaining by our deaths, by the deaths of all the people you've murdered?" Ski asked.

"A great deal, Captain."

"I don't understand. What good did it do you to embark upon a mission of sabotage?" Ski asked. "You killed a submarine crew, but the submarine itself lives on. It will just be manned by another crew. Other submarines of its class will be built and join the fleet, too. Surely, you don't think you can go around killing their crews indefinitely?"

"I had no intention of doing so. One dead crew was all I needed to make my mission a complete success," Grant said.

"But killing one Trident submarine crew wasn't going to stop the Trident submarine program," Ski rebuked.

"That wasn't my intention," Grant returned. "The overall success of my mission depended upon the program's continuance. The new fleet of Trident submarines are regarded as indispensable to the nation's future nuclear defense posture. The risk was that by my killing the prototype's crew, the program would be involved in additional controversy. But I thought the present administration wanted the new fleet bad enough to keep the program going regardless. And I wanted the construction of the remainder of the fleet to be put into more competent hands. According to what I've learned from Admiral Pulvey, I've managed to do just that."

"What does he have to do with all this?" Ski asked.

"Nothing, really. That is, he has no connection with my mission in any manner he's aware of. However, as I planned, he overzealously embraced the evidence I arranged for him to find so that my competition would be blamed for the *Trident* tragedy and thus be eliminated."

"Your competition?" Ski asked in astonishment.

"I'm the President of Salem Electric Boat Works in Virginia Beach, Virginia," Grant said. "My firm is the only other submarine builder capable of constructing the Trident submarine fleet. Now that I've caused Marine Dynamics to lose the contract, the remainder of the Defense Department's agreement with that firm will be transferred to Salem Electric Boat Works. I understand Admiral Pulvey's zeal accelerated the process, and I'm expected in Washington on Monday to discuss a smooth transition whereby Salem will be contracted to build the remaining nine Trident class submarines for the Navy. Marine Dynamics exhausted two billion dollars of the total award already, but there's still eighteen billion yet to be paid out by the Defense Department for the rest of the fleet. Even after costs are deducted for construction of the other nine subs, I'll see a handsome profit come out of my efforts.''

"All those men killed so that you could make money," Ski said softly.

"Please, Captain," Grant returned smugly. "I'm not the first man to be motivated by money, and I'm sure I won't be the last. The actions of my arch competitors at Marine Dynamics were motivated by financial gains when they resorted to underhandedness to steer the Trident submarine contract away from my firm and over to theirs. I submitted a realistic bid of two billion dollars per submarine, which was the lowest figure such a sophisticated vessel could be built for. And they knew it was. But they underbid me by submitting a figure of one point eight billion per unit. They did so with the assurance of the Defense Department politicians they bribed, that cost overrides could be submitted after the contract was awarded to their firm, which would allow them to recoup their point two billion dollar low balling bid. Surely you recall the subsequent cost overrides that Marine Dynamics submitted during production stages of the prototype on more than one occasion, Captain Kowalski?''

"Admiral Pulvey just recently acquainted me with the economics of the prototype submarine," Ski admitted.

"Well, that's what they were about, Captain. A recouping of the payola promised in return for favoritism, and in effect admittance that they underbid. Knowingly, at that. In doing so, they left my firm high and dry, with not even as much as a subcontracting share of the twenty billion dollar contract. It cost me a rather large sum of money to tool and prepare, just so I would be eligible to enter a bid. Even a small part of the huge defense project would have helped to defer those initial investments, but my rival was too greedy to turn a morsel my way. They saw the event as an opportunity to drive Salem Electric Boat Works out of business and thus eliminate their only competition for all time, and they jumped at the chance to do so. All I did was rightfully fight back and with *Scorpion*'s sting of justice, I delivered vengeance to their doorstep. A by-product of my justice was being in a position to have it appear as though Marine

Dynamics bigwigs caused the tragedy aboard the U.S.S. *Trident* out of greed. After all, they actually were guilty of greed by means of manipulation.''

"So instead of seeking redress to the injustice through a court petition, you took it upon yourself to render a remedy," Ski commented. "And in doing so you condemned innocent people to death. And that you call justice?"

"Come now, Captain," Grant snarled. "You're a military man, you can't be that naive. You've seen innocent people killed in wars, time and time again. Surely you comprehend that the fleet of Trident subs are nothing more than killing machines. Ten in all to be built and each one capable of unleashing total destruction on some four hundred and eighty cities without regard for whose guilty or innocent of war. The innocent often die along with the guilty in the name of a cause. And, in my actions and my cause, the same rules apply in my war against my enemies."

"You're a very sick man," Ski growled. "You're competitors may have stooped to cheating, but at least their hands are not stained with blood. Your hands are. You're a heartless murderer, and you belong in hell alongside the demon you came from."

Grant ignored him and turned to the line handler who was still holding his machine gun pointed at Ski and Dave. "Let the choice be theirs. Either they climb aboard the *Scorpion* willingly when the time comes or you shoot them down."

Ski watched Grant move to the boarding ladder set against the submersible's port side, climb to the top of the *Scorpion*'s rounded body, and descend through the open cockpit hatch. In another moment he saw Grant seated in the pilot's seat of the glass bubble bow, feverishly working to remove those components that could be reused. He glanced over at his XO and observed the despondent look on Dave's face. Out of friendship, Dave had agreed to help, and now he faced certain death as a result. He thought about the vicious woman who had gunned down Capobianco, now on her way to the yacht to do the same to Fay. That plagued him even more. He and Dave were acting in the line of duty. Fay was not. She was acting out of love and devotion.

## Chapter Forty-six

Fay put the yacht into neutral, then looked astern at the bright spotlight that was searching the sea some distance behind her. It was making short sweeping motions from left to right. She hoped it was Ski and Dave coming back, but she knew how unlikely it was that they'd be returning so soon. She looked around for binoculars, but couldn't see any, and didn't want to leave the controls long enough to look for them elsewhere.

"Launch from bridge," Horthorne said into the ship-to-ship radio mike as he stood over the radar operator. "Stay on your heading north. The yacht's less than half a mile ahead off your bow."

"Roger, bridge," Felicia answered from the cabin aboard the launch.

Just then the line handler who was standing between Felicia and the launch pilot settled the spotlight on the stern of the yacht. "There she is!"

"Catch up with her," Felicia ordered the launch pilot. To the line handler she said, "You come up on the forward deck with me." She and the line handler picked up their machine guns and climbed up through the forecastle hatch to the bow deck.

The launch pilot waited for them to get into a prone position on the bow deck, then, with the spotlight locked on the flying bridge of the yacht, he pushed the throttle full forward. The action raised the bow out of the sea as the launch lunged ahead.

Fay watched the launch pick up speed and begin rushing toward her. Increasingly worried, she decided to descend to the control station in the cabin. As she started climbing down the flying bridge ladder, a volley of machine-gun fire rang out from the bow of the launch. The windshield on the yacht's flying bridge shattered, and fragments of fiber glass sprayed over the forward deck. Fay ran inside the cabin, and as another volley of shots tore into the deck of the flying bridge that roofed the cabin, she got the yacht into gear and thrust both throttles full forward. She gripped the steering wheel as the yacht's V-shaped bow climbed skyward out of the sea. The twin propellers churned up the sea, raising a tall rooster tail astern.

Fay decided it was time to call for help. She picked up the radio mike and uncaring of proper radio procedures, she keyed on and shouted into the mike, "Calling the U.S.S. *Dart*! This is Fay Parks aboard the yacht Captain Kowalski called you from earlier. I am under attack and request assistance at once." She released the mike button to listen.

At the helm in the cabin, the launch pilot heard the mother ship radioing him. Fighting the steering wheel with one hand to keep the launch moving through the yacht's tumultuous wake, he keyed the radio mike with the other. "This is the launch. Go ahead bridge." He listened to the urgent message. "Will do." He tapped hard on the windshield, then opened one panel to speak to Felicia and the line handler out on the bow deck. "She's calling out for help. Aim for her radio mast."

Felicia gestured to the launch pilot to move the launch out of the yacht's wake so she could take aim. As soon as he had, she fired a burst at the yacht's flying bridge, using sweeping motions to strike the towering radio mast and rip it free of its deck mounting.

Also taking aim at the radio mast, the line handler fired a long blast from his machine gun. When he saw the mast topple over, he shouted, "We got it!"

Fay saw the top of the mast dangling from the flying bridge just outside the starboard cabin window and threw down the mike angrily. Another volley of machine-gun fire slammed into the aft cabin wall. Pieces of the aft cabin wall flew at her and the door was torn off one of its hinges. To make the yacht a more difficult target, Fay began turning the steering wheel from side to side. She wondered if Ski and Dave were dead.

Aboard the *Dart*, Commander Buel acknowledged the CIC room. "What is it, Mr. Lichenberg?"

Looking over the radarman's shoulder at the amber-faced scope, Lichenberg said, "Skipper, I think one of those small crafts is in deep gumbo. Both vessels are making highly erratic movements over the surface, as though they were involved in some sort of chase."

"Standby, CIC," Buel said. "Radio shack! Have you picked up a distress call?"

"Negative, Skipper. There was some brief transmission a few minutes ago, but it was too garbled to copy."

"CIC, what is that research ship doing?" Buel asked.

"Sonar is monitoring engine sounds from the ship, Skipper,"

Lichenberg replied. "But radar still shows it heaved to ten miles south of Montauk light."

"Standby, CIC," Buel said, and looked at Ensign Schmidt. "Kowalski said something about the big fish putting up a fight. I have a feeling the fight has begun."

"It'll be another fifteen minutes before we hold them visually, Skipper. Want to send the chopper ahead to investigate?" Schmidt asked.

"You're goddamn right I do," Buel said. "Flight deck from bridge. Scramble the Seasprite out to the vicinity of that research ship. Have the crew evaluate the situation between two small vessels in the area. If one vessel appears to be engaging the other in a hostile action, they are to order said vessel to cease and desist under threat of Naval intervention."

"And if the warning is ignored?" the air boss asked.

"Permission is granted to use force in obtaining compliance," Buel said. "Ensign Schmidt, send the following coded update of our disposition. Accelerated activity, possibly hostile in nature, ten miles south of Montauk light suggests research ship, *Brighton Explorer*, is involved in some form of subterfuge presently under investigation by New London Naval Intelligence. Scrambled *Dart*'s Seasprite, Navy one-one-nine, to fly ahead and assist Captain Kowalski. Due to port engine mechanical restriction, unable to attain flank speed. Proceeding two-thirds headway, ETA fifteen minutes. On arrival will advise state of disturbance and action to be taken. B. A. Buel."

"COMDESOPS, copy COMSUBOPS?" Schmidt asked.

"Affirmative," Buel replied, then stared out the forward bridge window as the *Dart*'s helicopter streaked out into the night sky ahead of the ship.

The launch pilot heard the mother ship calling and keyed on the radio mike. "Go ahead, bridge." He listened. "Great," he commented, then called out to the bow deck. "There's a helicopter heading toward us from the west!"

Felicia eyed the western sky and caught sight of oscillating red lights streaking toward the launch. Then the popping sound of a helicopter's rotor blades slapping the air could be heard. "Break off the attack on the yacht," she called out. "We'll deal with the helicopter first."

At the controls of the Seasprite, the pilot switched on his brilliant landing lights as he lowered in the sky to the west of the yacht. As he made a pass over the yacht, he observed the bullet-riddled flying bridge. To his two-man .30-caliber machine-gun crew situated at the open cargo door behind the cockpit, he said, "It's obvious as hell we're not after them."

The copilot had played his handheld spotlight beam on the pursuing cabin launch as they flew over the troubled yacht. "There isn't a scratch on those bastards."

"Load and report when you are manned and ready," the pilot said to the gun crew. He contacted the *Dart* and gave a full report of the situation.

"Roger that, Navy one-one-nine," Buel said. "Carry out your orders and report."

"Ready to open fire on your command, sir," the first class gunnersmate said.

"Standby for the order," the pilot replied. He pitched the Seasprite hard to the right and arced in the sky to come in astern of the pursuing launch. To his copilot, he said, "Give 'em a shout over the hailer."

The copilot removed his bullhorn from its stowage rack and leaned out his cockpit side window. As the Seasprite came abreast of the launch's port side, he keyed the hailer mike. "Aboard the launch! This is the United States Navy. You are ordered to cease your hostile action and heave to or we'll open fire."

On the bow deck Felicia said to the line handler, "You aim at the gunners. I'll aim for their rotors."

The two gunnersmates were forced away from their guns as straffing riddled the fuselage aft of the cockpit. More machine-gun fire riddled the rotors overhead of the cockpit and the rotor blades sang wildly.

"We're hit. We're going to have to ditch," the pilot shouted as he fought the controls through a spiraling descent.

"Mayday! Mayday! Mayday!" the copilot shouted into his radio mike. "This is Navy, one-one-nine, under attack and ditching." He had no more time to report anything else as the Seasprite struck the water.

"Grab the two-man life rafts and abandon ship!" the pilot ordered as he joined the others in an urgent effort to unlatch their shoulder harnesses and seat belts. Passing from the cockpit to the open cargo door after his copilot, he said to the two gunnersmates, "Hit the drink. We'll pass the rafts out to you." He worked frantically with his copilot to heave the two bundled-up rafts out the cargo door. As the gunnersmates received the bundles in the sea and pulled the charged inflation levers, he and his copilot dove out of the helicopter. "You get aboard a raft with one man and I'll go aboard with the other."

The copilot swam over to one of the rafts and crawled in.

Climbing into the other raft, the pilot asked, winded, "Did you squawk our position over the Mayday emergency band?"

"Affirmative," the copilot answered, taking short breaths. "But we'd better break out the emergency distress beacons anyway. It looks like we'll be carried further east by the prevailing surface currents."

The pilot nodded. "But don't use the flares till we see the *Dart* coming. We don't want to draw any more attention from that goddamn launch than we already have."

Standing angrily in front of his captain's chair, Buel keyed his mike. "CIC from bridge! Did they squawk their Mayday position?"

"Negative, Skipper," Ensign Lichenberg answered. "But we're copying two radio distress beacon signals."

"Well, we have survivors in two rafts then," Buel said to Schmidt. "Prepare to put lifeboats over the side when we arrive in their area."

"Aye, aye, Skipper."

"And, Schmidt!"

"Sir?"

"Call down to the engine room and tell my XO I want the snipes to put port engine back to flank. I don't give a damn if we burn the son of a bitch to a cinder! I want that chopper crew rescued. And I want those bastards who downed them in my gun sights."

On the bridge of the *Brighton Explorer*, Captain Horthorne looked at the large blip on ship's radar that the operator had called to his attention. "It must be that downed helicopter's ship," he said. "How long before it reaches us?"

"At its present speed I'd say they'll be within visual contact in about ten minutes," the radarman said.

"Captain!" the first mate called out from the starboard promenade deck. "That yacht is heading right for our midships."

"Where's our launch?" Horthorne asked as he joined the first mate.

"It's right on the yacht's tail, sir."

Overhearing news of the boat chase off starboard, the radarman took his attention off the approaching surface patrol ship to observe the launch's pursuit. By doing so, he missed noticing that the patrol ship had suddenly regained flank speed and would have the *Brighton Explorer* in visual contact in half the anticipated time.

Unaware that she was heading straight for the towering starboard side of the research ship, Fay kept swinging the steering wheel from side to side, peeking aft out the cabin door to watch the pursuing launch. She couldn't stay ahead of them indefinitely. She needed to take offensive action, but there wasn't much she could do without weapons. She smiled grimly. She could use the yacht itself and ram the launch, but that would be suicidal. Desperate for ideas, she looked around the cabin and saw the Very pistol and four spare flares mounted inside a glass enclosed distress equipment cabinet. She'd never fired a flare gun but in an emergency she could learn. She tied the steering wheel in place as best she could and eased back the throttles, knowing she was taking a risk in slowing down.

A few minutes later Fay crawled along the aft deck to the stern, then, holding the Very pistol with both hands, she rested her elbows on the flat surface of the transom to steady the heavy gun. She waited for the launch to come a little closer, and, as its V-shaped bow dipped down to slide over a wake trough, she squeezed the thick trigger and the gun kicked wildly in her hands. She laid it down and ran back to the cabin controls.

On the bow of the launch, Felicia and the line handler saw a puff of smoke blow over the stern of the yacht and heard a popping sound, then something whistling loudly toward their launch. The sound shrieked over their heads and turned into a shrilling noise inside the cabin, which erupted into a Roman candle, sending showers of sparks and flames shooting up in all directions.

"It's a fucking flare!" the launch pilot said, then rushed away from his controls, leaving the throttle set in its full forward position. He took down a handheld fire extinguisher from its wall mount and frantically began spraying the flames, but his clothes caught fire and he ran out the rear cabin door. Enveloped in flames, he screamed for help, then climbed the starboard gunwhale and dived into the sea.

Felicia took a step toward the forecastle hatch to attend to the controls, then slipped and fell backward, striking her head on the bow railing as she went down. The line handler on the bow with her tried to get her up, then, seeing the cabin turn into an inferno that threatened to devour the launch, he dove off the bow to save himself.

Fay watched the burning launch, delighted with her success, then turned to look forward. Her lips parted and her eyes widened in disbelief. Directly ahead of the yacht's bow was a slime-coated towering wall that was the *Brighton Explorer*'s starboard bulkhead. She whipped the steering wheel hard to the right. The yacht responded and sped along within inches of the ship. As the yacht streaked past the ship's towering razor-sharp bow and pulled ahead of the *Brighton Explorer*, crewmen perched along the ship's starboard bow opened fire with machine guns, riddling the yacht's aft deck and flying bridge. Once safely away from the *Brighton Explorer*, Fay looked back at the launch. Still aflame, it continued at full speed toward the side of its mother ship.

Felicia regained consciousness, but, still groggy, she rose slowly by gripping the bow guardrail. Looking straight ahead, she saw the ominous black slimy wall. Unable to get her legs to move, she futilely thrust her hands out in front of her and screamed.

Captain Horthorne looked in horror at the launch racing toward his ship. There was a thunderous roar and before his stunned eyes he saw the launch disintegrate, sending flaming pieces of deck and side board straight up like rockets into the dark night sky. They rained down onto the *Brighton*'s main deck like a fiery shower and sent the crew scurrying about in a frenzy. Horthorne ducked inside the bridge and shouted to the watch officer, "Sound the general alarm!"

Hearing the alarm bell resounding, the first and second mates, who had been firing at the yacht, dashed up to the bridge. "We gave the yacht's aft deck and flying bridge a good strafing, sir," the first mate reported to Horthorne. "I doubt she'll get much further."

"Well done, Mr. Wellington," Horthorne said as he watched the yacht some distance ahead of the *Brighton Explorer*'s bow. "See to mustering a fire brigade and get that falling debris extinguished." He looked at his second mate. "Mr. Thornwell, weigh anchor." To the bridge watch officer he said, "Get us under way at once, Mr. Graves. Full speed ahead on a westerly heading."

"Westerly, sir?" the watch officer asked. "But ship's radar reports a surface patrol ship is approaching us from out of the west. She's bearing two-seven-oh on a course of zero-nine-oh. Range is five miles and closing at twenty knots. She'll be here within ten minutes, sir. And with us going all ahead full in her direction, we could meet her in five minutes.''

"We'll have to run that risk, Mr. Graves. We can't allow the ship to find that yacht. We're going to run her over and send her to the bottom.''

A half-mile ahead of the *Brighton Explorer*'s knifing bow, the yacht's twin engines sputtered, then backfired one after another and fell quiet. The propellers stopped spinning and began dragging in the sea, slowing the yacht gradually until it lost all headway. Stopped and adrift in silence, unable even to steer the yacht, Fay moved both throttles back and forth anxiously. Remembering the strafing, she decided to look around on deck. Outside the cabin, she climbed the riddled bridge ladder carefully and inspected the flying bridge controls. Some of the bridge deck had been ripped up by machine-gun fire, exposing the cabin below. All the gauges on the dashboard were shattered. She tried turning the twin ignition keys off, then back on again, but there was no response from either engine. The dual throttles were torn loose from their housings and dangling to one side of their mounts by exposed wires and mechanical linkage cables. She was able to get them to move back and forth, but the action seemed lifeless to her.

She tried turning the steering wheel next, but it was jammed in place. Just then a brilliant light from astern illuminated the flying bridge, catching her by surprise. Looking aft, she saw the *Brighton Explorer* racing toward her. She grabbed the Very pistol she'd left on deck, ran to the cabin and reloaded, and went back aft. She knew she couldn't set fire to the steel ship the way she had the launch, but she was hoping to hit the bridge and cause some confusion. She propped her hands up on the transom and took aim, but before she could squeeze the trigger, she heard a distant thud and saw a flare go whistling up in the eastern sky. It exploded into a brilliant light that slowly danced back down toward the surface of the sea. She thought the flare could only have been fired by the helicopter crew.

Suddenly a second flare answered the first from behind her, and she looked toward the western sky as the flare rocketed up to the heavens with a whistling shrill. It thundered resoundingly out over the quiet sea as it erupted into a blossom of brilliant light. As Fay followed its descent, she spotted a ship's running lights. She glanced astern and saw the *Brighton Explorer* turning hard to port, taking up a southerly heading further out to sea and knew that the new ship must be the *Dart*. To help Buel find her, she pointed the Very pistol skyward, squeezed the trigger, and watched as her flare streaked to the heavens. Overjoyed by her rescue, she was suddenly saddened by the thought of Ski and Dave.

## Chapter Forty-seven

Buel was flanked by Commander Carwell and Ensign Schmidt as he gazed out the bridge windows at the flare the downed helicopter crew had shot off. Seeing another flare streak skyward closer to his ship, he said to Schmidt, "That one must have come from Kowalski's boat. Have a lifeboat lowered to rescue them as well as the downed chopper crew, Mr. Schmidt."

Carwell noticed the *Brighton Explorer* turning hard to port to head south. "Looks like they're going to make a run for international waters."

"I promise you, they won't make the continental shelf," Buel said. "What about our ship-to-ship radio calls, ordering them to heave to for boarding, XO?"

"They were sent out over all channels in seven different languages, including Russian," Carwell said. "Either their radios are off or inoperative—"

"Or they're deliberately ignoring our heave-to request," Buel finished for Carwell. "Then it'll be their ass!" he bellowed. "Get a well-armed boarding party mustered on the double, XO. Have 'em standing by additional lifeboats. Mr. Schmidt, is the rescue detail scrambled?"

"Aye, aye, Skipper."

"Okay, Mr. Schmidt," Buel said. "Now you're to make a notation in the ship's log as follows. At oh-three-thirty hours we came astern of the vessel, *Brighton Explorer*, believed responsible for the downing of our Seasprite. Vessel ignored directive to heave to for boarding. Vessel ignored warning that it would be fired upon for noncompliance. We have advised base that we are engaging said vessel in combat, but received no acknowledgment from COMDESOPS or COMSUBOPS. I am therefore—"

"But, Skipper," Schmidt interrupted. "We haven't advised base that we're engaging in combat yet." He got an acid glare from Buel that encouraged him to keep writing in the log.

"In lieu of a confirming or denying directive from base, I am acting on my own discretion and intend to commence firing. Sign the log, B. A. Buel."

"Roger that, Skipper," Schmidt said submissively.

Buel slipped on his headset and keyed the mike. "Bow turret fire control from bridge."

"Bow turret, aye," the fire control officer said.

"I'm engaged in a couple of surface rescues at the moment and need a few extra minutes to squeeze that detail in. We have every reason to believe the ship we're asking to heave to is ignoring us with intent to leave our jurisdictional waters. Now I don't want to put any undue strain on our limping port engine, so I'm going to have to use some long-distance persuasion. In plain English, see if you can drive a nice hot one right up her ass that'll get her heaved to for me on the double."

"Roger that, Skipper," the fire control officer said with a smile. "When shall we open fire?"

"Oh, immediately will do nicely, thank you."

The *Dart*'s cannon shot slammed into the rear of the *Brighton Explorer* with a thunderous concussion that caught everyone in the aft hold by surprise. The explosion tore both of the ship's propellers from their shafts, causing it to lose headway and drift slowly to a stop. The twin stern doors parted from their hinges and fell. When they hit the sea, they sent a tumultuous wave of foamy water inside the aft hold that sent everyone scurrying around frantically. Scaffolds were pushed off balance, toppling their occupants into the rushing water. As the ship's stern sank lower into the sea, a wall of water rushed in to flood the dry dock basin under the *Scorpion* and quickly climbed the submersible's rounded undersides.

Shaken by the sudden explosion and heaving sea that rushed inside the ship, the line handler guarding Ski and Dave was distracted. Ski reacted immediately. He rushed the handler and began wrestling with him fiercely for possession of the machine gun. Dave took a step to assist Ski, then found himself struggling with an engineering crewman brandishing a wrench. Ski brought his knee up swiftly to the line handler's groin, and the blow caused the man to squeeze the trigger of his machine gun. As he sank to his knees in ankle-deep water, Ski wrestled the gun from him and smashed him on the head.

Standing atop *Scorpion*'s rounded back was Chief Engineer Spragg who had just lowered a bucket by rope down the open bow hatch. As he stood by to hoist up the last-minute cockpit articles Dr. Grant was salvaging, the line handler's wildly spent machine-gun blast slammed into his face. He released his end of the rope and gripped his stinging face in a soundless grimace as the room around him turned to darkness like a drawn shade. He staggered rubber-legged for an instant, then collapsed onto the open hatch and brought it closed, pinning it shut with the weight of his lifeless body.

Seated in the pilot's seat in *Scorpion*'s cockpit, Dr. Grant hadn't heard the commotion taking place outside the submersible's thick-clad soundproof pressure hull. But when seawater began rushing inside *Scorpion* through the numerous scuttle holes burned and drilled all along the pressure hull, the sudden deluge plunged him into reflexed fright. He was sure someone had prematurely given the command to flood the dry dock basin benath *Scorpion* and shouted furiously, "Spragg! Stop the flooding at once!" Frantically he pulled himself out of the pilot's seat as the water climbed his legs without end. "Stop the flooding, you fools!" he grunted as he waded aft to the escape ladder. There he found Spragg's end of the hoisting rope draped over the bottom rung of the ladder, and the bow hatch closed above the top rung. He charged up the ladder and began pushing on it frantically, but it wouldn't budge. "Spragg! Let me out at once!" There was no answer to his plea, no response to comply. That fathomed his fear. He wedged his back under the hatch cover and in desperation he tried to force it open, but it still wouldn't budge. "My God!" he shrilled. "Those idiots have locked me aboard!"

In near tears, Grant descended the ladder and rushed through the fast-climbing seawater to the cockpit. He peered out through the wraparound glass-bubble enclosure and saw water surrounding *Scorpion* outside. There were crewmen struggling and scurrying about in waist-high water. With bulging eyes he gazed aft and got a glimpse of the parted stern doors and knew only too well what fate awaited him if he remained aboard the flooding submersible. It was the exacting demise he planned for the Navy intruders. He heard *Scorpion* make creaking sounds as it moved erratically while wedged between the launching cradle's locking jaws. He knew the added weight of the seawater pouring inside the pressure hull would put too much of a demand on them and the locking jaws would give away at any moment. Panic-stricken, he picked up the largest wrench he could find and began pounding on the glass enclosure. He delivered fierce blows to it as though he were expecting to break through the shatterproof and pressure-defying glass, but he knew even a sledge-hammer wouldn't free him from his imprisonment. He had to get help from outside to be freed and in seeing crewmen rushing past *Scorpion*'s bow, just inches away, he cried out, "Help me! Look this way you idiots! I'm trapped aboard! Help me!" There was no response to his banging, or his shouts for help. He knew there wouldn't be unless someone just happened to look his way and see him inside. In his genius he had made *Scorpion* sound-tight inside and out. He might as well be slamming the wrench against a rubber surface, might as well be screaming for help from his grave.

Ski fired a volley of machine-gun fire into the air and drove would be attackers off for cover. He appraised the steep slant the stern of the ship was assuming in the sea. There was no doubt in his mind that Davy Jones intended to claim the ship and all who remained aboard the vessel.

As they rounded *Scorpion*'s bow, Ski caught a glimpse of Grant staring wild-eyed out of the submersible's glass-bubble enclosure. The blows Grant was paying feverishly to the glass enclosure told him he was trapped aboard. The twisting and grunting the submersible was going through while atop its launching cradle suggested next that Grant knew his creation was about to break free of its berth. And the severe pitch to aft that the submersible was assuming spelled out that Grant was about to take the ride to crushing depths aboard *Scorpion* that he had planned for him and Dave. He gestured to the submersible. "I think our host needs help, Dave. Can you make it to higher ground on your own from here?"

"Ski, you're not going to try and rescue that bastard, are you?"

"He'd make a wonderful witness to turn over to Bull Pulvey," Ski said.

"He'd also make a wonderful candidate for hell," Dave said back. "Why risk your neck. Let him die and give the world a break by being rid of his kind."

"Believe me I'd like to, Dave. But . . ."

Popping noises interrupted Ski's rescue plan. He joined Dave in an astonished gaze as the launching cradle's locking jaws tore off their foundations and hurled into the air. For an instant the submersible hung by its bow cable before its braided steel strands peeled back like banana skins and snapped. As though catapulted backward, *Scorpion* rushed down the launching tracks and vehemently separated from its cradle. In an upheaving of foaming waves it crashed into the sea behind the ship's stern. Tumultuous bubbles erupted as the last few air pockets were forced out of the pressure hull with gurgling sounds. They caught a final glimpse of Grant still banging fiercely on the glass enclosure in head-deep seawater aboard the submersible, then *Scorpion* was devoured by the forbidding depths. In another moment the surface of the sea behind the ship turned calm again, waiting invitingly to swallow the submersible's mother ship next.

"That," Dave said, "could have been us, Ski."

"How well I know that, Dave," Ski said as they headed through the waist-high seawater for the starboard staircase leading topside. "But fate had it another way. It was payback time. And payback's a bitch."

The U.S.S. *Dart* was heaved to some fifty yards to starboard of the *Brighton Explorer* as the research ship sat powerless and sinking in the sea. On the bridge of the *Brighton Explorer,* as four lifeboats with armed Marine MP's and Navy SP's converged at the foot of the boarding ladder, Captain Horthorne regarded his first and second mates. "We must send the ship to the bottom after the *Scorpion,*" he said. He'd been told of the fate of the submersible and Dr. Grant.

The mates looked at each other and trained their weapons on their ship's master. "It's futile, sir. The crew is abandoning ship. We intend to surrender when the boarding party comes aboard."

Horthorne nodded. "Very well, then. Do what you feel you must. It's all over anyway, now that Dr. Grant has perished."

The first mate turned to the bridge watch officer. "Advise the destroyer that we don't intend to fight."

Ski and Dave saluted the *Dart*'s national ensign atop the destroyer's towering mast. Then, after saluting Buel, Ski said, "Permission to come aboard."

"Granted, Ski." Eyeing the man in handcuffs that two armed Marines had sandwiched between them, Buel said, "I gather this one is the ship's master."

"He is," Ski replied. "I hope you have a spot in the ship's brig for him."

"We certainly do," Buel said, and ordered the Marines to take Horthorne away.

Buel noticed Ski's and Dave's wet pants. "You told me you were going fishing, Ski. But it seems you also went swimming as well. I'll have my XO get you both some dry clothes."

"There's plenty of time for that, Commander," Ski said. "I'm most concerned about keeping that research ship afloat. It's a valuable piece of evidence." He stepped aside for four sailors moving huge pumps onto the boarding ladder.

"My boarding party will see to it that it doesn't get deep-sixed on you, Ski. We've radioed for tugs to tow it back to New London. And we also advised COMSUBOPS to expect it as evidence to sabotage. In fact, Admiral Pulvey is so taken aback by your investigation that he's flying out here by chopper to see you."

"Boy, is the Bull in for one hell of a surprise," Dave commented.

"We're going to have to raise that submersible that went down," Ski said.

"We're in about six hundred feet of water here," Buel told him. "That shouldn't prove to be too much of a task for Navy salvage people."

"How's Fay, the woman on the yacht I called you from," Ski asked anxiously. "You'll find Fay in the officers' ward room, sipping coffee. Considering what a shambles that yacht was in, it's surprising she survived without a scratch. From what I've heard of her story, she's one hell of a woman."

Ski smiled. "I'm shoving off for officers' country."

Fay was seated at the head of the officers' mess table with an untouched cup of coffee in front of her. She was aware that life boats were ferrying back and forth between the *Dart* and the *Brighton Explorer* and she had wanted to stay topside with Commander Buel in anticipation of Ski's and Dave's arrival aboard the destroyer. But there still was some uncertainty as to whether Ski and Dave had actually survived. That uncertainty had made her numb to everything beyond the warm blanket she was wrapped in. Even the cigarettes she'd kept lighting were smoked mechanically.

She'd just lit another cigarette when the ward room door suddenly opened. Filling the open doorway was Ski. She dropped her cigarette in the ashtray and rushed over to his extended arms. "Oh, Ski! I was so afraid . . ."

Ski smothered her words with an affectionate kiss on the lips. "It's all over now, Fay. It's all over." He hugged her tightly. "Now you can write that Pulitzer prize-winning scoop."

She returned his kiss enthusiastically and said, "Somehow that's not important to me anymore."

"What is important to you then?"

"You," Fay replied firmly. "Just you."

"Isn't that peculiar. You're all that's really important to me now, too."

"Where do we go from here?"

"I was thinking that maybe a trip home to San Diego would be in order."

"Roger that," Fay said, and melted in his embrace.